Praise for
THE STATUS REVOLUTION

"Witty and incisive . . . an entertaining and intelligent eye-opener."

—*PUBLISHERS WEEKLY*

"A very funny, surprisingly far-reaching attempt to determine what status means."

—*MEN'S JOURNAL*

"[*The Status Revolution*] is chock-full of fascinating revelations."

—*IN TOUCH WEEKLY*

"This will be hard for pop-culture readers to put down."

—*BOOKLIST*

"Thompson is an insightful, wry observer of our times, with a cynical eye for the most foolish of human follies."

—*KIRKUS REVIEWS*

"With plenty of laughs and mind-bending revelations along the way, Thompson is that perfect combo of dogged reporter and enthusiastic tour guide. In *The Status Revolution*, he connects disparate industries and unusual characters in the fun—and always surprising—way that makes him one of my all-time favorites."

—Sarah Knight, bestselling author of
*The Life-Changing Magic of Not Giving a F*ck*

"Chuck Thompson has tackled this slippery and ineffable topic with great aplomb, emerging with a book that is well-reasoned, beautifully paced, and a whole lot of fun. I feel improved."

—Henry Alford, author of *And Then We Danced*

"Fusing cultural anthropology, cutting-edge neuroscience and an impressive knowledge of Ferrari interior car design, Thompson has written a highly original book that is both eye-opening and hilarious. This is one writer who can keep a lot of balls in the air."

—Joe Queenan, *Wall Street Journal* columnist and author of *Closing Time*

"Buckle up and enjoy the hilariously curious, fact-packed global quest to understand why human beings still insist on outranking each other, from brain scientists to small-penis sports cars, purebred dogs, hiphop video directors, nudist hippie totem carvers, philanthropic tax evasion, and fame survivor Rick Springfield."

—Jack Boulware, cofounder of Litquake

ALSO BY CHUCK THOMPSON

Smile When You're Lying

To Hellholes and Back

Better Off Without 'Em

The
STATUS
REVOLUTION

THE IMPROBABLE STORY OF HOW
THE LOWBROW BECAME THE HIGHBROW

CHUCK
THOMPSON

SIMON & SCHUSTER PAPERBACKS
New York   London   Toronto   Sydney   New Delhi

An Imprint of Simon & Schuster, LLC
1230 Avenue of the Americas
New York, NY 10020

Portions of this text were originally published by *Gen/Medium* as
"The Rise and Spread of Excessive Wealth Disorder" and published by
Outside as "Totem Recall: One Chief's Mission to Reclaim the Past."

First Simon & Schuster paperback edition January 2024

SIMON & SCHUSTER PAPERBACKS and colophon are registered
trademarks of Simon & Schuster, LLC

Simon & Schuster: Celebrating 100 Years of Publishing in 2024

For information about special discounts for bulk purchases,
please contact Simon & Schuster Special Sales at 1-866-506-1949
or business@simonandschuster.com.

The Simon & Schuster Speakers Bureau can bring authors to your
live event. For more information or to book an event, contact the
Simon & Schuster Speakers Bureau at 1-866-248-3049 or visit our
website at www.simonspeakers.com.

Interior design by Lexy East

Manufactured in the United States of America

10 9 8 7 6 5 4 3 2 1

Library of Congress Cataloging-in-Publication Data has been applied for.

ISBN 978-1-4767-6494-8
ISBN 978-1-4767-6495-5 (pbk)
ISBN 978-1-4767-6496-2 (ebook)

*This and everything else
to The One and Only Joyce*

CONTENTS

The
STATUS
REVOLUTION

Introduction:
STATUS IN CHAOS

THE WOMAN ON THE RIVERBANK REALLY WANTED US TO KNOW it was bin Laden's dog.

Well, first she wanted us to know it was a rescue dog. Of course. No one can introduce you to their pooch anymore without letting you know four seconds into the conversation that good ol' Shasta or Quinoa or Sir Barks-a-Lot is a rescue.

I was a late adopter to the phrase. For several years after "rescue dog" became part of the popular vernacular, I assumed we were talking about animals that sniffed survivors out of earthquake rubble. Or charged twenty-five miles through blizzards and leapt through snowdrifts with mini-kegs of brandy around their necks. Gradually, I figured it out.

"Ohhhhhh! Rescue dog? You mean you got Crazer from the pound?"

Not long ago, people described dogs they picked up from animal shelters as mutts or mixed breeds. Somewhere along the line—mid-nineties, near as I can tell—people began attempting to confer a new kind of status upon themselves through the acquisition of orphaned animals. It still took me a while to sort out that the "rescue" bit refers as much to the owner's pedigree as the dog's. I mean, if that wasn't the case, wouldn't they more accurately be called *rescued* dogs? As in, "I, in signaling my empathy for all living creatures as well as a bottomless well of selflessness, *rescued* from barbarian euthanasia the princely beast presently interrogating your pants."

The lady on the riverbank, though? Her dog was apparently a noteworthy save.

This was along the North Fork Tongue River in Wyoming's Bighorn National Forest. I'd met up with my buddy Chris to do some camping and fishing. The woman was probably in her mid-fifties. Husband same. Both dangling with all the freshly unwrapped Smith/Simms/Sage gear you'd expect to find artfully strewn around an Orvis catalog shoot.

The dog looked like a medium-sized German shepherd. Deep fawn and mahogany coat. Powerful shoulders. Long, dark muzzle. Those half-feral, silvery eyes certain herding breeds have. The moment we'd gotten out of our truck, the inquisitive animal had raced over to sniff out any signs of trouble.

"She's the dog from the bin Laden raid," the woman called from across the gravel parking area. This salutation was unexpected. Were we meant to be intimidated or reassured by the dog's bin Laden bloodline?

The dog's owner ambled over to chat up Chris. She launched right into Bridger's backstory. Dog used in bin Laden raid. Rescue animal. Superintelligent. Great with kids.

I kept my distance. But as we headed toward the water, the woman's astonishing claim kept nagging at me.

Hold up a sec. This dog, this very dog right here in an obscure pullout along Highway 14A on the North Fork Tongue River, *this* is the dog famous for taking part in the 2011 Navy SEAL raid on Osama bin Laden's compound in Pakistan? The dog that helped take out the most notorious terrorist of the century? The dog the *New York Post* celebrated beneath the headline "Zero Bark Thirty"? A rescue? I know we treat our veterans like yesterday's trash in this country, but even a hero of this stature had been kicked to the curb? That dog was this dog? What were the chances?

The woman's story was a whopper, even for fishermen. I needed confirmation. I crunched across the lot in my rubber boots, keenly aware of the inadequacy of the forthcoming attempt to present myself as a fellow dog person.

"Excuse me, hi, hey, hello, whoa there poochie, nice doggie, good doggie, down girl," I said, brushing away a determined snout. "I couldn't help overhearing you saying your dog took part in the raid that killed Osama bin Laden. That's amazing." Though I didn't actually add the words "and total bullshit," the mirthless coda running through my mind was pretty clearly implied.

"Oh, no, no." The woman walked back the brag with a little smile. "She's a Belgian Malinois. That's the breed of dog that was used in the bin Laden raid."

"Ahhhh, okay," I said. "That makes more sense."

I stood there trying to pet Bridger, but she kept bobbing and weaving like a welterweight warming up in the locker room. I didn't really need any more information, but the woman was eager to embellish.

"She might have some German shepherd in her. And lab. We're not sure. She's a rescue," she said.

"Yeah, I heard that."

Okay. So one mystery solved. Not the actual bin Laden dog. Just the same type of dog. More or less. But larger questions remained.

Why would anyone in God's green acre (folksy idioms tend to roll off the tongue when you're in Wyoming) feel an appropriate way of breaking the ice with a pair of strangers would be to associate their pet with the architect of the most notorious foreign terror strike since Pearl Harbor? Were Chris and I simply in the presence of an unusual overreach at virtue signaling? Was this just typical pleased-with-themselves rescue owner braggadocio? Have pets finally replaced children as the fallback conversation starter of the times? Or was something more meaningful going on?

EVERYWHERE YOU LOOK, Americans are signaling status in new ways. We live in a time when "ugly shoes" (Balenciaga-issued Crocs, as of this writing) and flashy water bottles (VitaJuwel for the gym) inspire envy in the way a pair of Louis Vuittons or a Baccarat Harmonie crystal whiskey decanter might; an era in which your CEO might just as easily show up for work in baggy jeans and a hoodie as a set of snazzy Tom Ford separates or Louboutin heels.

Nothing is uniform. But it's not just a matter of replacing networks with Netflix or Testarossas for Teslas. Shifting tastes indicate shifting values.

Shortly after my encounter with the bin Laden dog, a pair of startling stories that appeared in news feeds across the country illustrated the point. They caught my attention for offering immeasurable new information about status; a commodity, I've always assumed, that's perpetually in short supply.

The first was from the Columbia Business School in New York. It made an astounding claim. According to a study conducted at the school, a "busy and overworked lifestyle, rather than a leisurely lifestyle, has become an aspirational status symbol."

Overwork as a status symbol? Hey, great news coal miners, hotel maids, and burned-out staff in every "streamlined" American workplace employing fewer people to do more work: you guys clocking sixty-hour workweeks, answering texts from colleagues on the john, and checking work emails in bed are moving on up!

The idea sounded preposterous. Weren't the study's authors simply retrofitting an optimistic aspiration—elevated social status—to the dismal reality that companies are working their employees harder while keeping wages stagnant and providing substandard benefits? By promoting a fantasy of grindstone prestige, weren't the Columbia professors complicit in corporate America's HR snow job of an increasingly powerless workforce? I tracked down one of the professors involved in the research to ask.

"Nowadays work has become more than when Charlie Chaplin used to go to the factory to work a shift and earn his wage and go home," Columbia associate professor of business Silvia Bellezza told me. "Especially for white-collar people, it's gone far beyond a workplace where you earn a salary and go back home. Work is where you build social bonds and receive other benefits from employment. The paradigm of spending money on expensive stuff or spending time on leisure as a status signal, they've basically become obsolete."

Bellezza's opinion isn't unprecedented. In her 2017 book, *The Sum of Small Things*, University of Southern California public policy professor Elizabeth Currid-Halkett extolled the "overworked lifestyle" more bluntly: "The leisure class no longer exists. . . . Abundance of leisure no longer indicates higher status."

EVEN HARDER TO get my head around was a second story, which publicized the latest ranking of America's most prestigious law firms. This is an annual list published by Vault, a Massachusetts-based career information company. As the *New York Times* reported, "In one of the most prestige-obsessed industries, the title of the No. 1 firm went—for the second year in a row—to Cravath, Swaine & Moore. The venerable firm had knocked its rival Wachtell, Lipton, Rosen & Katz off the top perch to No. 2."

This sounded about right. Two of New York's top law firms duking it out for prestige supremacy.

But here's the peculiar part. Vault never defined the parameters of "prestige." It provided no metrics, system, criteria, or explanation of the rationale behind its rankings. Neither did any of the many news outlets that reported on the survey. To put together its list, the company simply asked eighteen thousand associates at large- and medium-sized law firms to score firms other than their own on a ten-point scale, "according to how prestigious the firms are in the legal industry."

They didn't tell them how to figure what "prestige" meant or how points on the scale might be calculated. Not since those old Andre Agassi ads for Canon has the "image is everything" mantra been so dubiously applied. How, you might wonder, could you task eighteen thousand people to rate anything without providing common guidelines or means for gauging the subject?

The answer is shockingly simple: *It's because no one can adequately define prestige.*

"It is a little squishy," admitted Matt Moody, the Vault editor who oversaw the study. "We allow the list to maintain the slippery, nebulous essence that is prestige."

As with Bellezza, I'd called Moody shortly after his survey came out. Moody is a graduate of Georgetown University Law Center and a member of the New York Bar. In conversation he conveys a thoughtful, methodical personality. This made his "slippery, nebulous essence" answer, as well as the survey's non-methodical methodology, even more puzzling.

"The legal industry is very much a prestige-focused group, lawyers and law students alike," he told me. "Law firms are very much focused on where a given firm ranks and where they move year to year.

"Any movement of a firm up or down the list even a space or two gets heavily scrutinized. I get asked all the time why this or that firm got moved up or down. I really don't have an answer for that."

This cavalier approach to an empirical definition of status is a given in the $1.1 trillion global luxury industry. What other business worth so much would be so casual in defining its very essence?

"I'm astonished by the number of people working in luxury who don't have a clue to what luxury really is," says Robin Lent, whose guide to the modern luxury market, *Selling Luxury*, has been translated into six languages. "They simply don't know!"

This hasn't always been the case. As we'll see in coming chapters, basic arrangements of status have existed since the dawn of civilization. Judeo-Christian beliefs about prestige and luxury preceded the Enlightenment and informed Western thought into the modern age. In the twentieth century, these notions were broadly codified, if not calcified, within the context of mass consumerism. They've since become inextricably entwined with the foundations of contemporary society, including capitalism, the global economy, and social media.

Now, however, and for the first time since the Industrial Revolution, popular definitions of status, luxury, and, notably, privilege are changing—dramatically. It's true that time-honored markers of excess still illuminate a particular prestige path. Gucci didn't outfit Rihanna for a Christmas soiree in a pair of $1,300 crystal-studded socks for nothing. But in a world in which stray dogs and unpaid overtime have become symbols of virtue, it shouldn't be surprising that the notion of status now often as not conforms to the famous Supreme Court definition of pornography—you know it when you see it, and usually have mixed feelings about it when you do.

MY CALLS TO Bellezza and Moody were the start of an investigation into the people, concepts, and rules beneath the shifting sands of status. This inquiry went far deeper than I'd intended or imagined possible. One of the things I found most compelling were the odds-defying accomplishments of figures who remain virtually unknown to the general public, yet who have had immense influence in reshaping commonly held views of status, prestige, and privilege. Many of their stories appear in the pages that follow, examples of the cataclysm sweeping the luxe landscape.

Something else I hadn't appreciated before launching myself into this rarified arena is the size of the global industry working to evolve, promote, and sell status. We're all familiar with haute couture brands— Cartier, Prada, Valentino, Versace. Even uncultured brutes know what "haute couture" means (overpriced). But these names are mere blips on the radar of distinction.

As we career ever faster into a bifurcated world of have-lots and have-nots, our global corporate overlords have become obsessed with luxury. Business schools have dutifully followed suit. Colleges and universities around the world are filled with faculty and students cranking out market studies either at the behest of or to attract corporate underwriters. Inside the Columbia Business School, Bellezza told me, twenty to twenty-five people are actively researching luxury-related topics at any given time. Makes sense. A business school ought to know where the business is.

In any month of the year, from London, Paris, and Dubai to Shanghai, Las Vegas, and New York, you can for a hefty fee join a crowd of executives, middle managers, researchers, professors, publicists, consultants, data collectors, marketers, publishers, editors, and journalists at industry conferences such as the Monaco Symposium on Luxury (which focuses on the latest academic research), the International Conference on Luxury, Fashion and Design (fashion), Engage! (luxury weddings), the *Financial Times'* Business of Luxury summit (commerce), the IELP Expo (emigration and property advice for Asian high rollers relocating to the United States, Canada, and other Western countries), the Luxury Products Group Expo (prestige plumbing fixtures, no shit), and dozens more. Even as the coronavirus pandemic battered world economies and shut down countless events, gatherings of prestige connoisseurs continued to convene.

One of the big conundrums facing contemporary status makers is reconciling the fact that while a product's prestige is often based on scarcity and cost, in order to attain the global influence necessary to remain competitive within an increasingly saturated luxury market a consolidated brand must now attract a mass following. The concepts of scarcity and mass production are at odds. This wasn't such a big problem before women from Tallahassee to Terre Haute could order Sabina Savage scarves without ever leaving their trailers and the world became so saturated with Maersk shipping containers that people started building homes out of them. How is BMW supposed to retain its reputation for elitism when its cars are routinely piloted by middle school math teachers and Applebee's managers? Does BMW ownership elevate the status of working schlubs? Or does their allegiance to the product devalue the brand?

To address this problem, today's status leaders are promoting an idea that on the surface sounds like an oxymoron: *Prestige is proletariat, exclusivity is for everyone.* Like Orwell's infamous incantation—*War is peace, freedom is slavery, ignorance is strength*—the gestalt behind this new rule of status makes little sense to the neophyte. Spend time with prestige alchemists, though, and you soon appreciate the unabashed ways in which our ideas about luxury and status are being deconstructed and re-created.

Long before any of us were born, status has been considered a finite commodity in a zero sum game. If I had status that meant you and others had less. This paradigm is what the status revolution seeks to overturn. Status is no longer for the gilded elect. It's for everyone.

This might sound suspiciously communistic. In fact it's the opposite. It's a nakedly capitalist twist on the eternal values of *liberté, égalité, fraternité*. "Power socialism" if you prefer. It's an imperative driven in equal parts by corporate exigency, scientific inquiry, social wish fulfillment, and individual demand.

At first, the idea that "status is for everyone" made no sense to me. By definition, "status" separates the prized from the insignificant. Gradually, though, I came to understand this odd little axiom as the foundation of an entirely new system of status, prestige, and privilege, one that's been injected with the rocket fuel of the social and racial justice uprisings of recent years. Through the course of this book I hope to make you, too, understand the new and occasionally paradoxical rules of the status game.

IF ALMOST NO one has any idea what status and prestige are anymore, one thing is certain—the order they've traditionally provided is being disrupted. No wonder the country has become so dysfunctional.

You think our chronic social angst is a reaction to climate change, social upheaval, and a nation of educated adults that has somehow elected a government of children and dilettantes to lead it? Listen, we've survived rich, old white presidents before—this country was founded by a bunch of those guys—we'll survive this one. And the one after him. Natural disasters? Read up on the history of fires, earthquakes, floods, and catastrophic public school curriculum. We're gonna make it. Foreign threats? The United States has been fighting Islam since the marines invaded those infamous shores of Tripoli in 1805. We've been hammer and tongs with Russia for more than a century, starting with U.S. troops landing at Vladivostok to secure the American consulate there in 1908. North Korea? Truman weighed the pros and cons of dropping nukes on them in 1950.

The broader issue, the reason for so much hostility and existential anxiety across society, is that we no longer know how to measure our value and standing among our fellow citizens. Or, increasingly, the world. Every animal community arranges itself on a pecking order. For humans, the symbols of that order traditionally have been easy to recognize—the biggest brontosaurus burger, brightest tulips, frilliest collars and cuffs, flashiest Ferrari. The better that members of a society understand their position within the group, the more civilly they behave, the more society functions in a prosperous fashion. As Nobel Laureate economist John Harsanyi noted: "Apart from economic payoffs, social status seems to be the most important incentive and motivating force of social behavior."

Researchers have long understood the critical need for easily deciphered status markers. Lack of clear position cues, for one example, has been identified as a major problem for military veterans readjusting to civilian society. "In the military, you can walk into any meeting, do a quick scan of the room, and tell by looking at everyone's collar who outranks you, who's subordinate to you, who's on your level," says Todd Crevier, a U.S. Army Iraq combat vet who now runs a New England nonprofit that helps soldiers with PTSD recalibrate to civilian life. "In the civilian world that explicit indication of rank doesn't exist. You'd be surprised how disorienting this can be."

It's not just vets that get confused. As that Vault law firm survey shows, sorting out the terms of status practically requires a Nobel Laureate intellect. But it's important to do.

Some may argue that status is simply an artificial construct with no subjective validity. Technically, that's true. But it doesn't mean status is unimportant. In fact, among all the constructs in what historian and philosopher Yuval Noah Harari calls the "imagined order" that governs all human societies, it's the most vital, even more (with apologies to Professor Harsanyi) than the imagined value of money. Social hierarchies and the baubles that represent them are what allow human beings to cooperate on a mass level, from observing laws (also imagined constructs) to ordering copies of Harari's *Sapiens: A Brief History of Humankind* online and being confident in their delivery. Status establishes order; symbols act as proxies for that order; it's rarely fair, but if we want to avoid chaos it's necessary. As Harari writes, "We believe in a particular order not because it is objectively true, but because believing in it enables us to cooperate effectively and forge a better society.

"Sapiens," he goes on to say, "instinctively divide humanity into two parts, 'we' and 'they.'" But as the world marches toward global economic and political unity, we've arrived at an inflection point. The we/they paradigm is being blurred. Along with it, recognizable lines of status, rank, and prestige are dissipating—at least for those on the spear tip of progress.

This might all sound hyperbolic or frivolous. It's not. If social order is properly understood it can help save America by bringing it back from the brink of dissolution. The unprecedented (at least since the Civil War) conflicts we're now experiencing are plainly rooted in the uncertainty people feel about their position in an increasingly complicated society. The anxiety this causes reverberates through demographic schisms—race, gender, religion, geographic, urban-rural, mushrooms–no mushrooms, or any other fulcrum of communal friction you care to cite.

This is a peaceful revolution. Or should be. Like printing presses, electricity, telephones, cable TV, or Minecraft. There's no need to fight it. If we understand the new world of status and let the revolution play out, society will sooner rather than later reorganize on a more equitable plane.

One's place in the world need not be diminished simply because another's is being elevated. Fears of loss of rank are largely unfounded. The new rules of status assure us that those with status are none the poorer when others attain it; nor that those seeking to improve their position must do so at the expense of others.

Don't worry. I'm not going to spend the next two hundred and whatever pages preaching my politics, religion, environmental ardor, humanitarian empathy, or superior musical taste. While it's occasionally satisfying to shout at our benighted fellow citizens on social media, internet comments, radio talk shows, podcasts, and school board meetings, it's almost always counterproductive.

Cultural cohesion is just a subtext to this story. But it's an important one given the threats that social divisions pose to the country—and the world. A greater appreciation of the new theory of status can ameliorate a lot of problems. A key takeaway is the way our views of status, luxury, and privilege are changing, and how ultimately this should be a good thing for everyone.

A REQUISITE FOR understanding any subculture is communicating with the community in its own language. Following the murky practice of those in the biz in this book, I'm going to employ the malleable terms "luxury," "prestige," "status," and "elite" more or less interchangeably, while acknowledging their shaded differences. I arrived at the broad definitions below after consulting with Robin Lent; French brand strategists and coauthors of the industry bible *The Luxury Strategy*, Jean-Noël Kapferer and Vincent Bastien; and every toastmaster's trusty pals Merriam and Webster.

- "Luxury" applies to a durable good, service, or condition that adds comfort or status to one's life, while not being truly necessary—supersized drinks, $120 massages, and a 2010 Ducati Desmosedici GP10 that sold at auction for $325,430 all count.
- "Prestige" means the standing or admiration a person or product enjoys in the eyes of others. Unlike luxury, prestige isn't bought, it's earned or transmitted through reputation. However, on occasion I'll refer to a "prestige product" as a consumer item that signals prestige or status.

- "Status" refers to the social, professional, or other standing of a person or thing in relation to others. In the music world, Frank Ocean enjoys higher status than BlöödHag (actual Seattle band) or Anal Bleaching (gig-challenged UK band).
- "Elite" is . . . Well, you get it, right?

While each of these concepts is separate, each informs the other with a kind of gauzy, ill-defined logic. Hence: an invite to join Donald Trump Jr.'s elite luxury hunting expedition is prestigious and will affect your status within the community—discuss.

FOR MORE THAN a century our understanding of status has been rooted in the retrograde assumptions of religious institutions, Enlightenment ethics, and social science disciplines traditionally informed by Victorian-era ethos. Brilliant as they undoubtedly were, inveterate moralizers like Thorstein Veblen, John Kenneth Galbraith, and Vance Packard—famed status philosophers from whom we'll soon hear more—have cast a long shadow of derision upon the basic human drive for status and its sibling impulses for luxury and privilege. Synthesizing centuries of establishment distrust in humanity, their disapproving ideas about "conspicuous consumption" and "status seeking" have formed the cornerstones of popular censure.

Today, with far more sophisticated methods of research at their disposal, a vastly more dynamic and culturally inclusive array of scholars and entrepreneurs is challenging hidebound beliefs. Revolutionary concepts, many with origins in idealistic counterculture movements of the 1960s, have been able to flower only in recent years and are now convulsing ideas about luxury consumerism. Totemic notions of status—the most influential of which are still clung to by some in academia and popular media—are nevertheless being rendered obsolete.

This isn't a book about famous designer brands or orgies of overindulgence. Yes, the Fendis, Ferraris, and Ferragamos will inevitably appear—a few already have. But even if I cared about them, the preferences of the rich, famous, and gauche have already been covered more expertly and exhaustively than a guy in my tax bracket could ever hope to fake. Years ago I walked through St. Mark's Square in Venice, Italy. Looking around at all the designer shops that lined the historic piazza I thought, "Who comes all the way to Venice to buy the same overpriced business suit or necklace you can buy in Frankfurt, Nagoya, or Atlanta?" The fact is, bling bores me and always has. I never watched a single episode of *MTV Cribs*, nor regretted the hole left in my cultural fluency for not partaking.

It turns out I'm not alone. A rebellion against traditional measures of status, prestige, luxury, and privilege is underway. It's taken hold at all levels of society. It's swamping the status industry, from the academics who track and analyze it to the philosophers who explain it, the companies that manufacture it, the marketers that promote it, the retailers that sell it, the media that popularize it, and the consumers who buy it.

This book is about that rebellion. The social forces that brought it into existence (including efforts to assert social and judicial justice), the people behind it, how the public and commercial worlds are reacting to it, where it's going, and what it says about society.

I had to travel all the way to Wyoming to find the bin Laden dog owner—to that woman on the riverbank I dedicate this book—but I'd have to go much farther to find the true source of that memorable encounter. If the modern mavens of status had decreed that owning a rescue dog was suddenly a privilege to be savored like a Dalmore 62 (if you have to ask you probably won't like it), I figured that was a good place to start.

CHAPTER 1

The woman who invented rescue dogs:
STATUS AS VIRTUE SIGNALING

IN THE LATE 1980S, THE PENINSULA HUMANE SOCIETY HAD A problem. Despite robust education and outreach programs, it wasn't seeing positive results in its efforts to reduce the local homeless dog and cat overpopulation through adoption campaigns. Adoptions of what were then widely referred to as "shelter dogs" weren't unheard of, but when most people decided to get a dog, their first stop was a pet store or breeder.

"The statistics were flat," recalls its executive director at the time. "Numbers were just flat. We interviewed PR companies. We did various milquetoast-y campaigns like other shelters were doing. It was like, 'What else can we do?'"

PHS was (and still is) located in San Mateo, California, one of the most affluent and progressive parts of the San Francisco Bay Area. Meaning one of the most affluent and progressive parts of the world. Stanford University was twenty minutes away. With new tech already burbling in local garages and start-up back rooms, it'd soon become home to Silicon Valley titans like Franklin Templeton, Sony Interactive, GoPro, and SolarCity. After Facebook went public in 2012, turning hundreds of stock-holding employees into millionaires, San Mateo County became the richest county in America, with residents bringing home an annual average income of $168,000.

Even before that, every ingredient for a community supportive of animal welfare issues was in place—well-off, pet-loving people with yards who readily attached themselves to progressive causes. Yet no appeal PHS made on behalf of its beleaguered shelter animals could persuade its affluent, bleeding-heart neighbors to adopt a pet.

The situation in San Mateo wasn't unique. Despite growing public awareness of animal welfare issues, humane societies and animal shelters across the country were banging their heads against the same walls, running the same gratuitous spay and neuter campaigns, failing to move the needle.

Lots of dogs. Lots of dog lovers. Little community response.

Lots of frustration.

DOG OVERPOPULATION HAS been a problem in North America pretty much since the Spaniards arrived with purpose-bred "war dogs" brought to terrorize Native American communities. Their dogs ran rampant, leading to nasty offspring nobody wanted.

The Spanish may have been the country's original negligent pet owners, but they were hardly alone. In 1800s New York, the problem became so acute that packs of strays were rounded up on a daily basis, placed in iron-barred crates—some holding forty or fifty animals at a time—and drowned in the East River. A spot near the river on East Twenty-sixth Street earned the grim moniker "the canine bathtub." In a single morning there in 1877, 738 dogs and 20 puppies were cast into the water.

Cities like Philadelphia and St. Louis employed street thugs to chase down stray dogs and simply club them to death. According to one account, early in his Dodge City days, Wyatt Earp made a living as an animal control officer. The gunslinger was renowned for his ability to drop rabid dogs with a few quick rounds from long range.

By the 1940s and '50s, spay and neuter campaigns had come into fashion. Controversial at first, these efforts helped control animal populations. Public opinion swung around. In 1979, Bob Barker began signing off *The Price Is Right* broadcasts with the now-famous tagline "Always spay or neuter your pets." By the 1980s, however, it was evident that, even with the support of the daytime titan's sturdy mien, simply defrocking dogs and cats wasn't going to eliminate overpopulation. Both house pets and strays have a lot of time on their hands. They tend to multiply faster than humans can keep them in check.

FEW PEOPLE IN the country were more aggrieved by all this than Kim Sturla. As she was growing up, a dog lover from the cradle, Sturla's most treasured companion was her beloved Samantha Jane. Young Kim took the shaggy, mixed-breed poodle everywhere she went. This eventually included the campus of UC Berkeley, where Samantha Jane attended nearly every class alongside her master. All those dogs you see today tromping around Home Depot, Cabela's, Safeway, and your ex-favorite brewpub? Sturla was pushing that envelope long before anyone imagined you'd need rules telling people not to bring animals into places where they sell food and clothing.

After graduating from Berkeley in 1971, Sturla went to work for the Peninsula Humane Society, overseeing education programs. A long-practicing vegan, she, like a whole generation of budding animal rights activists, was inspired by two books: Peter Singer's 1975 *Animal Liberation* and Tom Regan's 1983 *The Case for Animal Rights*. Both are seminal tomes of the animal rights movement.

Sturla was especially impressed by Regan, a philosophy professor at North Carolina State University. Every page of his book underscores a simple message: "First, that animals have certain basic moral rights and, second, that recognition of their rights requires fundamental changes in our treatment of them."

Regan was appalled by animal euthanasia, the go-to method for dealing with unwanted creatures. In fact, he didn't even regard it as euthanasia, a word derived from the Greek meaning something like "good death."

"To persist in calling such practices 'euthanizing animals' is to wrap plain killing in a false verbal cover," he wrote. "It is no more true to say that healthy dogs and cats are euthanized when they are 'put to sleep' to make room for other cats and dogs at animal shelters than it would be true to say that healthy derelicts would be euthanized if they were 'put to sleep' to make room for other derelicts at human shelters."

Regan argued that changing the status quo would require a radical crusade. Prejudices die hard, he said, especially when they're entrenched in social customs and beliefs, protected by powerful economic interests, and enshrined in law.

"The animal rights movement is not for the faint of heart," he wrote. "Success requires nothing less than a revolution in our culture's thought and action."

After years of polite publicity efforts at the shelter, Sturla concluded Regan was right. Enough milquetoast. Real change would require militant tactics. The second catalyst for what was to become her revolutionary idea, however, ended up coming from a more mainstream source.

"I'll never forget, it was David Louie with KGO-TV in San Francisco," Sturla told me when I reached her at the Animal Place, a sanctuary for farm animals in Northern California that she cofounded. "I told him, 'I'm wracking my brains on how can we get better coverage on this issue.' He said something to the effect that every shelter in every city is faced with the same problem—'There's no hook, nothing new and sexy about rescue animals.'"*

Louie's frank assessment of mass messaging triggered something in

---

* David Louie, incidentally, is one of those mild-mannered, local TV institutions, a guy who's been covering the news for San Francisco's ABC affiliate since the mid-1970s. Not a dude Bay Area viewers might expect to channel Gavin Rossdale's "There's no sex in your violence" ethos on behalf of the nation's downtrodden brutes. Then again, how less interesting would history be without its unlikely supporting players?

Sturla, who had by now become PHS's executive director. If humane societies didn't have a hook for the media, she reasoned, they had the next best thing—a needle. Lots of them actually.

Thing was, no one had ever seen them. Sturla decided to change that. "Most shelters do a great job of protecting the public from the grisly aspect of dog and cat rescue," Sturla told me. "They sanitize the horrible, horrible reality of just killing animals because you ran out of room. Killing healthy, wonderful beings had become kind of the default. I wanted people to see firsthand the repercussions of their decisions."

In October 1990, under Sturla's direction, the Peninsula Humane Society purchased four-page advertising inserts in the *San Francisco Chronicle* and other local newspapers. The design and message of the inserts were outlandish, even by today's vulgarized standards. A screamer headline on the front page of the insert read: *This is one HELL of a job.* Inside, splashed across two full pages, readers were treated to an enormous photo of three industrial barrels filled to the brim with dead cats in various stages of rigor mortis. Above them loomed an accusatory headline: *And we couldn't do it without you.*

For the Bay Area's Sunday-morning coffee-and-comics crowd, the nightmarish depiction of the daily stray animal euthanasia toll hit like a sucker punch. It was sort of like waking up and finding . . . three barrels of dead cats in your house! And being implicated in the crime.

Adults were outraged. Children cried. Sturla answered the onslaught of angry calls and hate mail. Then followed up by inviting reporters to cover what one called a "public pet execution" of four kittens, a cat, and three dogs. TV cameras whirred as a veterinarian injected a quivering pup with a lethal dose of sodium pentobarbital. Within seconds it was dead, then dumped in a trash can atop a pile of puppies and kittens.

"One reporter cried, another began adoption proceedings, and a third left the room because the dog being killed resembled one he once owned," reported the *New York Times.*

Sturla's stunt turned into a national story. "You have to see it to experience the immorality of it," Sturla told the *Times* in defense of her ghastly tactics. Thirty years later, she recalled for me the emotional impact in vivid detail.

"One media person said to me, 'That seems so extreme!'" she said. "All I could say was 'You wanna see extreme? Follow me to the euthanasia room. Observe us having to take the life of this precious dog.' You kill them and you put them in the chill room until the rendering company can come by and pick them up."

NOW SEVENTY-TWO, STURLA can be found most of the time at Animal Place, a six-hundred-acre farmland animal refuge about an hour east of Sacramento. On the warm autumn afternoon I spent at her sanctuary, Sturla was dressed in faded blue jeans and a white long-sleeve T-shirt. Her shoulder-length straight hair is mostly gray, but with gold hoop earrings and stylish rectangular black-framed glasses she looks and moves twenty years younger than her age. In her sparsely furnished office—seventies wood paneling, a stand-up metal file cabinet, framed pictures of pigs, dogs, and chicks—she leaned back in a chair and propped her white Nikes on the desktop.

"That was a time when folks needed to be shaken up," she said when I asked about the *Chronicle* insert that changed the course of lapdog history. "I didn't care what people said about me. If I'm letting society guide what steps I'm taking I ain't doing my job."

From rescuing dogs and cats Sturla has moved on to a bigger battle. Ninety-eight percent of animals killed in the United States are farm animals. Animal Place takes in cows, pigs, sheep, goats, turkeys, rabbits, and other salvages, including about four thousand hens a year from the egg industry.

"To fight the agricultural industry, it's a borderline impossible task, but you still gotta do it," she said.

"Is your mission to make everyone vegan?" I asked.

"Sure. But more than that it's about fostering kindness and compassion," she replied. "Ultimately it's about inspiring a change of behavior. From understanding, empathy usually follows."

Sturla led me on a property tour, the same one that schoolkids bus out to Animal Place to take. This is the mythical farm where your parents supposedly took the secretly murdered Duffy the dog or Friskies the cat to roam away its days free and happy. Along the way I met Daffodil, an old, blind milk cow, and Wilbur, a pig the size of a prizewinning hog I once made my sister pose next to at the Ohio State Fair.

"Belly rubs and butt scratches, there's not a pig I know that doesn't love 'em," Sturla murmured as she knelt in the dirt to massage the reclining beast.

"I love you, too, I do, I love you, too," Sturla reassured him. Wilbur seemed to smile.

I know people who find this type of devotion to livestock bonkers—I'm sort of one of them—but for all her laid-back congeniality, when Sturla gets going her assertive manner makes her sound more like a fast-track movie executive than a good-hearted farmhand. She's unfailingly polite, but talking with her is tricky. I've interviewed thousands of people in my life—few have been better at making me feel inadequate or unprepared with a terse, one-word answer.

In the way of big personalities, of course, these were the precise qualities PHS needed to push through its agenda. Sturla's shock-and-paw (sorry, that one slipped through final copyedit) campaign turned out to be just the opening salvo of a broader war. Two weeks after the kitty carnage insert came out, PHS announced it had written an ordinance—meaning Sturla had written an ordinance—proposing a ban on the for-profit breeding of cats and dogs. The law even called for fining animal owners who simply allowed their pets to reproduce. The proposal was brought before the San Mateo County Board of Supervisors. Thought to be the first of its kind in the nation, the law, which eventually required owners of dogs and cats to buy a breeding license or get their pets sterilized, was aggressively opposed by professional breeders.

Sturla still fizzes with pride recalling the eventual adoption of her ordinance—which she lobbied for relentlessly—and subsequent legislative victories that have expanded on the idea that breeders and "puppy mills" are literal crimes against nature . . . or at least against the state of California.

"To get the media on your side you gotta give them a hook," she repeated to me. "So that was a big part of it. But I didn't want us to do any kind of campaign, hard-hitting or soft, that was gonna be business as usual."

After the controversial insert was published, most people did, in fact, go back to business as usual the following week. But a small group of literal "early adopters" had been awakened to something new—something exclusive, emotional, uplifting, and, most important of all, virtuous. And this was the key: to spread their message, to generate maximum positive impact, they needed others to recognize that virtue.

The act of rescue proffers nobility upon the rescuer. For Sturla, the transmission of that goodness was no less important than the rescue itself. From church tithing to baronial largesse, conspicuous do-gooderism has a long pedigree. But adding the salvation of man's best friend was like adding a motor to the wheel. Enhancing it with the virtuous expression of "rescue" was like putting high-octane in the tank—although Sturla can't take credit for that one.

"I don't know where the term 'rescue' was first used," Sturla said. "It just sort of evolved."

STURLA'S MESSAGE TRAVELED far. And fast. The term "rescue dog" had been around for decades—"re-homed" was tried by shelters, but it never caught on—but now it went coastal. Rescue dogs were in vogue. "No-kill" shelters began flourishing across the country. For trendsetters, a dog was no longer a pet. It was a badge of honor. A badge that said "I am a good person, I care about living creatures, I am virtuous, I am better than other pet owners." It conveyed status, but a new kind of status, one disconnected from wealth, talent, intelligence, success, religious or professional standing.

Pet euthanasia rates had been slowly declining since the 1970s, largely due to cheaper spay and neuter methods. But in the early 1990s, following Sturla's campaign, they began falling sharply, from an estimated 17 million a year in the mid-1980s to below 6 million by 1992, and down to 920,000 by 2021.

When the movement hit critical mass, the numbers started moving in the opposite direction. Dog-owning households increased by 36 percent between 2006 and 2020 to 49 million households—38 percent of U.S. homes now have a dog. (Cat ownership has remained largely unchanged over the past decade.)

The fastest-growing group of pets by far is rescue dogs. Adoptions surged in the midst of the coronavirus pandemic. According to one estimate, 8 percent of pet owners adopted a pet because of the pandemic, presumably because stay-at-home practices made doing so more attractive and feasible. In the early weeks of the outbreak Foster Dogs, Inc., reported a more than 1,000 percent increase in foster applications in the New York area. The marketing firm Packaged Facts estimated a 4 percent increase in U.S. pet ownership during the pandemic.

As Sturla will gladly recite for you, all manner of laws are now on the books to help facilitate the proliferation of rescues. More than 230 U.S. cities have passed bans on the sale of dogs and cats raised by professional breeders, whose fortunes have waned as the revenge of the mutts has become complete. In 2017, California passed a statewide law forbidding pet stores from selling any dog or cat not obtained from a shelter, humane society, or rescue group. Some rescue dogs might now be said to enjoy more legal protection than the rights of certain citizens to vote. Peak status was achieved in January 2021 when the Biden family's two-year-old German shepherd, Major, became the first shelter dog to take up residence in the White House—the First Rescue, so to speak.

Sturla profoundly influenced the way people think about dogs and cats. Her Bay Area rescue campaign turned into a movement that now spans the planet.

I HEAR THE murmur of skeptics.

"Interesting story. Never heard of Sturla. Seems like the proverbial 'piece of work.' But what do a moral crusader from California and a bunch of rescue mutts spared the ultimate needle have to do with prestige? This isn't what I picked your book out of the remainders bin and paid two dollars for."

To those who paid the full hardcover price after plucking the book from the "employee recommendations" shelf at their local brick-and-mortar, I respectfully respond: "Fair enough. I get that stray dogs don't immediately leap to mind when someone introduces the topic of luxury."

But that's the point. The whole idea of status is that in recent years it's been systematically subverted. Unexpected sources of elite standing are everywhere. Overtime is luxury, remember? When a sitting U.S. president can defend the virtue of Nazis and *Arbeit macht frei* becomes a rallying cry in the American workplace, you know the social strata is undergoing intense disturbance.

In the midst of these unprecedented changes, a British journalist named James Bartholomew was struck by the new way people were attaining status. Writing in the *Spectator* in 2015, Bartholomew popularized a term (likely coined in 2004) to describe it: virtue signaling. He described "an increasingly common phenomenon of what might be called virtue signaling—indicating that you are kind, decent, and virtuous."

Bartholomew understood a reach for status lay beneath all virtue signaling. "In the jargon of economics, the assertion of moral superiority is a 'positioned good'—a way of differentiating yourself from others," he wrote.

The rescue dog movement—and the virtue signaling mania it helped ignite—found a seamless handmaiden in another shifting social value. This one was articulated in a widely circulated book written by a Fortune 500 communications coach named Peggy Klaus called *Brag! The Art of Tooting Your Own Horn Without Blowing It.*

"Brag doesn't have to be a distasteful four-letter word," Klaus wrote in 2003, challenging centuries of consensus social morality. "To see bragging in this [positive] way, we have to start by wiping the slate clean and dropping our preconceived notions." In the cutthroat and message-saturated modern marketplace, she contended, self-promotion had become a critical survival skill, especially for business professionals.

What brought virtue signaling from the "discreet" collection-plate sawbuck to look-at-me mainstream acceptance was the notion of personal aggrandizement pushed by Klaus and others interested in self-esteem über alles. Popular culture became littered with self-touting success stories—Howard Stern, Rush Limbaugh, Jim Rome, Bill O'Reilly, Sarah Palin, Kanye. Immodesty morphed from vice to virtue. It reached its zenith with the presidential ascendancy of Donald Trump, the most popular and successful braggart in U.S. history since Muhammad Ali.

THE TIMELY CONVERGENCE of shifting values (virtue signaling, boastfulness) helped, but look closely and you'll find that Kim Sturla turned rescue dogs into status symbols not only by launching her crusade at just the right historical moment, but by employing principles straight out of the "positioned good" playbooks luxury and prestige marketers have been using for years to sell everything from Cire Trudon candles to Gulfstream jets. Sturla told me this wasn't done intentionally. But the parallels are noteworthy. Consider the following seven rules etched in luxury marketing bibles from Marin to Milan, and you'll find the real story behind rescue animals' unlikely rise to the top of the dogpile.

RULE #1: DEFINE YOUR CULTURE

"Luxury is culture." This three-word epigram serves as the running motto of the most influential book on luxury and prestige written in the last half century. *The Luxury Strategy: Break the Rules of Marketing to Build Luxury Brands* is the work of Jean-Noël Kapferer and Vincent Bastien, a pair of French marketing execs who have worked with Louis Vuitton

Malletier, Yves Saint Laurent, Oscar de la Renta, Fendi, and many of the other names that inspired the entire knockoff economy. Now professors at HEC Paris, one of the most prestigious (so they say) business schools in the world, Kapferer and Bastien held sway in the luxury world long before the 2009 publication of their book. The first edition of their guide taught businesses how to sell everything from Evian water to taking baths in Evian water—Serena Williams was the first to wallow in that $6,000 privilege at the Hotel Victor in Miami's South Beach.

One of the pair's main points is that luxury "must . . . be active at a cultural level." To achieve this, they advise those intending to create a sense of prestige around a product to first define themselves by creating a narrative that establishes their cultural identity. Then communicating that identity to a sympathetic community ripe for aligning itself with a brand whose products reflect its shared values.

Ben & Jerry's is a classic example. The company became an ice cream juggernaut in part by aggressively spotlighting its counterculture conscience and the numerous social causes it supports. This gives people a reason to feel good, not guilty, about adding a third scoop of Cherry Garcia to that waffle cone.

Sturla's efforts on behalf of shelter animals mirrored the same approach. After David Louie convinced her of the need for blunt communication, Sturla broadcast an appeal based on a collective cultural value. Like-minded others were galvanized around a simple message: animal murder is bad; animal rescue is good. Straightforward messaging. Clear statement of a dominant cultural principle. "It put the values on the table," Sturla told me, explaining her campaign.

Her appeal also played into another cultural tenet of prestige-culture building.

"Customers want to make a statement about who they are," wrote Robin Lent and coauthor Geneviève Tour in *Selling Luxury.* "At times, they make purchases to be seen as belonging to a certain group. Other times, the reason can be distinctly the opposite, they want their purchase to set them apart from everyone else."

Adopters of rescue dogs achieve both goals—group identity and individual recognition via virtue signaling. Lent and Tour might as well have been describing my Wyoming pal with the bin Laden dog.

RULE #2: IGNORE PRICE

A common misconception among the hoi polloi is that cost confers prestige. Not so, say Kapferer and Bastien: "Price on its own does not make something a luxury." Nor does it confer prestige.

Some confusion around this point is understandable. Most everyone knows a couple nights at an exclusive resort can cost more than the average homeowner's monthly mortgage. Plus car payment. Speaking of which, if your attorney pulls up to the courthouse in a Kia Forte and the other guy's arrives in an Audi R8, you know you're probably screwed.

But money is just one of many factors in the status equation. Consider a bishop or other religious leader who takes a vow of poverty yet attains a level of enormous esteem and lives a life surrounded by finery and luxury goods. Or authors. There's a reason they often say of writers, "He died penniless." But having a book published can land you on TV. At least a podcast.

You can earn prestige by merit, by work, or by efforts if they match the goals that society wants to reward, Kapferer has written. "There is a luxury industry because luxury does not mean anymore being accessible to a niche of richest people."

That last sentence is important. Kapferer calls this principle the heart of the modern luxury strategy. In part this has become true because luxury brands have worked hard to expand and diversify their market. Part of it is due to social movements (to be discussed in more depth shortly) aimed at breaking down barriers that have traditionally defined privilege. Kapferer's explanation is another way of saying prestige is proletariat, exclusivity is for everyone. Price matters, but not always.

Bernard Arnault, CEO of Moët Hennessy–Louis Vuitton, a group with more than sixty brands designed to make you feel inadequate if you let them, famously summarized modern luxury as "the ordinary of extraordinary people and the extraordinary of ordinary people." Arnault's point puts the "extraordinary" appeal of an "ordinary" product like an abandoned animal into proletarian context. It also helps answer the objection that cheap mutts couldn't possibly have a serious connection to the concept of prestige.

RULE #3: APPEAL TO EMOTIONS

Open any fashion magazine and the simulacrum of emotion are as understated as a strutting herd of Victoria's Secret Angels. Romance. Desire. Brooding precoital hollowness. Hollow postcoital brooding. FOMO. Neuromarketers have long understood and exploited the power emotions hold over our rational minds. Commercial appeals based on emotion are meant to provoke feelings of inadequacy, which often lead to the acquisition of products meant to boost self-esteem.

According to a study by Niro Sivanathan of the London Business School and Nathan C. Pettit of Cornell University, low self-esteem is a major factor—often the primary factor—in the purchase of luxury or prestige goods. Their work shows how "individuals whose self-worth was harmed sought affirmation in high-status goods." For prestige marketers, it's a simple formula—and kind of depressing, assuming you're not a prestige marketer—that never changes.

Sturla might have channeled atypical emotions for luxury consumers—outrage, indignation—but the strategy behind her campaign was identical to the one used to sell Hermès handbags and $58,000 golf cart hovercrafts (uh-huh, real thing): make someone feel lousy, then give them something to make them feel better. Studies have shown acquisition of goods with high price tags often make sad people feel happier, but the same principle is at play in ten-dollar-a-pitcher sports bars across the country where culture is strong: there are few economic barriers to group identity, and a small group of athletes stand in for the achievements of an entire community. Your team just got its ass kicked in the Tropical Smoothie Café Frisco Bowl? Have another Coors Light.

The concept is eminently malleable. How does this pile of dead pets make you feel? (Bad.) What if I told you you could save one? (Better.)

RULE #4: TREAT YOUR COMMODITY AS A PRECIOUS OBJECT

When Sturla described rescue animals as "precious" she was tapping into a particularly powerful sales concept. In *Selling Luxury*, Lent and Tour are emphatic that everything in a prestige brand's catalog exists on the same metaphysical plane as a Fabergé egg. Or, at least, that consumers be made to believe so.

The chapter titled "Handle everything you sell as a precious object" is devoted to the idea that "elegance and respect for the creation enhance its value." (FYI: In the artsy language deployed in the use of commercial persuasion, a "creation" means "anything you want to sell.") The point is illustrated with an anecdote of a sales ambassador who nails the sale of a luxury handbag to a mom and daughter by donning white gloves before she "carefully and securely picks up the handbag with two hands and sets it down gently on the tray" on the counter. Did the gloves protect the bag in any way? No, but they created an illusion of fragility, and therefore, luxury. After such an elaborate presentation, the plastic practically flew out of mom's purse in her haste to score the bag.

Suggesting as it does a commodity worthy of a special ops hostage extraction, the term "rescue dog" is an exquisite example of the dialectal embroidery used to inflate an object's preciousness and make its owner feel special for assuming the role of caretaker.

RULE #5: ACCENTUATE FLAWS

Counterintuitive, perhaps, but as any aficionado of British sports cars will tell you, if your baby doesn't come with a few cherished defects it can never be considered truly prestigious.

In the following excerpt from *The Luxury Strategy* section titled "Does your product have enough flaws?" Kapferer and Bastien discuss the difference between state-of-the-art watches and timepieces that denote true luxury. The parallels between purebred and rescue dogs are striking.

> *The aim of an upper-premium brand is to deliver a perfect product, to relentlessly pursue perfection. But it would take a touch of madness for it to be counted a luxury. Functionally, a Seiko watch is superior to many luxury watches—it is more accurate and shows the time directly and in a perfectly legible manner. . . . If you were to buy some of the famous brands of a luxury watch, you would probably be warned that it loses two minutes every year. The flaw is not only known, it is assumed—one could say that that is both its charm and its guarantee of authenticity.*

Who needs practical perfection? Vintage MGs have janky voltage stabilizers. Prized Japanese tea ceremony pottery has cracks. Rescue dogs have undocumented provenance. And, possibly, ringworm.

RULE #6: PROVIDE AN UPLIFTING EXPERIENCE

Kapferer and Bastien view luxury as an "improving force in society." Lent and Tour outline the way consumers buy prestige products to experience "an uplifting impact on their lives."

The classic example is the development of the perfumery business, in particular Chanel No. 5, in the immediate aftermath of World War I. Europe needed something to wash away the stench of gas, rot, and poverty of the Great War. It's no coincidence the country that suffered the worst of the war was the one to cover it up with the most panache. The same impulse drove mainland China into the welcoming arms of global fashion brands as soon as the handcuffs of Communism were removed and the country opened itself to the global market economy.

A more recent example is Everlane. Launched in 2011, the fashion company became a quick success by selling inexpensive "ethical" clothing. Low prices help, but what connects Everlane's legion of devotees is the company's commitment to fair labor—"We spend months finding the best factories around the world," its website boasts—and conspicuous environmentally friendly practices. The company that manufactures Everlane jeans reportedly recycles 98 percent of the water it uses. Led by an internal sustainability committee, Everlane strives to eliminate its use of virgin plastic. The virtue signaling generation has rewarded the brand with enormous sales. *Marketplace* called Everlane "a millennial fever dream."

Insofar as rescues go, nothing drives home the message of self-elevation through virtuous behavior like a visit to HumaneSociety.org. Even before you get to the main adoption page, a pop-up box features an aspiring rescue mutt—sorry, "mixed breed"—morosely imploring you with the question "Will you be my hero?" The site's top reasons to adopt a pet include "because you'll save a life" and "because of the bragging rights." The message of self-affirmation you're meant to walk away with after adopting an orphaned animal is far from subliminal. Perform a gallant act. Broadcast it. That's virtue signaling in a dog biscuit.

From the point of brand repositioning, Sturla's decision to transform a mundane transaction like buying a stray dog into an activity worthy of public admiration was a textbook move in creating an "uplifting" purchasing experience.

RULE #7: REDIRECT FROM THE COMPETITION

Whether you're selling hip-hop downloads to teenagers or Armani suits to Mafia dons, the first rule of image marketing is defining who you are not. Punk rock, for example, was first about hating fourteen-minute drum solos and the meandering bloat of corporate rock.

Bartholomew understood how anger and redirection fit into the new force of status he saw taking shape. "It's noticeable how often virtue signaling consists of saying you hate things," he wrote in that *Spectator* piece. "The emphasis on hate distracts from the fact that you are really saying how good you are."

This last point in the campaign to bring rescue dogs to mass-market popularity may have been the most important one. From its inception, the rescue movement pointed fingers—middle ones, usually—at the competition: purebred dogs and the people who raise them. "For anybody who has worked or volunteered with animal shelters or rescue groups, the focus has always been to redirect your adopter away from breeders and pet stores to your local shelter," Sturla told me. The movement redirected pet owners away from breeders (the competition) by showing "the inherent cruelty in purposely breeding animals in a puppy mill or small backyard breeder."

MANY VIEW STURLA as a heroine of the animal kingdom. For others, however, she's closer to heroin.

For three decades now, Sturla's most dogged critic has been a woman named Patti Strand. In 1991, as a reaction to what she saw as a misinformation campaign aimed at people like herself, Strand cofounded the National Animal Interest Alliance. She's still president of the organization. Over the years, the NAIA has attained a high profile in the animal welfare community for tracking legislation, lobbying on behalf of its members, and providing a media voice of advocacy for the breeding industry, all as a countermeasure to the agenda pushed by Sturla and her fellow rescue proponents.

Although the NAIA doesn't explicitly say so, its values are closely aligned with the American Kennel Club, the largest purebred dog registry in the world and the governing body for more than twenty-two thousand dog competitions and events a year. The kind of shows Sturla calls "nothing short of obscene." Strand served on the AKC's board of directors for sixteen years. Her accolades include an AKC Lifetime Achievement Award, being named Dogdom's Woman of the Year in 1993, and a Fido Award for advocacy of purebred dogs. No matter what you think of breeders, a Fido Award sounds like a pretty cool thing to stick on your mantel.

In the dog world, Strand represents old-school status. Since the 1970s, she and her husband, Rod, have bred Dalmatians. Their efforts have produced scores of champion show dogs. The couple has also developed one of the more prestigious bloodlines in breed history, known as Merry-Go-Round Dalmatians. Strand's enduring legacy, however, will be her decades-long battle against what she calls negative propaganda against dog breeders. In 1993, shortly after Sturla arrived on the national scene with pictures of dead cats and public executions of dogs, Patti and Rod coauthored *The Hijacking of the Humane Movement: Animal Extremism*. They billed the book as "a graphic portrayal of the tactics and terror of the various front organizations involved in the Animal Rights movement."

Strand considers Sturla and her confederates to be profit-driven ideologues. Also, domestic terrorists whose animal-loving radicalism is counterproductive to animal welfare. The NAIA's stated goals include "urging passage of strong laws that target vandalism, harassment, arson, bombing, and other types of domestic terrorism in the name of animal rights and environmentalism."

IF STURLA HAS been resolute all these years in defending her position, Strand has been just as tenacious. Talking to each side is like dropping into an arbitration hearing with Boeing and Airbus executives swapping complaints about unfair trade practices and corporate malfeasance.

"Dog rescue is a giant industry, nonprofit shelters are not accountable to anybody," Strand says. "The rescue groups don't have dogs to rescue anymore, they're just not there. So they've begun importing dogs. If not, they'd have to close their doors. They'd be in deep financial trouble."

On the rainy, windy day we meet in a coffee shop in Portland, Oregon, Strand arrives with reports, charts, and plenty of talking points.

Fresh off my Wyoming fishing trip, and having already irritated friends with numerous retellings of the bin Laden dog story, I get our coffee date off to a start by recounting events on the bank of the North Fork Tongue River.

Strand interrupts ten seconds into the story.

"Let me guess—the people you met in Wyoming were super nice and loved their dog and were really talkative and excited to share her story with you almost as soon as you met them," she says.

"That's exactly how it happened," I say.

"I've seen it a few thousand times." She shrugs. "That sharing-with-strangers is kind of like wearing a brand. Like how everyone started wearing Nikes in the nineties. It's called virtue signaling. It says, 'I'm a good person, I rescued this dog instead of adding more trouble to the world. I think about the world in this kind of way.'"

I hadn't brought up virtue signaling, but talking with Strand about the connection between rescue dogs and virtue signaling as a marker of status reinforced my belief that this was a new type of prestige. New generations require new symbols of sophistication. And new dogs.

"This is all the result of very well-done and sophisticated cause marketing by shelters on behalf of rescues," Strand continues. "These rescue groups are making a fortune. Some of the big groups have millions and millions of dollars."

She's not wrong. The Humane Society of the United States, for example, has an annual operating budget of well over $150 million. In 2020, its total net assets were $322.3 million. According to HumaneWatch.org, less than 1 percent of its expenditures consist of grants to pet shelters; and in 2016 CEO Wayne Pacelle raked in a salary of over $400,000, putting him within the fabled "top 1 percent" of American earners. In 2021, outlets reported that ASPCA CEO Matthew Bershadker makes more than $840,000 in annual salary and bonuses. Behind the inexpensive product it's clear there's big money and big status tied up in the rescue game.

Spend an hour with Strand and you start to see how something as apparently benign as picking up a pooch from the pound can boil down to a moral struggle. By the mid-eighties, Strand says, America's canine overpopulation problem had mostly been brought under control. Then Sturla came along.

"Kim Sturla started this marketing campaign, this San Mateo breeding ban," Strand tells me. "The campaign she did simply disparaged all breeders as evil. 'Here's a barrel of dead animals to prove it.'" It was classic conflict marketing: victim, villain, vindicator. "They call themselves animal welfare groups, I call them animal fundraising groups. It's been thirty years of constant marketing. Everyone has an emotional response to animals, so they've been able to easily distort the issue and facts."

Sipping tea and eating a scone inside a warm coffee shop on a cold day, Strand comes off as pleasant, down-to-earth, and sensible. And there are reasonable arguments for breeding dogs. Breeding for selective traits can produce police dogs or guide dogs, eliminate or diffuse certain health defects, and preserve rare breeds. You don't have to buy these arguments, but none of them seem inherently evil. Although she looks like the type of person prone to naming a dog "Lady" (worst dog name ever), I'd be shocked if Strand actually abused animals. She reminds me of my mom, that type of dog lover who shared ice cream cones with the family pets, even Spartan, the English springer spaniel with a tongue like a banana peel covered in spawning milt.

Strand opens her laptop to a chart showing that of the 5,000 shelter dogs adopted the previous year in Multnomah County (Portland is the county seat), about 3,900 came from outside the area. "I've been doing this for twenty-eight years, back when there were still dogs to rescue," Strand tells me, allowing that in some parts of the country, dog overpopulation remains an issue. Another chart shows golden retrievers imported from Turkey bringing a rare (in the United States) bacterial pathogen called Bartonella vinsonii into the country. Strand says U.S. regulations on imported dogs are among the most lax in the world. "The reason is nobody ever thought people would be crazy enough to import street dogs from countries that don't even have rabies under control," she says.

All of this might sound like just more dismal evidence that nobody in this country can agree on anything. Even fellow dog lovers inevitably divide into factions and go to war over purebred versus rescue. It's like the Mac/PC standoff, rival factions with identical interests battling over which side has the more catholic approach. But on a deeper level, the conflict comes back to Kapferer: "The evolution of luxury is a reflection of the fight between elites. Through luxury, elites try to impose their own taste, which is held as superior." Rescue dogs have disrupted an order once indisputably topped by purebred aristocracy—Strand resents Sturla for the same reason poodles resent pit bulls—and their acolytes have had predictably violent reactions.

To create the new elitist culture of rescue dog ownership, Sturla used the luxury industry's own insulating rules against it, employing classic prestige marketing strategy to topple the status quo. In doing so she brought prestige to a downtrodden group (stray dogs) while helping to make virtue signaling one of the new tenets of status.

More than this, she was a harbinger of emerging forces that would soon harness an entirely new set of ethics, technologies, and demographics to affect prevailing rules of status across a much broader front. Beyond undermining the position of kennel dogs, what greater series of values was she helping to replace? What made these entrenched values so powerful in the first place? And why were they becoming so vulnerable to attack, not just by people like Sturla, but a whole new tide of status disruptors?

CHAPTER 2

A rich yet tasteful history:
STATUS AS VICE

STATUS AND LUXURY HAVE OBSESSED HUMANITY FOR AS LONG as brightly colored stones have existed. The concepts have thrived because they're highly malleable. As history changes, so do fashion, symbols, and hierarchies. But one law is fixed: status is and always has been a decisive feature in every human civilization.

In order to appreciate the enormity of the change heralded by the new rules of status, it's necessary to review the old ones. In particular the events and figures that codified them in the consumer era, those forces presently under siege by a new army of status revolutionaries. Land, wealth, and attractive sexual partners have forever been associated with power and prestige. Probably always will be. We've all got that, right? No need to rub everybody's noses in their obvious shortcomings.

The Egyptians entombed their beautiful people in pyramids—ultimate status symbols of yore. Likewise, Ming emperors constructed elaborate tombs. Normans erected castles. American industrialists and NBA power forwards built mansions and sprawling estates.

Yet antiquity is littered with examples of less obvious baubles worth remembering. Cacao was a marker of status among Mayans. The first board games—such as a Mesopotamian game known as Twenty Squares, which looked a lot like backgammon—were so prized they functioned as diplomatic gifts. For a time in ancient Rome nothing said "You da man" more than, of all things, lemons. The first ones in Rome came from Southeast Asia via the Middle East right around the time of Jesus Christ. Pattern-welded swords were the pinnacle of "warrior luxury" among the Barbarian hordes that clawed out an existence beyond the borders of the Roman Empire. By the eleventh century, warhorses served the same purpose for knights and other mounted soldiers. Being rare at the time, books signaled advantage in fifteenth-century Europe. Owning a pineapple meant you'd definitely arrived in seventeenth-century Europe—which is why to this day a pair of gold pineapples top the towers on London's St. Paul's Cathedral.

But possessions are just part of the show. Denoting social rank, body scarification dates back centuries in Africa, particularly in the Congo Basin and among the Akan people of modern Ghana and the Ivory Coast. Aztec priests never washed their hair, reputedly signaling status by sporting copious amounts of dried blood to show the number of human sacrifices they'd presided over—prized life experiences of the time. Chinese women had their feet bound—bones broken, heels mutilated, growth stunted—to produce "golden lotus" feet connoting a life free of the rice paddy and ox plow and functioning as an indicator of candidacy for marrying into wealth. Western women sucked in their guts and squeezed into corsets to display that they, too, were above the coarse obligation of manual labor. Pacific Northwest Coast natives—Haida, Kwakwaka'wakw, Nuu-chah-nulth, Nuxalk, Coast Salish, Tlingit, Tsimshian, to name a handful—threw extravagant potlatches in which they gave away personal riches such as gold and animal skins to demonstrate their wealth and generosity.

Status anxiety has from the beginning been a problem in Western democracies whose superseding value system is an impossible and unrealistic ideal. Genetically speaking, as Yuval Noah Harari points out, "the idea that all humans are equal is also a myth. . . . Is there any objective reality, outside the human imagination, in which we are truly equal?" The universal chase for luxury and rank rudely demonstrates the fragility of the principle upon which any presumably egalitarian society is founded.

Governments have long attempted to regulate the problem away. In ancient Athens, status divisions were a significant political problem. Remembered primarily for attempting to legislate against moral decline (in vain, as it turned out), Greek statesman Solon sought to mitigate public displays of wealth by curbing the ostentatious funeral displays that became a custom among flashy aristocrats. The Chinese government attempted roughly the same thing in 2018 when authorities began cracking down on lavish wedding ceremonies favored by newly affluent couples. Such displays, insisted officials, eroded "socialist core values" and indicated "declining morality." A *Time* magazine story on the trend included a photo of a formally clad bride, groom, and wedding party dangling ridiculously by an expeditioner's rope from a cliff face off Chaya Mountain. How the Chinese, who in my experience have a pretty obsessive grasp on inauspicious omens, missed this one I have no idea.

University of Warwick classics and ancient history professor Dr. Michael Scott, known in the UK as the host of a number of BBC historical documentaries, argues the inequitable distribution of luxury goods in Athens evolved into a "crisis of privilege" that led directly to the founding of democracy. Essentially, Scott credits the entire concept of luxury with the origins of modern society.

The Romans picked up where the Greeks left off—adding an even more fervent attachment to enormous homes, fine clothes, lavish parties, and spa days with the girls (and boys), all of which remain familiar markers of luxury. Alas, good ol' buzzkill Christendom eventually came along to tsk-tsk everyone's good time. "For Christians, luxury was a dangerous roadblock on the path to heaven," says Scott. "Christians were told to . . . abandon worldly pleasures, to scorn material wealth."

Knowing they couldn't eliminate their flocks' invidious pursuit of the high life, religious leaders cannily redirected that energy into the service of devout collective projects hailing the glory of the church. These efforts resulted, most notably, in the massive, ornate cathedrals and art that stand as the centerpieces of modern European tourist itineraries.

Though never fully vanquished, the pursuit of status was renounced in the "capital sins" codified by Pope Gregory the Great in AD 590. It's easy to make the case that five of Saint Greg's so-called seven deadly sins, known as the basis of all transgressions, suggested divine retribution for the pursuit of status and luxury—lust, gluttony, avarice, envy, pride— leaving only "sloth" and "wrath" out of the equation. Catholic guilt and Puritan judgment followed in doses that'd ensure the enduring vigor of the personal therapy industry.

The takeaway here is that, allowing for shifts in tastes and resources, our basic understanding of luxury and status held more or less firm since the dawn of recorded civilization. Goods and services have always been part of the equation, but so, too, has an ethereal sense of attainment. Greek, Roman, barbarian, Christian, and pineapple-hoarding European attitudes fit together in a status tapestry that constituted Western understanding of privilege until the dawn of the twentieth century.

This is when two American social critics—their nationality no coincidence, given the country's emergence as the greatest consumer glutton in history—published the most insightful and influential books ever written on the subject. This pair of foundational status tomes—published in 1899 and 1959—stand as the definitive analysis of the modern drive for luxury and status. Whether you realize it or not, just about every opinion you have about status in the consumer age has its origins in these two books.

ALTHOUGH IN SOCIAL science circles he's still referenced all the time, Thorstein Veblen is no longer widely known outside of university curriculum. Even there, I suspect, he's one of those eminent fogies undergrads do their best to dodge. Veblen isn't so much read these days as he is skimmed.

This is a shame since few social critics before or since have summed up establishment attitudes toward the quest for luxury and status with such timeless lucidity. With his landmark 1899 book, *The Theory of the Leisure Class*, Veblen laid the foundation for the modern understanding of consumerism. His idea was that the system's survival wasn't predicated on manipulating and even creating desires for status, but for making its attainment "conspicuous" to others. Hence the term "status signal."

Part of the problem with Veblen is a dense and archaic prose style—a splendaciously coruscating exemplification shall well be made ere long—that critics in kinder moments have described as "elephantine," "fringe," and "obstreperous." Also "bitter," "deadpan," and "sarcastic." Veblen's writing reflected a notoriously difficult misanthrope. A university professor of "rough manners and unkempt appearance," Veblen was despised by his students for bestowing cruel nicknames on people, mumbling inaudibly, and apparently doling out Cs to almost everyone regardless of classroom performance.

Ever the futurist, the Wisconsin-born son of Norwegian immigrants was a firm believer in the power of technology to change economic and social systems. But after studying at Johns Hopkins and earning a PhD in philosophy at Yale, he was unable to find work in academia and spent seven years virtually unemployed. Mostly, he hung out at the family farm—eleven siblings!—and read like a maniac. Along with an irascible temperament, it didn't help his professional standing that he was an avid fan of Karl Marx, a blithe critic of capitalism, and an open agnostic, the latter being the most scandalous of these positions at the time.

Through an eminently patient mentor, Veblen finally landed a gig at the University of Chicago in 1892. Having had plenty of jobless time to ponder the fiscal value of his philosophy degree, the impoverished Veblen had looked long at the consumer world around him and arrived at some deep conclusions. These he was anxious to share.

Thanks to the success of his essays and books appraising modern society and economics, he'd go on to hold teaching positions at Stanford University, the University of Missouri, and New York's progressive New School for Social Research (today just the New School), where he was an original faculty member in 1919. Even so, he remained the "odd man out" in American economics of the time, according to the Library of Economics and Liberty.

Veblen died penniless and feeling defeated by life in 1929 in Menlo Park, California. It's too far a stretch to say the shamanistic professor might have foreseen the site of his death as the future headquarters of a tech-driven social revolution that would completely upend consumer behavior by driving it online. But it'd be interesting to hear what he might have to say about Silicon Valley's impact on conspicuous wealth signaling and social economics. It's likely he'd not have approved.

For all this, Veblen was a social mystic who nosed in just under the wire to write one of the most fascinating and prophetic books of the nineteenth century. For most of the twentieth century, *The Theory of the Leisure Class* stood as the touchstone critique of modern consumer society. In it, Veblen coined the phrase "conspicuous consumption" to describe an emerging status-driven citizen the world had never before encountered—a wanton spender for whom wastefulness was a virtue, not a mere by-product of wealth; a social statement to be slavishly mimicked by peers.

Despite being removed by more than a century, conspicuous consumption in Veblen's time didn't look all that much different from our own. Objects of his ire included overpriced underwear (seriously), specialty foods, leather shoes, general fashion ("a cheap coat makes a cheap man," he repeated with ironic spleen), gems, jewelry, "quasi-artistic accomplishments," literal silver spoons, and, wait for it . . . dogs! In a prescient turn that would have warmed Kim Sturla's heart, Veblen called out kennel dogs as useless "monstrosities" that served no practical purpose aside from showcasing their owners' alleged pedigree.

"The commercial value of canine monstrosities . . . rests on their high cost of production, and their value to their owners lies chiefly in their utility as items of conspicuous consumption," he wrote. Insolently dismissing feline powers of status, Veebs nevertheless revealed himself between the lines as a true cat man: "The cat's temperament does not fit her for the honorific purpose. She lives with man on terms of equality, knows nothing of that relation of status which is the ancient basis of all distinctions of worth, honor, and repute."

The Sumerians may have invented hedonistic philosophy. The Romans had their orgies. And no one knew how to spend at Palace Depot like Shang dynasty emperor Di Xin, who legend says ordered the construction of a Wine Pool and Meat Forest—that's right, a large pond of wine with an island on which skewers of meat hung from trees! But the one-two punch of the Industrial Revolution and social Darwinism had created a new kind of economy and brought a new kind of spending power to the masses. For his fellow Americans, not to mention designer undies and dog breeders, Veblen saw myriad dark implications, all of them rooted in a new status consumerism.

I'VE PAINTED A pretty grim portrait of Veblen, but that shouldn't be taken as an indictment of his ideas, which still have broad influence today. Raw genius is often concealed beneath a prickly skin. (I've tried this defense with some of my critics; doesn't often work; probably helps to be dead.)

For Veblen, the whole point of the leisure class was leisure, and nothing less. Wealth by ownership, consumption for consumption's sake, and scads of free time were the coin of the realm among the emerging gang of Americans for who "pecuniary strength" was everything. He asserted that the upper classes' exemption from employment "is the economic expression of their superior rank." Amplifying this idea throughout his text, he called all labor "debasing," "repugnant," and "vulgar."

The beaver-felted top hat, fashionable at the time, was another target of one of his eloquent gripes: "It is extremely doubtful if any one could be induced to wear such a contrivance as the high hat of civilized society, except for some urgent reason based on other than aesthetic grounds." Dedication to the ludicrous head cover of the times was, like bound feet, a desire to display one's freedom from the shackles of common labor. Ever tried baling hay or fixing a leaky pipe under the sink wearing a top hat?

Because he was writing before the invention of such modern marketing staples as focus groups, social media blasts, and talking geckos, Veblen based most of his conclusions on sheer observation, Age of Enlightenment–style reasoning, and magnate confidence. As a result, he aggravates modern scholars for failing to cite any sources, studies, or academic references whatsoever to support his many claims. A lot of his ideas simply don't hold up to scrutiny. Or to the evolution of American life, which, as we've already seen, no longer has an identifiable "leisure class." Even rich people now work hard at getting richer.

But Veblen did correctly predict all manner of developments: the ubiquity of branding on apparel; the Me generation's campaigns for self-esteem; cheap knockoffs of famous brands (Veblen seemed to understand Thai night-market forgeries decades before the modern country's existence); endless warfare driven by industrial concerns (a decade and a half before World War I and half a century ahead of Eisenhower's warning about the military industrial complex); the near-pathological push to protect elite schools as the exclusive provenance of the upper classes; and, especially, the consumer impulse that would metastasize into a neverending, buy-buy-buy-waste-waste-waste status pyramid scheme.

Veblen argued each social stratum would strive to mimic—in fashion, behavior, and material holdings—the one just above it, thus creating a ceaseless whirlpool of unrequited need. In doing so, he articulated what would become known as "status anxiety" and the "aspirational consumerism" so prevalent in travel and fashion magazines, TV programs celebrating gaudy lifestyles of the superrich, and celebrity blogs like *Goop* functioning as guides to the good life. "The possession of wealth confers honor" in a consumer-based society, and the "motive that lies at the root of ownership is emulation," he wrote.

For a nineteenth-century guy, Veblen was impressively woke about the subordinate roles of non-whites and women in the nascent consumer society. He was reportedly fired from his position at Stanford for loudly defending the rights of Chinese laborers. Some of his grandest political magniloquence was imparted on behalf of the disadvantageous position of women, against which he railed with excellent stuffed-shirt bile. "Women and other slaves are highly valued," he inveighed with gallows sarcasm. "There need be little question but that the basis of the industrial system is chattel slavery and that the women are commonly slaves."

Veblen accurately foresaw that American women could not forever be denied the right to vote—a basic status marker in a democracy—as well as other routes to equality. Had he foreseen the power of the sound bite—or at least been capable of writing down to the fourth-grade level of the narcissists he saw all around him—he might today be hailed as one of the great muckraker-prophet heroes of his day, alongside Ida Tarbell and Upton Sinclair, if not Twain and Mencken. Alas, he was inclined to shroud simple ideas in loquacious ascents of as many ivory towers as he could manage before pausing for a comma. Behold the following typically overloaded passage of Veblenian density:

> *The pressure exerted by the environment upon the group, and making for a readjustment of the group's scheme of life, impinges upon the members of the group in the form of pecuniary exigencies; and it is owing to this fact—that external forces are in great part translated into the form of pecuniary or economic exigencies—it is owing to this fact that we can say that the forces which count toward a readjustment of institutions in any modern industrial community are chiefly economic forces; or more specifically, these forces take the form of pecuniary pressure. Such a readjustment as is here contemplated is substantially a change in men's views as to what is good and right, and the means through which a change is wrought in men's apprehension of what is good and right is in large part the pressure of pecuniary exigencies.*

Eloquent, perhaps. But Veblen might more effectively have just said "Money changes everything" and gotten on with killing and field butchering the next pecuniary exigency in his path. Or at least found an editor with the wherewithal to rein in that "it is owing to this fact" redundancy, which, yes, appears twice in one sentence in the original text.

VEBLEN'S GREAT RECURRING theme, and the conspicuous consumer's cardinal "virtue," is waste. Again proving himself a century ahead of the game—or perhaps just illustrating that no matter how badly millennials want to believe they invented everything from sex to small-batch whiskey, there's really nothing new in human existence—Veblen articulated his "law of conspicuous waste."

Annual and seasonal changes in fashion and style, he said, were a perfect example of the need for waste—last year's toy, jacket, or gadget being thoughtlessly discarded—in a system reliant upon conspicuous consumption. This was a criticism of capitalism, but Veblen also couched it in terms of status. He saw the global order changing through the rise of capitalism and a newfound pursuit of status through heedless material consumption. He turned out to be murderously accurate about that, too.

Though he didn't live to see it, the highest global expression of the law of conspicuous waste arrived with the all-hands-on-deck American "arsenal of democracy" effort in World War II. American soldiers in that world-shaping conflagration were certainly brave, resilient, and patriotic, although, in reality, no more so than most of the soldiers from the countries they fought against or alongside. They won because they were better supplied. Simply put, Americans had more stuff with which to annihilate the world.

If two things can be said to have definitively won World War II—ignited, incidentally, by German and Japanese efforts to redress a humiliating loss of global status vis-à-vis their Western counterparts after World War I—they are overwhelming Soviet soldiery* and overwhelming

---

* Before you begin shouting about my socialist, America-hating rhetoric, consider that of the estimated 13 million German casualties in World War II, more than 10 million were sustained fighting Russkies on the Eastern Front. The USSR lost 27 million lives in the war. The official American death toll was about 407,000. In a purely American sense, it was the power of the status-driven consumer production apparatus that carried the day.

American production. To grasp the extent of that production—and to appreciate the influence of "waste" on status—consider the postwar testimony of a Japanese officer stationed in the Philippines who summed up his country's hopeless plight by relating a story about watching a single Japanese soldier on a beach being shot at by huge American naval guns trained directly on him: "Machine guns, even mortars, yes, but naval guns against a single enemy straggler? Incredible! The enemy must have equipment and ammunition to throw away!"

Veblen hadn't specifically foreseen those hapless Japanese soldiers hoarding rice and bullets while being shot at by battleships and destroyers. But it's safe to say he wouldn't have been surprised by their plight. And that he would have seen in the demise of their culture the fulfillment of his dark vision about the frenzied race for national status unleashed by the Industrial Age.

NOTHING CHANGED STATUS in the United States—the world for that matter—like World War II. Over just two decades following the war's end in 1945, the U.S. economy more than tripled, from a nominal GDP of $228 billion in 1946 to $742 billion in 1965. Think traffic and parking have become a nightmare in your city? Imagine four times as many cars and drivers clogging your roads just ten years from now. That's what happened across America between 1946 and 1955, when automobile production quadrupled.

The war begat the home-tech revolution. In 1946, fewer than seventeen thousand TV sets existed in the country. By 1960, 75 percent of all U.S. households owned one. Fourteen years. That's all it took to glue the vast majority of American faces to screens. It took the personal-computing industry twenty-four years to pull off the same trick—8.2 percent of Americans owned a home computer in 1984; the number didn't hit 77 percent until 2010.

World War II also consolidated the corporation, even more than government, as the defining force in American life. In the early 1800s,

80 percent of Americans were self-employed, engaged mostly in farm labor on family plots. By 1950 it was just 25 percent. The number eventually shrunk as low as 10 percent, though thanks to the gig economy it's rising again, possibly as high as 30 percent, depending how you define "self-employed." The point stands: World War II turned America into a nation of servicemen and then into a nation of service workers. According to the U.S. Bureau of Labor Statistics, 80 percent of Americans now work in service-providing industries.

Even a man of Thorstein Veblen's powers couldn't have foreseen the scale of the greatest production and consumer boom the world had ever created. Or the new status-consumed society that rose from it. By 1956, for the first time in U.S. history, the majority of workers held white-collar jobs.

THE FLOWERING OF Western affluence produced endless contemplations of capital and wealth, and updated iterations of Veblen's themes. Like the mighty public intellectual who wrote it—who stood six feet, eight inches—John Kenneth Galbraith's 1958 *The Affluent Society* towers above most peers. Like Veblen, Galbraith could be entertainingly uppity in an anachronistic way. The august Harvard economist updated Veblen's themes by using "jewel-encrusted bosoms" as the outstanding contemporary symbol of wanky showboating, complaining that such vulgarities had been devalued now that they could be afforded "by a television star or a talented harlot." By making them affordable to dilettantes, mass production was beginning to cheapen the value of established status symbols—Galbraith was displeased. This is also the book in which Galbraith coined the phrase "Conventional Wisdom," so ubiquitous now it usually comes in lowercase. An international bestseller, *The Affluent Society* was named by the New York Public Library as one of its Books of the Century.

Great thinkers they might have been, Galbraith, French sociologist Pierre Bourdieu, and a raft of other status academics consistently aimed over their targets' heads. This explains why the heir to Veblen's throne would eventually come not from the towers of academia but the mean streets of mass consumerism, to which the daily grind for status had shifted in midcentury America.

Like Veblen, with whom he shared a number of traits, Vance Packard was an unlikely figure to make sense of America's new tidal wave of status. Born on a Pennsylvania farm in 1914, Packard also spent much of his life as an outsider. He sympathized with socialist movements and the Soviet experiment. Employing a phrase gone missing from modern discourse, what friends he had described him as a "parlor pink." They called that "limousine liberal" in the seventies. For a while in the 2000s it was "Feel the Bern!"

Unlike most men of his generation, Packard had no military experience. He spent World War II as a reporter on the home front for the Associated Press. After the war he wrote human-interest features for magazines.

Like Veblen, however, Packard's outsider status made him a potent social observer. Unlike Veblen, his ability to write punchy, easily understood sentences—and cite sources and stats along the way—made him a national celebrity. No one grasped the implications of the postwar economy on the American psyche like the gimlet-eyed journo, in particular the way it would reshape privilege, status symbols, and social rank.

Between 1957 and 1960, Packard produced three bestselling books explaining America's binge for material wealth and social gain. A study of the psychological tactics used by advertisers, 1957's *The Hidden Persuaders* launched his career as a social critic. Published in 1960, *The Waste Makers* was a blistering assault on the age of consumer gluttony that picked up on both Veblen's pet theme of waste and the impact of World War II.

Americans nowadays make no pretense of living in a classless society. We're well aware of the .01 percent; the 1 percent; the 10 percent "new American aristocracy," outlined in demographic detail by Matthew Stewart in a 2018 *Atlantic* article; and the endless regional, racial, sexual, political, and multifarious demographic designations designed to plot us against the mean. Yet the myth of an egalitarian, class-free system—for so long a way Americans distanced themselves from their European cousins—remained powerful in the 1950s and '60s.

Packard saw it as his job to smash this fallacy. The 1959 publication of his book *The Status Seekers*—a phrase Packard coined—sealed his legacy as Veblen's heir. Egalitarianism, he noted in kicking off the book, was disingenuously embedded in the national folklore. "Such a notion unfortunately rests upon a notable lack of perception of the true situation," he wrote. Class lines were actually hardening in the 1950s. "Status straining has intensified. . . . Classes are based on such prestige factors as occupation, schooling, address."

Everywhere he looked, Packard found hidden hierarchies. Status defined the nation, from the corporate boardroom to the downtown street corner, where he reported on the rigid occupational ladder of prostitutes the way Joe Friday might grill a busted john. "Call girls" managed by their "old man" (pimp) were the aristocrats of the profession. They lorded their lady status over "house workers," "street girls," and "chippies" (promiscuous amateurs).

Overconsumption—waste—had become a national norm. Cars. Boats. Houses. Home furnishings. Clothes. Vacations. Gas fireplaces. Bad TV. Arguably a natural reaction following the deprivations of the Great Depression and an all-consuming war effort, Packard nevertheless saw in the mechanics of systematized consumption a quiet influence that had escaped the attention of the common rabble—the postwar militarization of American society. And the strict codification of rank and status that descended on the workplace like a natural phenomenon following the near-universal military experience of World War II. Adapting wartime experiences to the peacetime economy, big corporations were implementing military-style hierarchies to "exquisite extremes." A society based on a foundation that aped the military's entrenched hierarchy of 1 percent generals, 9 percent officers, and 90 percent rank and file was taking shape.

"Employees are usually expected to comport themselves in conformity with their rank, and generally do so," Packard wrote. "Industrialists are noting that the military experience millions of our younger generation have had has made them more accepting of rank." The implication was that workers were more apt than ever to strive for the stripe on the sleeve one level above their own. A nation of GIs had become a nation of employees, with roughly the same aspirational attitudes.

"Our class system is starting to bear a resemblance to that which prevails in the military services," Packard noticed. "In the services there are, of course, status differences between a private and a corporal and between a lieutenant and a captain. The great division, however, is between officers and enlisted men, with only quite limited opportunities for acquiring, while in service, the training necessary to pass from one division to the other."

The military-style social hierarchy Packard described calcified. How's this for a crazy statistical parallel that shows Packard's clairvoyance and modern America's slavish replication of the military status ladder? According to the 2021 Bureau of Labor Statistics, 82 percent of U.S. military personnel were enlisted; 10 percent were officers; the remaining 8 percent were warrant officers, or "technical and tactical experts," basically the equivalent of today's IT class, who hold a status that's critical yet still outside the social norm.

The ballyhooed 1 percent, .01 percent, and .001 percent that make up today's economic and political elite? In 2022, sixteen four-star generals sat atop the entire army and eight admirals ran the navy. That makes generals about .001 percent of army personnel and admirals .002 percent of navy people. Military populations provide an eerily similar counterpart to civilian society's top .001 percent—Packard called them "upper uppers"—who've drawn the attention of everyone from *Forbes* to *Vanity Fair* to economists at Harvard, NYU, and the University of Chicago Booth School of Business. Wanna know where our whole increasingly imbalanced have-and-have-not social stratification started in the modern era? World War II is your answer. Vance Packard is your soothsayer.

THE STATUS SEEKERS was the nation's top-selling book for four months. It remained on the bestseller list for more than a year. It touched off a national identity crisis.

Like Veblen, Packard was nostalgic for a less status-driven country. His tone throughout *The Status Seekers* is that of a crusader. Condescension is a go-to device. He could be particularly discourteous with the junior varsity. On the newfound mania for antiquing as a way to feign a connection to old money, he dissed: "The lower classes have never grasped the subtlety of honoring the long-used object. Perhaps they have had too much forced experience with hand-me-downs."

Packard meant his books to be a clarion call against the dangers of status seeking and the accumulation of grotesque amounts of wealth. Affluence, he concluded, was a bigger threat to social cohesion than poverty or racism. The street protests that convulsed America in 2020—and their visual embodiment in that porcine couple in St. Louis who stood in front of their mansion waving guns at passing protesters—at least partially proved him right.

Packard spotted other trends and made accurate predictions about how status would look in the employee era of class stratification. Anticipating that Columbia Business School study about overwork becoming a status symbol, he noted that for employees, leisure time was losing "most of its potency as a status symbol." He observed with wry humor the growing penchant to confer nobility in the workplace with euphemisms and new job titles that bordered on the absurd. A campaign by the country's twenty-five thousand undertakers to rebrand themselves "funeral directors" in a formaldehyde-free bid to convey executive dignity caught his eye. The broad success of this kind of language softening would pave the way for the dialectal sensitivity that embalms modern discourse.

Though his primary focus was fixed on his middle-class, white audience, Packard was, again like Veblen, acutely aware of the disadvantaged status of non-whites and the untenable nature of that injustice on economic and moral grounds. He touted the contributions of Armenian and Korean immigrants, ascribing them "early settler" status in California. He railed against white flight from cities to suburbs, citing statistics that debunked the widespread myth that incoming African American neighbors lowered property values. And half a century before it became a ubiquitous call to feminist arms, he was all over the gender-pay gap. He framed the issue in terms of indentured sub-status, which Veblen would have appreciated. "An example of irrational discrepancy is the fact that men typically are paid more than women for performing the same job," he wrote. "Usually there is no pretense that men can do the job in question any better than women."

Packard's succinct style, social empathy, and reference notes—all improvements on Veblen—assured his rank as a leading arbiter of status until his death in 1996. In *The Status Seekers* he covered a list of one hundred jobs scored in terms of status in 1947 by the National Opinion Research Center. Doctors, scientists, and college professors landed near the top of the list. Street sweepers and shoe shiners held down the bottom tier. The NORC repeated its survey in 1963 to '65, 1989, and 2012, eventually including 860 occupations. Some were of the type you expect to see in one of those *Onion* "American Voices" bits: seed analyst, loom fixer, skip-hoist operator, hod carrier, panhandler, drawbridge tender, nut roaster, tombstone carver, and time-motion analyst. The Harris Poll got in on the act in 1977, conducting its own job prestige survey. This would lead to a 2014 Harris Poll that put doctors at the top of the cachet heap and led to this headline in *Slate*: "The American Concept of Prestige Has Barely Changed in 37 Years." *Slate* should have said the concept of prestige hadn't budged since Veblen's day at the turn of the last century.

Veblen and Packard left a formidable legacy. In the public consciousness they embedded direct connections between status and leisure; capitalism; conspicuous consumption; waste; martial-style ambition; occupational rank; race- and gender-based injustices; and, perhaps most important, a deep and abiding opprobrium that framed consumerism and the pursuit of status through consumption as a moral failing.

What *Slate* didn't appreciate, what almost no one yet appreciated, was that within a year, a book based on a revolutionary type of new technology would be published that would signal the biggest change in ideas about status and prestige in a couple millennia. And that just a few years before, in one of the most affluent neighborhoods of Atlanta, a random group of teenagers brought together by a frustrated rock guitarist were already charting the path of that change.

CHAPTER 3

Music, wine, and sex appeal:
STATUS AS NEUROLOGICAL IMPERATIVE

GREG BERNS IS ONE OF THOSE PEOPLE WHO ARE CURIOUS about almost everything. Genetic variations in New Zealand sheep populations. Child psychology. Average height of NFL placekickers. The reason the piece of toast you dropped always lands butter-side down. Bring up a topic and chances are he's thought about it. (It's because you buttered the wrong side, by the way.)

What Berns is most interested in, however, is the brain—specifically, what the brain does when it's interacting with other brains. In fact, Berns knows so much about brains he's the Distinguished Professor of Neuroeconomics and director of the Center for Neuropolicy and the Facility for Education and Research in Neuroscience at Emory University in Atlanta.

Careful readers will note I don't say Berns is interested in "human brains." That's because he's fascinated with all types of brains. Like most dog people, he might even prefer canine brains over human brains. His books include *What It's Like to Be a Dog: And Other Adventures in Animal Neuroscience*. Berns likes to put dogs in MRI scanners and read their minds. The hardest part of this, he says, isn't getting the dogs to remain completely motionless for ten minutes. That takes a few days or weeks of training. The tough part is to keep them from howling at all the rumble and noise created by the scanner.

In November 2006, shortly before he began scanning dog brains, Berns took his love of music (he's also a pretty good guitar player) and love of brains and did something no one had done before. He devised an experiment using new technology to find out whether functional magnetic resonance imaging (fMRI) could be used to predict the future popularity and sales of a common consumer product: music.

"Being popular is a marker for social status," Berns wrote at the time. He identified music preference as a reliable indicator of popularity, i.e., status, among adolescent populations. Berns wanted to see how their peers' opinions about music changed kids' own opinions. Essentially he was interested in herd mentality.

To do this he and a graduate assistant slid twenty-seven Atlanta-area kids ages twelve to seventeen into an MRI scanner and recorded their brain activity as they listened to fifteen-second snippets of twenty songs from six genres: alternative/emo/indie, country, hip-hop/rap, jazz/blues, metal, and rock. Fourteen girls and thirteen boys of mixed ethnicity listened to songs in genres they'd preselected as their favorites. In order to minimize prior exposure to the music—Berns wanted subjects with as yet unformed opinions—songs were culled from new releases by relatively unknown artists. Over a two-week span in October to November 2006, Berns had his grad assistant download 120 songs from the most popular music portal of the day—Myspace.

Although he wasn't thinking of it in these terms at the time, Berns had done something unique: he'd created the world's first neuromarketing focus group.

"The original idea was to use music to study the effects of social conformity on kids, especially teenagers," Berns says. "What happened after that wasn't planned."

THE EXPERIMENT BERNS devised required kids to rate each song on a one-to-five scale. After a period of time elapsed, they heard and rated the same songs a second time, only this time they were shown the aggregated rating the rest of the group had given each song. Berns originally just wanted to find out if knowing how their peers rated a song shifted individuals' opinion toward the group consensus. It did. The study generated proof of the insidious power of group thought.

Interesting as this was, it merely confirmed what many earlier studies had shown—that anxiety created by the mismatch between one's own preferences and that of a group tends to motivate people, especially teenagers, to modify their thinking in the direction of the consensus. People have a measurable predisposition for conformity. This sheds light on all sorts of inexplicable cultural phenomena, including everything Kardashian, Republican dating sites, those little nose rings that look like dangling boogers, flavored vaping, and "Bohemian Rhapsody," which, sorry, was a chore when it came out and is an even greater burden on the millionth exposure. Again, though, none of Berns's initial findings was groundbreaking.

The truly worthwhile results of the study came only after all the kids had been dismissed and Myspace began to crater. One afternoon, long after the study had been completed and for no reason in particular he can recall, Berns came up with a different way to look at the data he'd collected. During the test he'd asked subjects to rate the songs they heard. At the same time, he was measuring how their brains were reacting to each snippet.

Research at the time strongly suggested activity in reward-related regions of the brain—particularly the orbitofrontal cortex, ventral striatum, and nucleus accumbens—might be predictive of future purchasing decisions. Berns wondered if what kids verbally reported as their preferences or the "hidden" activity in their brains' pleasure centers would be a more reliable predictor of the future popularity of a given song, and, thus, its sales success. He did this by spending the next three years tracking the commercial success of each of the 120 songs used in the survey. He got this data from Nielsen SoundScan, and took into account sales of singles, albums, and compilations. Finally, he compared these sales figures with his test group's subjectively stated preferences and then against their brain activity.

The results rocked his world. Although the one-to-five ratings of new songs verbalized by subjects showed no correlation with how the songs would eventually fare in the broader marketplace, Berns found that "signals in the reward-related regions of the human brain [were] predictive of individual purchase decisions." And modestly predictive of national sales.

By this time (2009), some in the nascent field of neuromarketing were making claims that people's brain functions were more reliable indicators of their future purchasing decisions than their mouths. Berns had come up with hard data to prove it.

What was going on here? Why did people say they liked one thing even as their brain scans said they liked another?

Berns posited that asking someone how much they like something requires a number of cognitive operations, from processing the initial stimulus (listening to a song snippet) to predicting its future utility to projecting how the answer will position them vis-à-vis their peers. In other words, before people state an opinion, a lot of things have to happen in the brain. And, as we know simply by listening to half the population's opinions, a lot of things can go wrong once people start thinking too much, then opening their mouths.

"In contrast, brain responses in reward-related regions are likely to reflect subconscious processes and may yield measurements that are less subject to cognitive strategies," Berns told me. "While the act of rating something requires metacognition, the brain response during the consumption of goods does not, and the latter may prove superior to rating approaches."

Berns's initial conclusions were superficial and confirmed what researchers already knew—that most people move to the mean public opinion regardless of whether or not they actually like something. But as creator of the world's first fMRI focus group, he blazed what has since become a deeply grooved trail leading to neurological-based insights into status and prestige unavailable to previous generations of researchers and philosophers.

AS A FLIP-SIDE bonus, more than a decade later Berns's study resonates with a number of curious notes for the dedicated pop musicologist. As I happen to be one of these, I'll ask you to stick with me for a second here. The overwhelming majority of songs used in the study failed to register any significant sales at all. Only three tracks ended up certified gold (five hundred thousand unit sales). Turns out it's not only tough to write and record hit songs, it's no breeze trying to predict them. The most successful song in the survey turned out to be the OneRepublic mid-tempo, botched-relationship moper "Apologize," which hit number one in the United States and fifteen other countries, became one of the biggest radio airplay tracks in the history of the North American Top 40 chart, and was certified multiplatinum in the United States with nearly 6 million unit sales. I'm not sure what my orbitofrontal cortex, ventral striatum, and nucleus accumbens think of it, but I can say for sure no matter how many times I hear this dead horse beaten on the radio I'll never care for it.

Another future heavy hitter was Dethklok's novelty skull-crusher "Duncan Hills Coffee Jingle," which got a boost when it was featured on the Adult Swim cartoon *Metalocalypse*. Perhaps unsurprisingly, artists with names like Absynthe Minded and Papoose failed to impress Berns's Atlanta teen judges. Finishing near the bottom of the bandstand with an overall rank of 101 out of 120 was a poorly regarded track called "City Is Mine" by an obscure Canadian rapper named Drake. Well, nobody's perfect.

That goes for the creators of the study, too. A few older, well-known songs slipped into the mix—including Mark Wills's 1998 country megasmash, "Don't Laugh at Me," and Leon Russell's 1972 Top 20 classic, "Tight Rope." Which goes to show you can't even rely on grad students at prestigious universities to do their homework.

One more note, just because it allows a spotlight to be shined on one of the forgotten heroes of American music: among other findings, Berns concluded there is "a positive correlation between likability and familiarity" in music. In other words, the more you hear a song, the better the chances you'll like it.

To which Todd Storz no doubt would have said, "No shit, Sherlock."

In the mid-1950s, Todd Storz was the owner of KOWH-AM. The last-place radio station in Omaha, Nebraska, it featured a hodgepodge of programming. Holding court in a bar over the course of a long night, as the story goes, he observed customers playing the same handful of songs over and over again on the jukebox. The kicker, however, came when the bar was closing up. That's when Storz noticed one of the waitresses with a mop in her hand plunking her own coins into the jukebox. To his amazement she chose a song she'd already heard ten or fifteen times over the course of her shift.

A power chord surged through Storz's mind. He went back to his station, ditched the general-interest programming, and began playing the same set of songs in a confined rotation that came back around every few hours, day and night. Thus did Storz invent the Top 40 radio format. KOWH rocketed to number one in the Omaha market. Imitators followed.

Although for decades this was the accepted story of the birth of the Top 40 format in radio circles (Casey Kasem, among others, repeated it on the air), some radio scholars now refute it. These wet blankets insist Storz came up with the idea by drawing on his experiences as an army soldier in World War II, watching people repeatedly drop money into the jukebox to hear the same tunes repeated over and over. Same story, just not as fun.

Regardless, by the early 1960s, the top station in nearly every market in the country was following Storz's repetitive format. Without it, the Beatles and countless other acts would never have attained the level of status and cultural power they eventually attained. Following some form of logic, we can thank that Omaha waitress and her mop for everyone from Elton John to Billie Eilish. Of course, we can also blaspheme her for the careers of Chris Brown and Justin Bieber.

Pop culture minutiae notwithstanding, Berns's music study was vital because it laid hard data beneath an emerging suspicion about how the brain functions. Even though his original experiment was focused elsewhere, its conclusions cracked open the door to a rapidly developing appreciation of how the mind processes external stimuli. Namely, that its primary wellspring comes from a deeper neurological function that's closer to instinct than choice.

Now all someone had to do was come along and kick that door open. Preferably someone who liked kicking in doors with a pair of Saint Laurent Lukas python-skin boots (retail price: $1,595).

WHEN HE STARTED writing what would become his rule-changing treatise on status and consumerism, Dr. Steven Quartz wasn't looking to disrupt accepted orthodoxy. He'd read Thorstein Veblen and Vance Packard and found their conclusions reasonable.

"I didn't have an ideological axe to grind," he says. "I was sympathetic to the money-can't-buy-happiness thing, to the general ideals of anti-consumerism."

Since 1998, Quartz has been a professor of philosophy and cognitive science at the California Institute of Technology. Caltech is where the field of "neuroeconomics" was developed around the turn of this century. When I meet him on the campus in the middle of an extremely wealthy neighborhood in extremely wealthy Pasadena, California—there are few places in the world where you can feel major funding this palpably— Quartz tells me his interest in the interplay between luxury commodities and status came about by chance.

"Lisa Ling asked us to do an experiment about consumerism and 'cool' for her [*National Geographic Explorer*] TV show," Quartz says. "I hadn't thought much about consumerism. I was working on brain plasticity at the time."

Ling's request sent Quartz's mind in a new direction. He began looking at some of the issues that had possessed critics of modern consumerism. But Quartz had a new tool with which to work—MRI. He was also familiar with Berns's work. "Greg and I did our postdocs together at UCSB," he tells me. Like Berns, he was anxious to find out what the new technology might reveal about deeper-seated consumer tendencies.

What he discovered upended centuries of thought on privilege consumption. The result was a book he cowrote with Anette Asp called *Cool: How the Brain's Hidden Quest for Cool Drives Our Economy and Shapes Our World.* Really, though, "cool" is just a sales hook. Replace "cool" with "status" and you get a more accurate title. With the book's 2015 publication, Quartz immediately became both debunker of and heir to the intellectual legacy of Veblen and Packard, the modern world's chief arbiter of status and what it means in a contemporary consumer context.

Though clearly writing with new centurions in mind, Quartz shares traits with Veblen and Packard. He's politically progressive and at least sympathetic to socialist causes. He has an abiding interest in the effects of mass consumerism on society and national identity. And he began critiquing these forces of social transformation in the midst of a colossal wave of economic prosperity. Veblen wrote *The Theory of the Leisure Class* at the tail end of one of the most rapid economic expansions in history, a time when the United States had tapped into the immense potential of the Industrial Revolution to surpass Great Britain as the world's leading manufacturing economy. Packard attained his notoriety during the unparalleled postwar economic miracle that made the United States the spearhead of global capitalism. Quartz not only had the digital economy at his back, but the rise of U.S. megacorporations into virtual nations unto themselves.

In fundamental ways, however, Quartz represents a seismic break from his intellectual predecessors.

"Our beliefs and behavior have transformed profoundly over the last fifty years," he says.

One thing that sets Quartz apart from other prominent twentieth-century status critics is that he does his own lab research. This is what led him, in the course of inspecting consumer behavior for Lisa Ling, to his breakthrough epiphany. Regarding status and prestige products, some-

thing happens inside the brain that no one before had the ability to see—
and it refutes every high-handed assumption moralists from Aristotle to
Veblen to Packard to Grandma Moses ever made about the iniquitous
pursuit of material or personal luxury. For centuries status seeking and
wealth signaling have been appraised as morally pernicious impulses
manufactured by marketing devils to separate unsuspecting naïfs from
their well-earned wages. Status was sin. And artifice.

By peering into the brain at the exact moment of consumption,
Quartz unearthed a more complex reality. Neither a product of peer
pressure nor artificially created social anxiety, in the eternal quest for
status—and specifically in the pleasure generated by a set of hedonic hot
spots within the limbic circuitry—he discovered a measurable biological
foundation.* Rather than mock the pursuit of status and luxury, this
led Quartz to believe we should accept it in the same way we accept our
need for oxygen and sexual gratification. Maybe even celebrate it in the
same way.

"A major barrier to understanding consumption is the idea that our
status concerns are artificial, or worse yet, pathological," Quartz and Asp
write in *Cool*. "This is a historically monumental mistake, one that has
resulted in decades of misleading consumerism critiques. Once we recognize the biological reality of consumer motives . . . the prescription
to deny them becomes as feasible—and right-minded—as the Victorian
demand for chastity."

Quartz offers an entirely modern response to Veblen and Packard:
Stop hatin'!

"Many discussions of consumer culture today are deeply tinged with
moralism and focus more on condemning it than on understanding it,"
Quartz says. "The result is a void in our understanding of a basic force
shaping our world." This approach to understanding status doesn't just
overturn the applecart pushed by Veblen and Packard. It's a rejection of
canon that goes all the way back to the ancient Egyptians, who regarded

---

* Cells in many brain regions respond to reward. The mesolimbic dopamine pathway is thought to
play a primary role in the reward/pleasure system.

the brain as so meaningless they rudely disposed of it by extracting it through the nasal cavity before mummifying their exalted figures. Quartz puts paid to the ancient idea that the heart is where important decisions are made. To him it's all about the brain.

Cool revels in heady status consciousness. From the opening page, it explodes with festive references to Gucci, Prada, Fendi, Bijan, Dolce & Gabbana, and some already-defunct brand's $800 jeans. Quartz demolishes the idea that the pursuit of status is ephemeral or unnatural. "We intrinsically care about status," he and Asp write.

At his most excitable, Quartz sounds like a brand ambassador for Big Luxe, proselytizing about ways the world can be saved by conscious and even conspicuous consumption, especially if we're intentional and thoughtful about what we buy. In a radical break from the tradition that regards all consumerism as morally suspicious, Quartz is bullish on the ethics of status and corrective morality of consumption. For example, "[buying a] Prius isn't signaling wasteful spending," he and Asp write. "It is signaling prosocial traits, including altruism and environmental concern."

Electric cars are good examples. So are rescue dogs. But at his core, Quartz remains a philosopher and historian. And consumer.

"There's a strong biological basis for our consumer behavior and status signaling," he tells me at an outdoor table on the Caltech campus, sipping from a bottle of Fiji Water, describing a vacation he'd taken to France, and getting ready to head home to his house in Malibu. "Veblen got his evolutionary history wrong."

Veblen assumed consumer behavior was based largely on external cues. Unlike Quartz, he had no way of knowing how much of it is bred in the bone.

QUARTZ'S THESIS IS supported by numerous studies. The most convincing, the one that for me best presents the new empathy for our preoccupation with status and luxury, was conducted in 2007. It centered on three bottles of cabernet sauvignon picked up in a moment of inspiration at Trader Joe's.

The study was led by a then–Caltech researcher and pioneer in the field of decision and consumer neuroscience named Hilke Plassmann. She's now the Octapharma Chair of Decision Neuroscience at INSEAD, the self-proclaimed "business school for the world" in France.

Plassmann's Caltech study pivoted on the age-old derision of self-styled wine aficionados. In test after test it's been demonstrated that without the benefit of a label even experienced wine snobs can't tell the difference between a $250 estate-bottled Chilean Carmenère and a $4 bottle of Missouri altar wine. Blindfold taste tests, of course, have traditionally been Kryptonite to even highly regarded connoisseurs. Who doesn't enjoy seeing pompous pricks defrocked when their alleged expertise is body-slammed in an actual test?

To test a hunch that *perceptions* of quality can actually animate neural pleasure centers, independent of a product's intrinsic qualities and molecular composition, Plassmann devised a crafty experiment. It was one that could be carried out only in the era of MRI.

To my way of thinking, the best lab experiments have a diabolical edge to them. They involve a fake-out—the guy administering the punitive electric shock doesn't realize he's the sicko who's the actual subject of the exercise. Timeless.

Plassmann's study is a good example. Using fMRI, Plassmann and her team scanned the brain activity of twenty adults while each sampled different wines administered with electronic syringe tubes fired by computerized pumps. Subjects were told they were going to taste five different wines as part of an experiment intended to measure the effects of degustation time on flavor. Unbeknownst to the subjects, they were tasting only three different wines, not five. And no one conducting the test gave a shit about degustation time. That was a ruse.

Two of the wines were administered twice. The first time, each wine was identified at a high retail price—$45 and $90 a bottle, respectively. The second time around, tasters were given the same wines, but this time they were told they were tasting wines costing $5 and $10 a bottle, respectively. The figures represented real prices with a 900 percent markup ($5 was the real price, $45 was the fictitious price) or a 900 percent reduction ($90 was the real price, $10 was the fictitious price). A third control wine was truthfully and consistently identified as a $35 bottle.

The broad results were predictable to anyone familiar with hints-of-pumice-and-artisan-pottery snottery. The higher the given price, the more subjects reported they enjoyed the wine. Der. A clear-cut case of elitist intimidation, right? It's expensive ($45), so it must be better than the cheaper one ($5), and I'll look like a fool if I say otherwise.

But Plassmann noticed something else going on. What the fMRI results showed wasn't just illuminating. It was groundbreaking. Each time participants were told the wine they were tasting was getting more expensive, activity in several of the brain's known pleasure centers heightened. A lot of that pleasure-center activity was created by a rush of dopamine, the brain's primary reward chemical. Upon drinking the "high-priced" wine, increased levels of dopamine were sent from the nucleus accumbens to the medial prefrontal cortex and other areas, measurably changing the biology of the brain.

The implications refuted centuries of accepted wisdom about luxury consumption. Plassmann proved that, independent of taste or other physical properties, expensive wine actually is more enjoyable to drinkers. It really does make them feel better. Just not for the reasons previously assumed. It's not the wine itself drinkers most enjoy. It's not even (completely) the alcoholic effect. It's the perceived value—and the *perception of status* that value confers—that literally gets people high by releasing dopamine and other chemicals in their brains. This flood of happy chemicals in turn generates what scientists call "experienced pleasantness," or EP.

"Whereas there is ample behavioral evidence that various marketing actions [i.e., pricing] are successful in influencing EP of individuals, that they can modulate neural representations of this signal had not been reported before," concluded Plassmann and the experiment's coauthors.

The lesson for Quartz—now well on his way to synthesizing his own growing body of research into a wholly new understanding of status—is that we need to stop making fun of people who get off on expensive wine. Or take Evian water baths in outrageously priced hotels. Or consume brand-name goods with criminally jacked-up prices. Even if not for the reasons they might profess—quality, craftsmanship, superior flavor—even if their taste buds don't know the difference—consuming extravagantly priced goods and services literally does make people feel better because of the dopamine that doing so releases into their brains.

The premise that consumerism relies on instilling false or superficial needs—the linchpin of most critiques of status seeking—is based on prim judgment. From their battleship of empirical fact, researchers like Plassmann, Berns, and Quartz have blown that opinion-powered dinghy of an idea out of the water. "Although [Packard's] explanation of postwar America's consumerism remains popular, it's wrong," wrote Quartz and Asp, calling out Packard's bestseller *The Hidden Persuaders* by name.

Quartz is right about the Veblen and Packard view of consumerism being particularly stubborn. In 2010, a study by University of Colorado Boulder and Cornell University researchers titled "Stigmatizing Materialism" found "modern materialism is widely viewed as detrimental to society." Eighty-eight percent of respondents said Americans are too materialistic, 93 percent believed Americans are too focused on money, and "87 percent said that consumer culture makes it difficult to instill positive values in American children."

Reliably reposted across the internet each holiday season leading up to New Year's celebrations, a 2015 *Vox* piece with the by-now-predictable exposé title "Expensive Wine Is for Suckers" focuses almost entirely on those tired old, blind taste tests that fool industry critics and competition judges into rating cheap wines higher than expensive wines. Its producers either weren't aware of, or weren't impressed by, Plassmann's discovery that flavor profile isn't what people are buying when they're buying wine.

At least among the scientific community, opinions are changing. Like climate change, it may take the general public longer to accept the proposition that status isn't an illusion. It's a real need. And that consumption of luxury goods is one of the fastest ways to fulfill it.

In London, a pair of doctors is using MRI to drag this revelation out of the soporific halls of academia and embed it into the mainstream consciousness. After visiting with Quartz in California, I called and asked if I could come have a look to see just how they were doing that.

JOE DEVLIN IS a fifty-two-year-old Philadelphia-area native who earned a PhD in artificial intelligence from the University of Southern California in the late 1990s. After graduating, he went to work for Lucent Technologies in Columbus, Ohio. Eventually he moved to London—England, not Ohio—where he landed a job teaching at Cambridge University. He now teaches neuroscience at the University College London (UCL). In 2016, he launched a side business called Applied Consumer Neuroscience Labs (ACN).

John Hogan is Devlin's UCL research and ACN business partner. After growing up in the small town of Newmarket, just outside Toronto, Hogan graduated from the University of Toronto with degrees in psychology and cognitive science. After following the woman he would eventually marry to London, he earned a PhD in neuroscience from UCL, where he met Devlin and formed an immediate bond.

One of the first things people notice about the forty-four-year-old Hogan is that, like Devlin (who holds a black belt in jiujitsu), he stays in excellent shape. His outsized biceps and thickly veined arms indicate a fair amount of time in the weight room. Maybe even some GNC products. Recently, he's taken up soccer to help maintain his cardio.

All of these personal details about Devlin and Hogan I divined in a comparatively short amount of time using a long-honored data-research method—the in-person interview. To certain marketing professionals—particularly the overlords of modern industry interested in tapping into the subconscious desires of consumers—this method of gathering psychographic information is seen as woefully primitive. Its archaic roots make it laughably inadequate to compete in the data-driven and universally connected algorithmic sales and marketing environment of the twenty-first century.

Because marketers lust for new psychographics the way teenage boys lust for . . . I was going to say teenage girls, but video games is probably the safer bet these days . . . they come to ACN for help. Along with a tight community of researchers scattered around the world, Devlin and Hogan are regarded as modern-day witch doctors. Within their power, they hold, or so the hope goes, the ability to unlock, influence, and manipulate your mind. My mind. Everybody's mind. And in the process release the riches of Croesus upon their benefactors. Or at least help meet next quarter's sales goals.

Even within the supremely heady fields of neuroscience and neuromarketing, Devlin and Hogan—who I'm going to refer to collectively as DevHog from here on out because it's easier, shorter, and amusing—are doing something almost no one else is. They're drawing back the curtain on what's traditionally been a closely guarded, proprietary, and nearly inaccessible world of neuromarketing research.

Open to the public, their customizable UCL Neuromarketing Workshops in London include time with a magnetic resonance imaging (MRI) scanner gathering functional magnetic resonance imaging (fMRI) data—closely related to MRI, fMRI is the actual technique of measuring brain activity. Anyone with a few thousand bucks to spare can attend a workshop and learn the secrets of the trade.

This may sound like a significant money drop to John Q. Science Buff. But it's chump change to places like Caltech, Stanford, and MIT, to say nothing of Google, Amazon, and Facebook, all entities that have employed neuromarketing to better understand SEO, test consumer impressions, track ad effectiveness, and consolidate their dominion over humanity. Our massive tech khans intimidate a lot of us. But DevHog is demystifying the data they and others use by walking clients through the process by which it's collected and analyzed.

The bulk of their research takes place on the UCL campus inside a block-long monstrosity of 1970s poured concrete known as the Institute of Education building. Drab and Soviet, the five-story gray Goliath has been called one of London's finest examples of Brutalist architecture. The design sets a tone best described as midcentury Checkpoint Charlie. From the outside, it hardly looks like a place where neuromagic luxury-market telepathy occurs.

A big part of what DevHog see as their mission at UCL is debunking scientific myths. One of their favorite slides in a PowerPoint presentation they give on neuromarketing dissembles a Mercedes-Benz print advertisement illustrating the left and right hemispheres of the brain. The ad's message is that driving a Mercedes produces the ultimate cerebral experience because its frighteningly strict Teutonic engineering stimulates the "rational" left hemisphere of the brain, while its balls-out performance on every road between Flanders and the gates of Moscow fires up the "creative" right side of the brain. The ad features a gorgeous illustration with a groovy Einstein-snorts-oxycodone-then-drops-the-needle-on-a-Hendrix-deep-track vibe. Some graphic designer somewhere looked at the final proof of it and no doubt said to herself, "Goddamn, I deserve a raise."

Unfortunately, according to DevHog, the science the ad co-opts to sell prestige cars is bogus.

"The whole left-right brain thing is total crap," Devlin says. "The brain is bilateral."

"Everything happening on the left is happening on the right," Hogan adds, allowing for minor exceptions.

Naturally, they're correct about misconceptions surrounding brain hemispheres. The left-right brain story line got going in 1861 when a French physician named Pierre Paul Broca performed an autopsy on a male patient nicknamed "Tan," because "tan" was one of the only words the poor man could articulate. Broca opened Tan's skull and found a large lesion on the left side of his brain. He believed the lesion was responsible for impairing Tan's ability to speak and concluded that because it was located on the left side of the brain this must be the side of the organ that controls speech. The left frontal lobe of the brain has ever since been known as "Broca's area." Technically known as "lateralization of brain function," the Frenchman's left-right brain theory has since been resoundingly discredited.

Its popularity, nevertheless, lives on. Observant fans of the TV version of *Game of Thrones* who can get past all the superb cudgeling, raven mail, and brothel tittery will notice a scar creasing the left temple of the dim-bulb giant Hodor, so-named because "hodor" is the only word the unfortunate simpleton can summon. The scar and Hodor are an homage (intentional or not) to Broca and Tan.

The relevant connection here is that all sorts of companies—not just Mercedes-Benz—are selling status and prestige in the name of debunked science. Because the debasement of facts can sometimes lead to dark consequences, DevHog considers this antithetical to their duty as scientists. Back in the early 1800s, for just one example they cite, German scientist Franz Joseph Gall founded the pseudoscience of phrenology. The half-baked theory, which became wildly popular in Western countries, used skull size and shape, as well as "readings" of various contours on the scalp, as indicators of intelligence and cultural advancement. In then-influential displays, the skulls of people of African descent were placed on a continuum between the skulls of apes and white people.

"The scientific community knew phrenology was utter horseshit, but they didn't do anything to engage the public," Devlin says. "This led to Francis Galton, unfortunately right here at UCL, to popularize eugenics and turn this into a 'scientific' justification of white supremacy. This came about because the academic community didn't engage with the communities around them."

"Through its inaction, the academic world bears some of the responsibility for that," says Hogan.

It's important to DevHog that academics call bullshit on any perversion of scientific truth. "There are neuromarketing companies today that claim they use AI to process their data," Devlin tells me. "We have yet to speak to anyone at any company who actually knows what they do with that data, or how they apply it.

"They have pat phrases. 'We use such and such technology.' We'll say, 'Oh, yeah, what is that?' 'Oh, it's proprietary, we can't share that.' We say, 'No, it's not proprietary. It was published in the 1970s.' They look like deer in the headlights. There are people who have no idea what their data is. And they're selling it."

"These are the biggest neuromarketing brands in the industry," Hogan says. "It's shocking stuff."

I'm glad I wasn't around these two in high school. Not only are they built like linebackers, they have roughly the same tolerance for nerds, who they're smart enough to give a metaphorical pantsing on the Algebra II final.

ALL OF THIS background led me, after a brief chat in a Brutalist conference room, to volunteer to be loaded into the narrow tube of a 5-foot-long, 5.9-ton Siemens Magnetom Avanto magnetic resonance imaging scanner—an MRI machine. I'd asked DevHog to have a look inside what I hope to God turns out to be a healthy, tumor-free brain.

Aside from a mild headache induced the night before with some local friends, I feel all right. One thing about London, people there tend to drink a lot, then settle on a bag of potato chips for dinner after missing the last train home.

"Your hangover won't affect the results," Hogan assures me.

I'm going to be a sample participant in an experiment sponsored by a British beauty blog meant to test my reaction to women's appearance in a variety of stages of makeup. Combined with the responses of others, my reactions will help quantify how makeup influences perceptions of attractiveness. Am I more attracted to women who've just rolled out of bed? Or those who are fresh-faced in the produce section examining avocados? Or who are coming out of the bathroom at a nightclub after applying a fresh layer of golden-ocher eye shadow? Beauty blogs urgently need this information. Fortunately, I've got a great many opinions on women and am excited for the rare, guilt-free opportunity to provide them under the cover of scientific inquiry.

"Try to stay as still as possible," Hogan says in a soothing way I'm guessing he's practiced in front of the mirrors in the weight room. Seriously, dude is jacked, and not just for a neuroscientist. It's distracting. I can't get used to it.

"This thing isn't gonna give me cancer, is it?" I ask.

Devlin's voice crackles over a speaker from a control room behind what looks like a bulletproof window where he commands a small bank of computers.

"Not that we know," he says.

"Perfect," I say.

"I've spent a couple hundred hours in the scanner myself, so I hope not," he says. "Having a ten-minute scan is like having a ten-minute cell phone call."

The scanner is exactly like the ones you've seen on all the TV hospital shows. Or in actual hospitals. It's a molded-plastic cylinder with a hollow core in the center. Since it's all white and you see only the top half when you're on your back, being inside kind of feels like killing time in the entryway of an igloo. Hogan positions my head between a pair of cushions in a tight little basket and affixes a grilled apparatus over my face that makes it look like I'm staring through a football helmet. A rubber squeeze ball on my chest will activate an alarm in the event I wig out inside the chamber, which offers no range of movement for arms or legs.

"It's gonna be loud in there once the scanner gets going," he says. "It's gonna sound like bad techno music."

He's referring to the steady rhythm kicked out by the spinning of a heavy core magnet that drives the scanner's cooling system, or "chiller." A by-product of the function is a loud, repetitive four-four beat with a deep bass whoomp on the one and three, accompanied by a squishy, Bauhaus snare on the two and four. Once engaged, the actual scanner adds a penetrating buzzer noise on top of the beat that sounds more or less like what you'd expect to hear during a meltdown event at a nuclear power plant. This sonic blast intrudes in alarming, arrhythmic spasms. Hogan might have his act together in the lab, but he's wrong about one thing. This aggressive mechanized cacophony doesn't sound like bad techno music. It sounds like *good* techno music.

While I'm tripping, DevHog activates the scanner. This records a model of the brain activity that controls my emotional and intellectual re-actions. The more still I remain, the clearer the scan will come out. I try to zone out to the beat. Flat on my back, immobilized in the pulsing cham-ber, I stare into a small screen as various images of the same eighteen young women of various ethnicities are presented to me in three-second intervals.

Sometimes the women appear disheveled—puffy eyes, skin blem-ishes, rumpled collars, grumpy faces. In other shots, the same women look the way you'd expect to see them walking into the office at nine a.m.—clean, put together, ready to manage the company's social media accounts or negotiate a merger. Other times, they're clearly ready to hit the club, and by the looks of their makeup, a cooler one than I'm usually allowed into.

For all the effort, the experiment is mildly disappointing. At least for me. I'd expected an updated Four Lads, standing-on-the-corner-watching-all-the-girls-go-by kind of experience. But there really isn't much to engage with.

I try, as instructed, to focus on the overall attractiveness of each woman in various situations. But there's little variation. And zero eroti-cism. Most of the models seem to have been chosen for their plain looks and moody dispositions. Anyway, in my estimation, women care a lot more about makeup and bed head than guys do. Thinking I might be asked questions later, I pick a favorite out of the bunch—shoulder-length blunt cut, outdoorsy vibe, brown eyes. I name her "Audra."

AFTER THE SCAN, DevHog gives me a computer-image tour of my brain, complete with neon cross-section images sliced wafer-thin. It's colorful and cool, but it looks pretty much like every other brain scan I've seen in places like *Scientific American*. Looking at the thing on a computer screen all I really want is for someone to say, "Your brain looks healthy, no signs of disease or premature aging," which, thank God, DevHog do, though not without prodding. My test results are filed away without comment. No follow-up questions about Audra.

Having flown to London already convinced by people like Steven Quartz that, beyond oxygen, food, and water, nothing motivates people like status and success, I figure I might as well try to pry some helpful marketing advice out of the masters before I go back to the States.

"I'm writing a book about status," I remind the guys. "As neuro-marketers, what kind of marketing plan would you craft to immediately connect the concepts of 'Chuck Thompson' and 'prestige' in consumers' minds?"

DevHog falls silent. For the first time in the six or so hours I've been with them the conversation falls flat. Devlin literally scratches the back of his head. I know linking me and luxury is a heavy lift, but I try to prod some neural activity in those big scientific brains. How can I use fMRI insight to attract readers? I ask. Maybe we can devise a study that would offer subjects different book covers to look at and gauge their neurological responses.

The guys instead start talking about devising a simple questionnaire test. Something that could be administered online.

"You test your prediction that way, that's a straight psychology test," Devlin says. "Low cost, low effort."

"But I want to use the scanner," I say. "What's the point of all this fMRI insight if I can't use it?"

The main reason DevHog tell me I don't want to use fMRI to create my marketing plan is that it's incredibly expensive. Cranking up the scanner costs $500 to $1,000 an hour, depending on various factors. This seems bonkers to me. The machine's right here. How expensive can it be to hit "power" and take some pics?

"This scanner itself costs about two million dollars. A new one might cost about three and a half million," DevHog says. "They have a life cycle of about ten years, so you have to amortize the cost. There's two hundred thousand dollars a year in Siemens service maintenance. Things go wrong all the time and when they do your tech support is a physicist."

Hellacious cost is the reason companies are always looking for the "holy grail" of neuromarketing—being able to use the results of a small study, say thirty scanned subjects, to accurately forecast the luxury-buying patterns of millions. It's what Berns was groping toward with his music focus group. It's what the beauty blog was up to.

As big an obstacle as cost is accuracy. Despite widespread paranoia about marketers using fMRI to crawl into the deepest crannies of our minds—and with 86 billion neurons firing 10 trillion synapses across 1,000 miles of axons there are a lot of these to crawl into—the reality is far more banal.

"Our ability is actually still very crude," Devlin says. "We can't read minds. We can measure brain activity, but that doesn't necessarily mean we know how to translate it. Can we put someone in a scanner and read their dreams? No, we cannot."

The biggest takeaway from my time with DevHog, Quartz, Berns, and the rapidly expanding host of experts changing the way we view ourselves in relation to others is that status is real, at least insofar as what's happening in the brain makes it so. It may take another generation or two before the message goes mainstream, but repressive Judeo-Christian reactions to status seeking are becoming obsolete. Recognition of the essential human need for status—often as not delivered by prestige and luxury goods and services—will likely change the consumer game in ways we cannot yet fathom. That's because status can always be sold. Even if it's camouflaged as working more or owning less, there'll always be a hook, line, and sinker to reel us in to the dopamine rush released by consumption of privilege and prestige.

But something else was also taking shape in my mind. It was a concept planted by Sturla, then confirmed by the emerging pontiffs of neuroscience. The evolving ease with which these eminences of brain sciences were able to test their assumptions had inspired me. With all of this research technology and technique now within reach of the public, maybe I could test, perhaps even debunk, one of the most enduring status legends of the past century. And, along the way, take part in the twenty-first-century approach to status reconstruction for myself.

You can read books and talk to experts all you want. The best way to learn is by doing.

CHAPTER 4

Sports cars and small penises: STATUS AS INCLUSIVITY

I'VE NEVER EMPLOYED A CHAUFFEUR, DRESSED DOWN A LAMBO PR flack while picking up a $400,000 sports car from the factory in Italy (more on this in a sec), or catcalled at women out the window of my 2002 Buick LeSabre. But I have had at least one memorable experience with the intercourse of cars, status, and the internal combustion male rut. In the early 2000s, my college buddy Russell and I flew from his home in Beaverton, Oregon, to Florida to pick up a restored 1965 Plymouth Valiant convertible he'd bought off eBay. I rode shotgun and occasionally spelled Rusty behind the wheel on the cross-country drive back home, partly because I've always enjoyed his company, but mostly because that's the kind of time freelance writers have on their hands.

Though not as muscular as some of its 1960s Detroit peers, the Valiant is nevertheless a pretty sleek and sporty little classic. In his memoir, *Shoe Dog*, Nike founder Phil Knight writes that the first car he bought after college was a Valiant. Maybe it's a Beaverton guy thing. "The salesman called it sea-foam green," wrote the future CEO and shoe savant of his new car's color. "It was actually the green of newly minted money."

Being in Russell's car for a week gave me perspective on what it must be like to go through life as a beautiful woman. Guys hooted and whistled as we passed on the street. No matter where we stopped—gas stations, restaurants, Walmarts—they just couldn't stop themselves from staring. Some took pictures.

Young and old, inevitably one or two would break from the pack and walk over—some shy and shuffling, others brimming with confidence and cologne—looking for a clever way to break the ice. How old was she, they always wanted to know. How many miles on her? What's under the hood? How fast was she? We always escaped before any of them could pin us down for a ride, though it was pretty clear that's what they all had in mind.

If like ships cars are traditionally anthropomorphized as female, they've also acquired a not-so-subtle reputation as proxy for the sexual endowment of their gentleman owners. The prevailing assumption is the showier a man's car, the more likely it's being used to compensate for an inadequate crankshaft. Even if teen driving and car sales are in decline—globally down 5 percent from 2017 to 2019, then plummeting another 22 percent in pandemic 2020, before a slight rebound in 2021—the old punch line hasn't lost its juice. In 2019, Bill Maher used it in his signature bit while riffing on a coffee mug emblazoned with the catchphrase: I ♥ coffee.

"New rule, you don't need to write 'I love coffee' on a coffee mug," Maher said. "We get that from the mug itself. Because you filled it with coffee. It's like writing 'I have a small dick' on your Ferrari." Accompanied by a doctored image of a Ferrari with a little weenie painted on the hood, the line received lascivious guffaws and knowing applause from the studio audience. Everyone understood the lurid association between hot cars and micro-peens and knew how to respond to the suggestion.

Guys, of course, are even more preoccupied with the size of their genitals than with the price tag of their rides. In the free-porn era—loads of enormous cocks everywhere—anxiety over penis size has swollen to epidemic levels. Guys google more questions about their penises than any other body part or function.

SO, WE ALL assume by now that guys who buy sports cars do so at least in part to overcome sexual shortcomings. But is that really true? Short of lining up one hundred Ferrari drivers, having them drop their pants, and moving down the line with a tape measure, how would one even go about finding out if the popular myth was rooted in truth?

My first attempts at tweezing out an answer involved putting the question directly to experts: Do men who drive sports cars really have small penises?

"Luxury is an appearance business. As such it is linked to seduction," wrote Jean-Noël Kapferer, coauthor of the industry bible *The Luxury Strategy*, responding by email. "In terms of Darwin evolutionism, exhibiting a Lamborghini is a way to select females by showing off one's attributes, at least symbolically." This sounded like eminent French wisdom, but it didn't really address the question.

In Michigan, the director of the Society of Automotive Historians, Bob Elton, offered no proof, but laughed and said that like most jokes there was probably some truth to this one.

Rick Springfield,* who I believe resides in the top one percentile of guys on the cars-and-girls† portion of most standardized measures, was more equivocal. Springfield will figure more prominently later in this book. Initially, he was merely a go-to source for hot rod op-ed.

"The thing about dick size, I bought this car fifteen years ago when dick size didn't matter to me anymore," he tells me in the breezy outdoor courtyard of the Malibu Starbucks. The legendary rocker, known for such hits as "Don't Talk to Strangers" and "I've Done Everything for You," and now well past sixty, is referring to a 1963 Corvette Stingray. He shows me a photo of himself and ex–Van Halen frontman and self-styled Red Rocker Sammy "I Can't Drive 55 in Any of My Ferraris and Many Other Sports Cars" Hagar posing in front of the vehicle.

---

* And, yes, here I'm referring to the Rick Springfield of 1980s "Affair of the Heart" and "Love Somebody" fame.
† And, yes, eighties college radio aficionados, that was an intentional reference to the immortal Paddy McAloon.

"Women don't like this car," Springfield continues. "If I was into fifty- and sixty-year-old guys I'd be getting laid all over the place."

I tell Rick (once frank dick chat makes its conversational appearance, I figure I've been carried across the celebrity first-name-basis threshold) my Valiant story, and we concur on the point that most sports cars are actually pretty uncomfortable to ride in. They're small, cramped, and low to the ground.

"It's a guy thing," Rick reiterates. "There are certain guys who get the Ferrari and always have girls around. Do women just maybe like fucking successful guys? Women respond to confidence. Success affects the way you carry yourself into a room. A car might signal that."

These were all fascinating conversations, but they weren't getting me closer to the truth about superior cars and below-average dicks. I realized nothing shy of a rigorous academic study could solve the ultimate car status riddle. I began to think in terms of those clickbait-y headlines you see in your news feed like "Researchers in Scotland Say Four in Five Cavemen Were Bisexual" or "Study Finds Playing Soccer Makes You 35 Percent Less American."

I started fishing around for a visionary academic who shared both my keen curiosity about male genitalia and down-market sensibilities. This proved tougher than expected. Networking with a couple of college professor pals turned up some leads, but these quickly went cold. A few researchers at U.S. universities were kind enough to reply to my emails, but only to tell me in so many words that my idea belonged alongside the Ministry of Silly Walks. Then, just as I was about to give up, an email arrived from Joe Devlin at the University College London: "Dear Chuck, I spoke with a colleague about your interest in penis size and he had an interesting idea."

Not precisely the way I would've put it, but God bless 'em, no one does eccentricity like the Brits.

DANIEL RICHARDSON IS that university prof whose class stressed-out undergrads look forward to. He's witty, even-tempered, bright, and just different enough from his colleagues to function as a subversive element within a parochial system. Also, he's not afflicted by delusions of academic grandiosity.

"Some people want to use science to construct big theoretical explanations for the universe. I'm happier thinking about science to answer small questions," he tells me shortly after the introduction from Devlin. "My career has been driven by the weird little things that catch my eye."

At forty-six, Richardson looks like what you'd expect an experimental psychology professor to look like—open-faced, glasses, beard that seems to come and go, neither in shape nor out of shape, no evident sartorial ambitions.

One of his early experiments began when a female student told him a story about being the only woman in a room filled with prominent male psychologists at Stanford University. During the meeting, someone cracked a joke about women drivers. Everyone laughed. Then everyone stole a glance at the young woman.

Why did they do that?

Richardson suggested it was a simple matter of visual association. As benign as if someone mentioned the color green and someone in the group is wearing a green shirt and your eyes automatically drift over to the green shirt.

A female colleague disagreed. She posited the look was a means of "social referencing." A classic example is the way a baby looks at its mother's face for visual cues to gauge her pleasure or displeasure with its behavior.

The two decided to test their assumptions. They constructed an experiment in which someone in a largely Caucasian group says something vaguely race-baiting about affirmative action in the presence of a sole Black male (a confederate in the test). In one condition the Black man could plainly hear the offensive comment. In another condition the Black man was visible to the group but clearly could not hear the racist comment.

Following the insulting statement, the number of looks over to the

Black man differed significantly between the two conditions. When the man was privy to the offensive remark, more people looked at him, apparently in an attempt to assess his reaction.

"Proving that she was right and I was wrong," Richardson says.

One thing I like about Richardson, he's perfectly fine having his assumptions disproven. He's not a pain in the ass about being right. He just wants to know why things are the way they are. This makes him good for my experiment. When I tell him I'll be just as happy if we can prove or disprove a correlation between sports cars and penis size, or even come to no conclusion at all, he seems to make the same judgment about me.

WHEN THE FIRST horseless carriage chugged out of Karl Benz's workshop in Germany on New Year's Eve 1879, the world's measure of status changed forever. Automobiles were the quintessential communion of technology, craftsmanship, beauty, form, function, and personal wealth. The upshot was a status bonanza the ancients could never have imagined. Personal mobility made cars the ultimate status symbol. You can't park a million-dollar home, a gold watch, or even a trophy wife downtown for everyone to gawp at. Particularly for males, cars have been the universal symbol of success and status ever since.

In the 1924 film *The Navigator*, comic stunt hero Buster Keaton exploited the already well-worn trope. Playing a fatuous playboy millionaire, he famously had his chauffeur drive him in a stylish convertible from his mansion to his girlfriend's house directly across the street. The hundred feet or so that separated the homes made for too banal a walk. Bipedalism? So nineteenth century. Keaton was a genius. You can watch that scene twenty times without getting bored.

Roughly a century after Keaton's gag, internet stunt antiheroes Jake and Logan Paul filmed their own send-up of privileged car douchebaggery, freaking out like Ritalin addicts after being denied the right to film inside Lamborghini headquarters in Italy while picking up Jake's new customized Huracán Performante. The Paul bros may be canny but they're not geniuses. Unless you're a particular kind of dual-clutch so-ciopath, it's a scene that's challenging to watch in its entirety even once, though millions have.

Car culture is arguably on the wane. Today, only about 25 percent of American sixteen-year-olds have a driver's license. In the early 1980s, 46 percent had a license. But the connection between cars and status remains embedded in the Western psyche. In a *Psychology Today* article, evolution-ary psychologist Dr. Gad Saad proved a point by referencing a study that found women rated men more attractive when they were sitting behind the wheel of a Bentley Continental as opposed to a Ford Fiesta.

"Endowing a man with a potent status symbol triggers an endocri-nological response," Saad wrote with charged imagery. "The social status of the car that an individual is driving affects the likelihood that he'll be bullied (less likely if driving a high-status car) or will bully others on the road (more likely if driving a high-status car)."

As cars morphed into society's consensus signifier of wealth, power, and status, it was only a matter of time before they also came to stand as a broader barometer of personal and cultural virility. Babes on bumpers became fixtures at car shows. Posters of Hemi-friendly vixens splayed across the hoods of Maseratis and Mustangs appeared as cornerstones of dude dorm room feng shui. America's "muscle cars" defined a global power at its apogee. As China and other Asian countries have caught up to the West in terms of material excess, citizens of the "bicycle kingdom" abandoned their legacy of cycling to compete with Western ideals of suc-cess. Car ownership has become the benchmark of arrival for which its populations most ardently reach.

THE WORLD DOESN'T want to hear about the labor pains, it only wants to see the baby. That may be true for new moms and Ikea kitchens, but most of the motivation for embarking on this irreverent enterprise was to see how a real academic study worked from the inside. (Although, naturally, I was curious about the results.)

In the world of status and prestige a virtual army of researchers and analysts in every corner of the world is slogging away all the time—it's Zoom o'clock somewhere—to uncover shards of wisdom that might give their corporate underwriters an advantage in the battle to win the hearts and credit cards of luxury consumers. Commissioning a study and teaming with a legit social scientist to carry it off would give me a 360-degree view into an indispensable part of the status machine.

Richardson suggests running the study as part of a student lab section he's leading. Using students means we can tap into a pool of free labor from which to draw the grunt work. Having myself served in this capacity as an undergrad—one of my journalism professors was notorious for molding nearly all of his classes into work parties to obtain election polling data he used to promote himself to national media—I have no compunction about this whatsoever.

Because the aforementioned lineup of pants-less car owners is tricky to pull off outside a navy boot camp or porn casting call, and because self-reporting is notoriously unreliable, we settle on a next-best-thing approach.* Richardson devises a simple survey experiment designed to manipulate subjects' self-esteem based on what they believe about their own penis size relative to others. Once subjects are made to feel less sexually substantial than their peers, they'll be presented with questions about sports cars.

The manipulation piece is a little mean. It'll be achieved by providing subjects with a string of "facts," some true, some false. Some of the "facts" will be red herrings. One we come up with: "The first known written instance of 'OMG' is in a letter to Winston Churchill in 1917." Unless you're a web philologist, that's a pretty inconsequential fib. Other "facts," however, will be specifically designed to induce low self-esteem. These will include information stating the average penis size is larger than it actually is.

The reasoning behind the ruse is that, on average, once study males

---

* Richardson argues our method is "not second best at all," saying it's actually more scientifically interesting than simply pantsing people.

are made to feel that relatively and subjectively their own schlong is lacking, they'll be primed to place a higher value on sports car ownership. Or not. The facts and questions pertaining to personal meatpacking will be buried among other unrelated items in the survey (OMG, Churchill!), thereby masking the study's hypothesis from participants.

If the "manipulate self-esteem" basis to the experiment feels a little weak to you, it did at first to me as well. However, this is a standard approach to academic experiments in which you want to see how a person's self-esteem changes their behavior. Richardson provides an example about an experiment in which people are given information that they either aced or failed an IQ test. Following this, the subjects are shown a video of a job interview and asked to rate the candidate.

"The candidate has a Jewish-sounding name," explains Richardson. "If, and only if, they have had their self-esteem lowered, then they are more likely to use racially toned and stereotypical, negative descriptions of the candidates. And the degree to which they are racist boosts their self-esteem when measured at the end."

There's lots of peer-reviewed research behind the method that shows it is in fact pretty easy to manipulate people's feelings about themselves and that feelings expressed in lab settings—inferiority, confidence, joy, anger, narcissism—have a real-world correlation. It's one reason so many mental health professionals felt confident observing Donald Trump's public behavior, then worked backward to make clinical diagnoses that shocked half the country and appeared comfortingly familiar ("That's Dad!") to the other half.

Almost immediately after agreeing to the project, we encounter our first hurdle. Richardson stops replying to my emails. After several weeks of apparent ghosting I begin wondering if the noncommunicative prof is the right guy to partner with after all. Then one day Richardson writes: "Our progress has so far been hampered presumably because of the repeated references to penis length." The university's email filters, he explains, have been blocking or diverting my emails to a spam account Richardson rarely checks.

I devise a set of code words. Penises attached to sports car owners will hereafter be known as "Hagars," after the man most associated with Ferrari audacity (Enzo himself notwithstanding). In emails the project will be referred to as the Johnson & Johnson project. We firm up a few other soft spots and carry on.

MY FIRST MEETING with Richardson and the student assistants at University College London is done via Skype video. Three p.m. in the UK, seven a.m. on the West Coast. The team is gathered in Richardson's drab university office. White walls, scattered books, dying plants on cheap shelves. Flanking Richardson are three graduate students he's recruited as research assistants—Rea, Luyi, and Annie.

Rea is twenty years old and by her own admission "raised in a very luxurious environment." Growing up she spent time in Beirut, Dubai, Milan, Los Angeles, and Egypt. Along the way she did some child modeling for Ford, Nokia, and Pizza Hut. Speaks five languages. Lots of energy and confidence.

Born in Japan, raised in Shanghai, and having spent a couple years at Penn State, the laid-back Luyi has a similarly polyglot background. She's nineteen. When I ask what luxury products she owns or cares about she replies, "None."

Annie, whose parents emigrated from China, grew up in Vancouver, British Columbia. She's a third-year student on exchange from the psychology and sociology program at McGill University in Montreal, where she's specializing in criminal and deviant behaviors. These feel like solid credentials to bring to our experiment, though I'm not exactly sure why.

I feel good about the student group right away and consider a variety of ways to refer to them in easy shorthand, eventually settling on Team Hagar.

After introductions, Richardson opens the meeting with some general comments about an experiment that will use "various measures of self-esteem to assess generic purchasing decisions." The phrase "generic purchasing decisions" disappoints me. I interrupt to remind everyone the sole objective of our experiment is to prove or disprove the notion that in disproportionate numbers men with small penises buy sports cars to compensate for their perceived sexual inadequacy. There's nothing generic or nonspecific about what we're up to here.

"Yes, yes, we're simply trying to be as creative as we can with the language without having to be constantly referring to . . . penises," Richardson says, making me feel like an uncultured chimp.

I can't be sure if Richardson is simply a terminally repressed Brit, if he's mortified at the prospect of extended penis chat with a klatch of studious young women, or if his vocabulary is merely constrained by the close-minded proscription that's made college seem so much less interesting than when I was in it. Perhaps all three factors—embarrassment, political correctness, academic censure—are working on his mind. I ramp up my use of euphemisms and begin to employ strict medical terms (genitalia, glans, frenulum) where necessary.

Team Hagar witnesses this tortured negotiation with mute interest. All three women appear unfazed by two middle-aged men fumbling around with penises in the least upsetting way possible. Perhaps they're old enough to have already been disappointed by the male members of the species.

FOR MONTHS I'D been examining the way status and prestige are studied, measured, analyzed, explained, marketed, sold, bought, and enshrined in everything from pineapples to top hats to rescue dogs. One fact kept recurring. For the past century or more, virtually everything we accept to be true about status has emanated from the perspective of white males. In particular, with the exception of Vance Packard, from white male university professors.

Before moving on with this line of thought I want to say I don't find anything inherently offensive in the white male point of view, which has come in for a lot of criticism lately. I believe I'm open-minded enough

that I'd say that even if I weren't a member of this widely defamed cohort. White males have done a lot of great things in this world; white
males have visited a lot of unspeakable horror upon this world; just like
males of every color. I wish more people felt this way, including white
people. If the American political left had spent less time shaming away
one of its most reliable voter bases with relentless bashing I'm pretty
sure we wouldn't have had to endure four years of Donald Trump in the
White House. I'm just talking strategy here, not morality. Blind fury is as
self-defeating on the left side of politics as it is on the right.

That said it's obvious the white male career academic point of view
produces a less-than-comprehensive perspective on any given topic. It's
tough to make a case for its universal application. This is basic intellectual
honesty that shouldn't have to be noted, but such are the times in which
we live. *C'est la guerre.*

Like society at large, academia has caught up to the idea that diversity and inclusivity aren't just morally righteous, they are profitable.
Inclusivity has always been fine for the social justice warriors in the Ethnic Studies Department. But guess what? It also produces more accurate
results in the lab. Bonus: effective results tend to make companies that
underwrite research eager to underwrite more of it.

Simply being a woman didn't enable Hilke Plassmann to demonstrate
that perceptions of luxury trigger pleasure centers in the brain. Including women as wine-guzzling test subjects, however, made her findings
relevant across the consumer spectrum. In the same way, Greg Berns's
multiethnic cast of teenage subjects made his findings about music representative of the diverse U.S. population.

This isn't to say academic or commercial entities with an interest
in status have always been the exclusive provenance of narrow-minded
white men. Just that often as not the test results they've used to make
global assertions have been based on a constricted demographic. Not always, but very often in the formative past, when women or non-whites
were used as subjects it was as part of tests limited exclusively to studies
of those groups.

All of this has changed. For one example, the gender gap that once skewed the social sciences at American universities is effectively obsolete. Each year since 2006, women have earned more than half of all doctoral degrees nationally. They've evened the field among ranks of faculty as well. Between 1999 and 2018 at degree-granting postsecondary institutions the percentage of female faculty increased from 41 percent to 50 percent, according to the National Center for Education Statistics. Inequities still exist at elite levels within universities. In 2019, at schools with tenure systems, the percentage of full-time faculty with tenure was higher for men than women, 54 vs. 40 percent. There's debate whether that gap is narrowing, or moving in the reverse direction.

I don't have corresponding figures from Veblen's time, but given that his sister was the first daughter of Norwegian immigrants to graduate from an American college, I feel comfortable saying there probably weren't a lot of lady sociologists working alongside the old grouch. When the idea for the Sociologists for Women in Society was first floated in 1969 (the organization was formally founded in 1971), there were no women on the American Sociological Association's eleven-member Executive Committee or thirty-member Council. Of the six officers on the ASA's 2021 Executive Committee, five were women. The only man on the council, and the ASA's president, was Black. Not a single white male was part of the group's primary leadership committee. That's a huge shift over the course of a single generation. Its implications should not be considered small.

Likewise, students from all over the world have reoriented American research institutions. The top five countries of origin for foreign students enrolled in U.S. universities in 2019 were China, India, South Korea, Saudi Arabia, and Canada. Combined, students from China and India account for more than half (52.1 percent) of all international students at American schools. This is a lot different from the turn of the last century when status-research templates were being devised. Changes in the complexion of social scientists and, as importantly, the projects they deem important and conclusions drawn from them, are a by-product of the tectonic demographic shift in the halls of academia.

The international makeup of typical test subjects also represents a big change from just a decade or two ago. The instantaneous global reach enabled by digital communication makes it possible for researchers to canvas the planet from their offices or even bedrooms. In the 1960s, social psychologist Henri Tajfel gathered boys from the same school in Bristol, England, and rested his famous conclusions on group identity and peer pressure upon this confined data set. By contrast, many of today's most important studies base their conclusions on respondents from multiple countries and cultures.

Digital technology provides easy access to data sets that weren't imaginable a decade ago. The internet has put original data collection, automated computation, and instant analysis on a global scale within reach of underpaid associates beavering away in offices from community colleges in Schenectady, New York, to land grant institutions in once-backwater places like Tucson, Arizona.

As Seth Stephens-Davidowitz explains in *Everybody Lies: Big Data, New Data, and What the Internet Can Tell Us About Who We Really Are*, statistics gathered with tools like Google Trends, social media aggregating apps, and internet polls have radically expanded our ability to understand humankind. "New digital data now shows us there is more to human society than we think we see . . . making possible important, even revolutionary insight," he writes.

It seems almost unfair that a dilettante like me should have access to such powerful tools of research. One wonders what great minds like Veblen, Packard, Tajfel, or Max Weber would have done with such might at their disposal. Likely not started by looking down their pants.

AT OUR SECOND meeting, Richardson has some positives to report. The undergrads have spent the last couple weeks scouring the academic literature to see if anyone has previously attempted to find a link between sports car ownership and penis size. We're looking for anything similar from which to compare questions or borrow overlapping methodology. But we don't want to replicate someone else's work.

"Good news—no one seems to have done anything exactly like this at all," Richardson says. This doesn't come as a surprise, but it's good to verify. "That also means we're on our own with this, we're defining our own parameters. But this territory appears novel enough to do something interesting with."

Team Hagar has unearthed a few relevant studies. One looked at the relationship between self-esteem and how much people would be willing to pay for a car. An intriguing 2009 experiment found sports cars appear to have a direct and specific effect on males: driving a Porsche Carrera increased testosterone, whereas driving a station wagon decreased it. That study was coauthored by Dr. Gad Saad, whose scholarship in the field of "the proverbial sexy car" (his term) I'd already encountered in that Bentley Continental/Ford Fiesta study. My confidence in Team Hagar increases.

An even more promising study, conducted in the UK in 2014, found that 30 percent of sports car owners claimed to have larger-than-average penis size; their female partners however estimated that only 12 percent did, and that 42 percent of these males were actually smaller than average. In part the discrepancy can be explained by sheer male bravado, since even those without a sports car also made a more generous estimation of their endowment than did their female partners. But the difference in estimates as larger was 18 percent for sports car owners, with only a 3 percent difference for those without. Since it relied on self-reporting, the study is of limited value to us. But Richardson says it suggests a possible relationship between sports cars and feelings of male prowess.

As already mentioned, all of my favorite psych experiments pivot on a ruse. Richardson has come up with a devious one for ours. Instead of being told we intend to find a link between wedding tackle and flashy cars, subjects will be informed they're participating in an experiment measuring how well people multitask while doing online shopping. Imagine yourself at work, we'll suggest, feigning your way through various employee obligations while at the same time buying a pair of cross-country skis off Amazon.

In alternating sets, our experiment will simulate this scenario by presenting news items about various topics interspersed with consumer goods. The news items might include articles about the effects of climate change on saltwater marshes, a political scandal in Ohio, a new report on average penis size, the latest NASA deep space findings, the mating habits of Indonesian frogs. Juxtaposed against these will be a selection of consumer items to purchase—laundry detergent, vacation packages, sports cars, desk lamps. The only correlations we actually care about are those between the cars and stick shifts. All the other items are filler and controls.

I'm delighted by the subterfuge and tell Team Hagar I'm always impressed by the sneaky brainiacs who come up with ways to throw psychology test subjects off the scent of the trail. "We wake up in the mornings thinking up ways to lie to people," Richardson jokes, getting into the swing of things.

A number of issues still need to be resolved. What will our set of stimulus purchase items be? Meaning, exactly what models and makes of cars, watches, vacations, laundry soaps, whatever, will we show test subjects? What age groups do we want to include? Richardson says we can make things easier on ourselves by finding out the average age of men who make sports car purchases and limiting ourselves to that group—say thirty-five- to fifty-five-year-olds.

But, this being a university, for every good point there are a couple hundred equally strong counterpoints that need to be argued over for hours. While middle-aged or slightly older men might make the majority of sports car purchases, sports car owners might form crucial emotional attachments to those vehicles much earlier in their lives, maybe in their teens or twenties, when penis-size anxiety is at its height. The middle-aged purchase, then, could be seen simply as the fulfillment of an adolescent ambition. Richardson cites the Kevin Spacey character in *American Beauty* who, after being fired from his job, begins a midlife spiral by going out and buying a new sports car.

"Nineteen seventy Pontiac Firebird, the car I've always wanted and now I have it. I rule!" says Spacey to his peeved wife, Annette Bening (totally at the top of her game here).

The Firebird reference erases any doubt in my mind that Richardson is the guy for this mission. He gets it. In the end we decide to canvass men between eighteen and fifty-five.

Although penis size doesn't change much as men age, status and self-esteem markers such as income, number of sexual partners, and body mass index do. Rea thinks presenting men with information about the number of sexual partners is a good way to influence sexually related self-esteem. She makes an astonishing claim that she's seen a study saying the average number of sexual partners for eighteen-year-old men is between zero and one.

"That can't be right," I say. "Where was this survey taken, a fourteenth-century monastery?"

"The UK," she says.

Already I can see how fraught with culture, gender, race, and every other type of bias these kinds of studies are open to.

Regardless, the overall idea is to manipulate subjects' self-esteem prior to making a purchasing decision. We'll attempt to get some of them feeling they're hauling inadequate equipment into battle by showing them a news story claiming the average erect penis is about seven inches long. Others will have their ego boosted by being exposed to a story claiming a new study has determined the average hard Hagar is just four and a half inches long.* Then we'll see how or if this information affects their feelings about new car choices.

We also need to determine how large our data set (i.e., the number of test subjects) will be. Ability to reach a large pool of respondents is essentially determined by how much money you're willing to spend and how long your survey takes to complete.

---

* The results are in! According to a report published in the *British Journal of Urology International* that synthesized findings of seventeen penis-related studies and took in measurements of more than fifteen thousand men around the world, the average flaccid penis is 3.61 inches in length and 5.16 inches erect. Corresponding girth measurements are 3.66 inches for a limp willy and 4.59 inches for a firm wonka. Please never ask me to do that again.

Subjects will be motivated to take the survey by receiving a small payment. The longer the survey, the more time it takes to complete, the higher the payment. My total budget is $2,000. Richardson ballparks that with a five-minute survey my bankroll should get us about two hundred respondents, which he believes are enough for a meaningful result.

"In a scientific study we normally ask the same question twenty different ways," he says. "In this case, we've just got the one shot. If we keep going back to penis size over and over, subjects will catch on pretty quick." Team Hagar nods sagely.

RICHARDSON STARTS TO build the survey. Team Hagar gets busy with logistics. They'll recruit subjects from a research company called Prolific Academic, with others coming from social media and sports car community chat sites. Participants will carry out the experiment using the online platform Gorilla.

I get going on the list of cool cars to use in the study. Since I was never one of those guys with the hot-lady-on-the-hood posters in my dorm room I'm going to need help. My first call is to my nephews Erik and Chuck 2.0. Both have spent the bulk of their professional lives in car sales in the Maryland/Washington, DC, area. A formidable hermano-a-hermano automotive enterprise, the guys have done everything from selling on the lot to overseeing online marketing to being the guy in the back room that upsells you on fabric protection and extended warranties to managing whole sales teams.

Erik and Chuck 2.0 look over my initial list of status cars and nix the 1970 Pontiac Firebird and 1966 Shelby Mustang. Guys who buy muscle cars tend to be motivated by different factors than guys who buy look-at-me cars, they explain. Nostalgia for one. Guys for whom *Smokey and the Bandit* was a cultural touchstone often go in for older cars because they can repair and restore them themselves.*

---

* Add neighborhood mechanics and Yankee ingenuity to the list of things computers have ruined forever.

In the end, the nephews and I come up with a list of cars designed not only to get the blood of survey respondents racing, but one that covers a range of makes and countries of origin. Don't assume just because they wear greasy ball caps and Carhartt overalls with stains from the 1990s that car guys don't #CelebrateDiversity.

These are the vehicles (with manufacturer starting list prices) that will be presented on a rotating basis to study participants when asked how likely they would be to buy a sports car.

- Aston Martin Vanquish S ($298,000)
- Tesla Roadster ($200,000)
- Ferrari Testarossa (a lot)
- Audi R8 coupe ($169,900)
- Corvette Stingray convertible ($59,995)
- BMW M3 series ($69,900)

The BMW is a late addition. Its MSRP seems too low for top-flight German engineering. I insert it after a conversation with my real estate appraiser buddy Brian. A lifetime Beemer owner, Brian assures me the M3 series is the standard "entry-level douchebag car."

I WAS ENJOYING all the texting with the nephews and Skyping with Team Hagar. But after a couple months of planning, researching, and strategizing, I was antsy for results. Which is why it was so exciting a couple weeks after the test had gone live online and the gang in London began analyzing incoming data when Richardson sent an intriguing email: "Every which way I look at the data it looks good. We seem to have found something."

In the annals of discovery it wasn't exactly "Dr. Livingstone, I presume?" But when you find yourself on the cusp of a major scientific breakthrough—even in the social sciences—time slows down. You see the world the way Tom Brady sees a football game. All possibilities are open. Long shots look close. Nobel podiums and MacArthur Foundation grants appear before your eyes.

What we'd found was this, taken verbatim from the study summary Richardson composed and submitted to a respected academic open-source journal called *PLOS One*: "Males, and males over thirty in particular, rated sports cars as more desirable when they were made to feel that they had a small penis."

There it was. Confirmation—sort of—of the correlation between hot rods and small rods.

This was big. Maybe not Nobel or MacArthur big. But possibly enthralling enough to land me a spot on Bill Maher's show. Not the panel. Maybe just the opening-segment guy who comes out and lets Maher push him around a little for the privilege of promoting his new book. Hmm. Well, maybe BuzzFeed would pick it up.

Either way, the scientific community would demand something more concrete to support such a bombastic claim. They'd want us to show our work. Our report summary gave it to them: "Our primary hypothesis was confirmed," the report announced before laying out the John Thomas particulars. Among responses that had come from guys around the world—the United States, the UK, Italy, Russia, India, South Korea, several other countries—ratings for sports cars increased by approximately 11 percent when male participants were manipulated to believe that they had a relatively small penis.

That was a good number, but there was an even more important wrinkle. The difference in overall ratings was driven entirely by men over thirty. Younger males rated the sports cars almost identically in the two conditions. Men over thirty rated them 24 percent higher when they were made to feel they had a smaller penis.

In fact, and this was the really interesting bit, participants in the low-self-esteem condition were 94 percent more likely to give higher ratings to the sports cars. Our study produced no evidence that younger participants changed their ratings according to the "penis-threatened condition," a term Team Hagar deployed with gusto in the term papers they'd

eventually write summarizing the study. But at 98 percent, older participants showed strong evidence of an effect of ween-esteem on car ratings.
"Is there a specific link between how men feel about their penis size,
and how they feel about sports cars?" our report reported. "That possibility is supported by our data. . . . We can conclude that having a relatively
small penis leads older men to value sports cars specifically as more desirable, and can cautiously speculate that it may have broader effects on a
range of luxury items for men of all ages."

THE EXISTENCE OF data connecting sports cars with small dicks was
good enough for me. For those who wanted to go the extra inch (give or
take), Richardson put in a lot more work writing a thoroughgoing case
study. Technically speaking, I was coauthor of the report that summarized our experiment. The original idea was mine, and Richardson was
cool about sharing credit, invoking a sort of Lennon-McCartney spirit to
matters of attribution. But since Richardson produced the overwhelming
bulk of the study and academic report—reducing me more to Ringo
status—I'm compelled to put quotation marks around the lengthier sections of our report. This is how the writing process goes with a lot of
those academic studies that list three or four coattail authors at the top.
    "Why should it be—jokes and jealously aside—that there is a con-
nection between sports cars and penis sizes?" we (Richardson) wrote.
"The psychological literature suggests two possibilities. Firstly, it has been
shown in general that there is a relationship between self-esteem and purchasing luxury goods. People seek out luxury goods when their self-worth
is low (Braun and Wicklund, 1989).

The second possibility is that there is something about luxury
goods that is specifically linked to male mating strategies. Be-
fore cars existed on a mass scale Veblen (1899) wrote about
the phenomena of "conspicuous consumption," in which peo-
ple buy and display goods not for their virtue or enjoyment,

*but as a signal to others that they can afford luxury goods
with no practical purpose.*

*More recently, evolutionary psychologists have put for-
ward the argument why men and women might differ in
their conspicuous consumption. The seeds of these ideas are
present in Darwin's (1871) original work. He remarked
on the peculiarity that a male peacock has evolved a substantial and elaborate display of feathers that confer no
functional advantage in feeding or surviving; indeed, they
would appear to hamper both. The function of these costly
displays is purely to attract a mate. The fact that a particular peacock can invest the biological resources into growing
his tail feathers, and invest the time to show it off, is an
indirect signal of health, and therefore, reproductive value.
Indeed, those with the most impressive tail feathers do attract more mates* (Miller, 2009).

Richardson's analogy was the most satisfying one to end on. Like
the peacock's feathers, our study was absurd, awkward, indiscreet, vulgar,
outrageous, flashy, mildly profane, a little embarrassing, dirty to drag
around, and tough to justify over the long haul. To the knee-jerk critic it
exists for no better reason than to attract attention.

None of this is untrue, but the audacity merely shrouded a deeper
objective. The project wasn't really about cars and penises. Those were
just entry points into a process of evolution—in this case the evolution
of how status and prestige are tested, measured, and understood by society at large. In many ways, that process starts with a single individual,
perhaps hunkered over a textbook in a dorm room or cogitating over
data sets in a windowless university office. Not long ago, it was simple
to conjure a physical image of that contemplative figure—he might have
worn glasses, maybe he had shaggy hair, probably his skin was pale from
a lack of exercise and sunlight.

Today's image of the academic trailblazer is far more colorful. It's no coincidence the three student assistants Richardson drew from a notice he'd posted on a university job site were women. The now commonplace inclusion of women and non-white ethnicities in subject populations tends to make research conclusions more broadly applicable to an increasingly integrated planet. Perhaps more important, the empowerment of diverse project leaders imbues experiments with a more universal perspective than campus studies conducted even twenty-five years ago could have hoped to attain. Poking around cars and penises was a hoot, but the real value of our gaudy investigation was the view it provided into how status research has changed, and the people who are changing it. Their influence in turn leads to shifts in how all of us view status. This is the quiet mechanics of the status revolution in action.

Trouble was, working with Richardson and Team Hagar really had got me thinking hard about cars. In decline or not, automobiles are still a ubiquitous projector of status familiar to everyone. But I didn't feel like taking a business trip to Detroit.

CHAPTER 5

The King of Comfort:
STATUS AS SOCIAL JUSTICE

KNOWN IN EUROPEAN CAR CIRCLES AS THE KING OF COMFORT, Paolo Scudieri didn't break into the Italian auto industry in typical fashion. Partly this was due to the circumstances of his birth, which put him at a career disadvantage vis-à-vis more privileged peers. This situation produced in him a burning want for social status and chip-on-the-shoulder chutzpah with which to pursue it.

Even armed with these weapons of social battle, however, but for a nick-of-time performance on the part of the notoriously inefficient Italian postal service, Scudieri's unlikely ascent to captain-of-industry status might never have come to pass. And the car world would be drabber as a result. Indeed, had Poste Italiane not saved Scudieri with the overdue delivery of a fateful invitation, the interior of the car you drive today might be a lot less slick. And its seats less comfortable.

The car seat you now sit on is made primarily from polyurethane. Among the most versatile of plastics, polyurethanes are used to form various types of foams and solid forms. In cars, they're fabricated into seat cushions, fabric backing, door panels, dashboards, steering wheels, headliners, and bumpers. They're also made into parts that absorb sound and energy, dampen vibration, and encapsulate windows.

With or without Scudieri, the material the industry refers to as PU would have found its way into your vehicle. Just likely not without the same éclat. In the quirky way history has of unfolding, though, the recipient of that letter from a now-forgotten but divinely conscientious Italian postman went on to become one of the people most responsible for the look and feel of modern automobile interiors.

Paolo Scudieri is a stylish sixty-two-year-old Italian tycoon who in his spare time likes to paint and race cars. One of his paintings sold at auction for $90,000. His company's logo, which the soft-spoken gallant designed himself, features a baby eagle seizing the earth in its claws.

Long before he became known as the King of Comfort, however, Scudieri was known as something else: Terrone. It was not a designation that earned him respect in Italy, particularly within the automotive community he one day hoped to join and, as his company's logo now attests, go on to conquer.

PAOLO SCUDIERI WAS born and raised in the country town of Ottaviano, just east of Naples. The large region that starts south of Rome and ends in Sicily is known as Mezzogiorno. Ottaviano is a small burg in the Campania region of Mezzogiorno. To Italians, Campania represents deep southern Italy, which equates to deep sticksville. "Terrone," or its plural Terroni, is deeply insulting slang for Mezzogiorno's presumably bumpkin residents.

One of the startling discoveries American travelers in Italy make is how the cultural divide between the country's historically industrialized north and historically agrarian south feels so familiar. For negative stereotyping, Italy's "Deep South" has a lot of parallels with America's Deep South. Then as now, Mezzogiorno ("the South") was noted for joblessness, bleak standards of living, widespread crime, substandard education, and stubborn social conservatism. Many northern Italians consider it a cultural and economic backwater nobody with an Armani suit would want anything to do with—unless they happen to be Mafia, which is the other thing Mezzogiorno is known for. In the popular Italian comedy film *Benvenuti al Sud* (Welcome to the South), a cultured but dishonest Poste Italiane middle manager is punished by being relocated from his home in the north to a two-year posting south of Naples. He regards the transfer as a death sentence.

Compared with their northern countrymen, southern Italians are widely portrayed as racist, sexist, uneducated, poor, culturally retarded, politically reactionary, easily angered, and ultrareligious hicks. A Second University of Naples academic paper explaining regional conflicts in the country—these have been exhaustively studied since the uneasy 1861* unification of politically divided states into the sovereign Kingdom of Italy—uses the word "backward" no fewer than nine times to describe the prevailing view of "Terroni." The best quote I came across from one of dozens of "Italy insider" travel blogs goes: "Most of the people I know in the south are religious as fuck." There are a lot of implications in these statements, most of them as familiar to Italians as to Americans on both sides of the Mason-Dixon Line.

On the plus side, like their Dixie counterparts, southern Italians are esteemed for their magnificent cuisine, devotion to their mothers, old-fashioned public manners, and fun-to-imitate accents. Even so, for a variety of centuries-old, Hatfields-vs.-McCoys type of reasons, northern prejudices against southerners are even more malevolent and unambiguously acknowledged in Italy than in the United States.

On his first attempts to break into the car business, Paolo Scudieri ran into them all. Italy's major automakers—Fiat, Alfa Romeo, Lamborghini, Ferrari, Maserati—are all headquartered in the north. For an unknown southerner, getting a foot in the door as anything more than a poorly paid laborer was nearly impossible. To hear Scudieri describe it, in early 1980s Italian automotive circles he enjoyed all the status of a stray dog.

---

* Same year the U.S. Civil War began. Another weird North–South parallel.

"At that time the prejudice was much worse, much more open," Scudieri says. "Factories and companies wanted to exclude me and my company because I was from the south. They said it to my face. They said, 'We're just not interested in doing business with a company from the south.' I demanded to know why. I talked with managers, chief operating officers, international executives. I received no satisfactory answers." Mafia connections were feared, though only tacitly acknowledged.

"One manager I approached was quite rude and aggressive with me," Scudieri says. " 'Who brought you here? What are your credentials?' he asked me. I answered, 'Technical competence.' That was my strategy. Be better than the others, be the most competent at what you do."

Scudieri despised the disrespect he felt he'd suffered for no reason other than his connection with the least-developed part of Italy. He returned from his interviews in the north not just personally aggrieved—for the first time in his life, he felt insulted on behalf of his entire region. His devotion to cars evolved into a social mission. He vowed to do something to uplift not just his own status but the status of his fellow "Terroni." As a hammer is to a carpenter, so would status be to Scudieri.

ONE OF THE fundamental things I learned while profiling status sovereigns is that their origins are frequently humble. Almost none of the prestige mavens I spoke to during the more than three years I spent researching this book started out as luxury consumers. Most entered the world poor or middle-class. Few grew up with outsized privilege. What they did grow up with was a burr in their saddle for being denied a status borne unto others.

History's greatest example is the United States of America. In his 2004 book, *Status Anxiety*, Swiss-born British philosopher Alain de Botton writes that, more than any event in Western history, America's War for Independence "altered forever the basis upon which status was accorded. . . . The theoretical impulse towards political equality and more equitable social and economic opportunities for all, after being in the ether for a century and a half, finally found dramatic, concrete expression in the American Revolution of 1776."

The universally celebrated pluck of the colonists' status revolt in part explains why it was two Americans—Thorstein Veblen and Vance Packard—who became the world's most influential arbiters of status. (Americans are not, as a people, renowned for philosophy.) It also says a good deal about the hidden underpinnings of upheavals in ideas about what status and privilege are and who gets to be associated with them.

Consider hip-hop videos. No matter what you feel about the way bitches, hos, basketball jerseys at formal events, and gold rope chains have altered the nation's moral fiber, it's impossible to deny the global impact of these mini-masterpieces of visual gluttony. The classic rap video template was pretty much the creation of a man named Harold "Hype" Williams. As a young music fan, Williams was bothered by the retrograde imagery of rap videos.

"The stuff that was being done at the time was so shitty, it just felt like I could do it much better," Williams said in 2018. "It just looked bad all the time. There was rappers in junkyards and shit like that."

A Queens-born graffiti artist, Williams decided to upend the form with images conveying high status and luxury lifestyles. He made groundbreaking videos for LL Cool J, Tupac Shakur, DMX, Snoop Dogg, Wu-Tang Clan, Missy Elliott, TLC, Jay-Z, Beyoncé, and Kanye West. But, along with a Harlem kid soon to be renamed Puff Daddy, he basically invented the big-pimpin', orgiastic genre with up-from-the-gutter, mid-nineties videos for the Notorious B.I.G. The pair's video for "Big Poppa" features Sean "Puff Daddy" Combs sipping champagne in a bubble bath alongside a gaggle of hoochie mamas. Directed by Combs, "Juicy" was shot in a twelve-thousand-square-foot Setsuo Ito–designed mansion on a hilltop in the Hamptons.

"At one point rap music was a joke, it's like everybody thought it was nothing," Williams has said. "You have to really understand that. All these people, all these great artists, they proved them wrong, they proved everybody wrong."

The hysterical reaction of critics was predictably hypocritical, as though this was the first time a bunch of rich misogynists had gotten high and defiled the flower of young womanhood at a private party in the preferred getaway of New York's coke-straw plutes. Then again that was part of the point. As French luxe maven Jean-Noël Kapferer reminds us: "The evolution of luxury is a reflection of the fight between elites."

It's unlikely Williams read any luxury-industry instruction manuals prior to setting up those early video shoots. But flip back to chapter 1 and you can't miss the way his status-drenched videos followed the how-to path laid out by prestige gurus—define your culture, appeal to emotions, accentuate flaws, provide an uplifting experience.

Rags-to-riches tales like Biggie's litter the luxury landscape.

Champagne began as a fizzy mistake, fermented soda pop, insofar as French sophisticates were concerned. Then aristocracy took a liking to it. A reputation was born. A market formed. Barriers to competition erected. An exclusive provenance secured. The global champagne market is now worth $6 billion and still growing. Booze industry forecasters say it'll be valued at $7.4 billion by 2026, led in consumption by France, the UK, the United States, Australia, and Japan.

Seventy-five years ago, the Japanese weren't drinking much champagne. From the literal ashes of World War II, the country was in fact rebuilt on the backs of status losers. So deprived was former military officer Kihachiro Onitsuka in the late 1940s that he created the original molds for his revolutionary Tiger shoes by pouring hot wax from Buddhist temple candles over his own feet. Those shoes led to a partnership between Onitsuka and a middling distance runner from Oregon named Phil Knight. Without them, Nike, the most prestigious global brand in sports, which Knight would go on to found, would not exist.

The unlikely start of Sony, for decades the most hallowed name in personal electronics, is even more fantastical. It includes the exploits of twenty-two-year-old Nobutoshi Kihara—future inventor of the Walkman—who in 1948 used a badger-hair brush and homemade rice glue to affix magnetic particles of oxalic ferrite he'd cooked down in his kitchen skillet to a section of ticker tape, thereby producing a crude form of magnetic recording tape. He first tested his handiwork by running the tape across a head using two 78 rpm turntables as feed and take-up reels. His goal? Attain the level of audio prestige enjoyed in prewar Germany and postwar America.

There are, of course, silver-spoon exceptions. But the backgrounds of most people on the front lines of the 1 percent armada aren't all that dissimilar from Milton Pedraza, the Colombian-born, Queens-raised CEO of New York's Luxury Institute consulting firm. "Though I work in luxury I'm still proletariat at heart," Pedraza says. Luxury, he explains, is not a machine. It's an ecosystem that's constantly reinventing itself, usually as a reaction to disruptions from its lower tiers. This helps explain the current status revolution, which is fueled by technological, commercial, and other advancements, but also by global social upheavals of the past decade.

Like Pedraza, most status makers I met were plebeian warhorses. Talking to them and digging into their backgrounds demystified the origins of luxury. Most had this in common: a desire to lift a downtrodden group or community to a social station above the one they'd historically occupied. Colonial Americans, defeated Japanese, Black kids from the projects—each weaponized status, privilege, and prestige as means to a larger communal aim.

"In terms of self-identity and status, for most people what's more important than how you define 'me' is how you define 'us,'" Joe Devlin told me at University College London. "I suspect any argument you make for individuals is equally if not more valid for groups. If you have trust in your group, you can do more things than you can as an individual."

"Prestige reflects on community," said John Hogan. "It's all about groups."

In his book *American Dreams: Lost and Found*, Studs Terkel interviewed a cabdriver in St. Louis who defended America's prosecution of the Vietnam War. "We can't be a pitiful, helpless giant. We gotta show 'em we're number one," the cabbie insisted.

"Are you number one?" Terkel asked him.

"I'm number nothin'," the cabbie answered.

MEZZOGIORNO CAN INDEED be tough. But Scudieri chose his parents wisely. He was born into money. Honest money. In the 1500s, one of his ancestors had invested in silkworms. For centuries the family devoted itself to a highly successful silk business. During World War II, Paolo's grandfather made clothing from the silk parachutes abandoned by American soldiers.

Following the postwar collapse of the silk market—synthetic fabrics and cheaper Asian alternatives obliterated Italy's traditional silk industry—Scudieri's father turned the focus of the family operation to clothing and furniture. In 1956, he founded a company he called Adler, the German word for "eagle." Papa Scudieri made a good living stitching shirts, as well as cushions for household sofas and chairs.

Young Paolo's future looked secure. As ranking scion, he was poised to take charge of the family business. But Paolo had an artistic streak. He was more attracted to drawing and painting than to plackets and box stretchers. Nothing about peddling shirts and furniture appealed to him. Though he eventually went off to the University of Basel in Switzerland to earn a degree in industrial engineering, from an early age his passion was design.

And cars. Especially cars.

"The big problem with family businesses is, every generation it has to have a turnover, in my case from the father to the son," Scudieri says. "I realized I could not continue to innovate or be myself in my father's business. My father was a big oak."

Despite these reservations, following university Scudieri dutifully joined the family operation. He was twenty-three, and, though he'd at least been off to school, like George Bailey toiling away at the old building and loan, he was itchy for his own story to begin. By this time, his interest in cars had developed into an obsession. The sexy, aerodynamic designs were an antidote to the rigid lines and function-over-form mandate of Adler seats and cushions.

SCUDIERI DID HAVE some positive interactions with the family business. As a child he loved playing with the long rectangular tubes of expanded polyurethane strewn around the floor of his father's small factory, which he's called "my daily playground."

Developed in the 1930s by a German chemist named Otto Bayer working for IG Farben—the German chemical maker that, among other notorious acts of industrial evil, produced Zyklon B for Hitler's gas chambers—polyurethanes weren't widely available until the mid-1950s. Some of the first commercial applications came as padding for household furniture, so it was natural that Scudieri would be exposed to the new wonder material in his father's shop.

After home products, automobiles were the next logical step for PUs. General Motors installed the first car seats made with PU cushions in 1958.

Not everyone was in a rush to abandon tradition. Seats in the first automobiles were simply leather-covered benches with cotton stuffing supported by large coil springs mounted directly to the frame. Ford Model T seats were stuffed with horsehair and other natural fibers. Starting in 1932, when they were installed in London public bus seats, latex foams, some embedded with springs, some interwoven with horsehair and other organic materials, became the yardstick for seat comfort.

Latex was such a big deal that early car companies charged extra for it. Makes like Hudson sewed tags on the outside of seats—"Goodyear Foam Rubber Cushions"—so owners could show them off. Latex foam would dominate car seat design into the 1960s.

Chances are you take car seats pretty much for granted. But carmakers—particularly luxury carmakers—spend as much time thinking about them as they do any other part of the vehicle. All cars are designed around what's called the H-point, or "hip-point." This is the theoretical location of the average driver's hip. Calculated according to dimensions that have become standardized in the industry, H-points determine the interior geometry of every car on the market.

"A chief engineer at BMW a while back told me that seats were the second most important part of the car, second only to the engine," Michigan-based director of the Society of Automotive Historians Bob Elton tells me after I begin sniffing around old car seats. "When you walk up to a car the first thing you see is the exterior. The first thing you feel is the door handle. But the first thing your body interacts with is the seat."

Now retired, Elton spent fifty years in the car business working for Chrysler, GM, and various suppliers. He spent the last thirty years of his career engineering seats and interiors.

"I find seats one of the most intriguing technical and aesthetic challenges," Elton says. "One company that seems to have done a remarkably poor job with seats is Tesla, in the Model S. There are multiple reports of structural and mechanical failures in front seats."

For its blend of innovation, style, green technology, and association with wunderkind Elon Musk, Tesla has vaulted to the top of the prestige list of American carmakers. That doesn't mean the company always knows what it's doing.

"I found the trim sort of cheap feeling, and the seats not particularly comfortable," continues Elton. "I also read that Tesla engineered and built the seat themselves, and I suspect that they underestimated the difficulty of building a good seat."

With the exception of BMW, Elton says, every major carmaker has outsourced seat manufacturing to third parties. That's because the perfect seat has long eluded the auto industry. Polyurethanes were a game changer, but not a final solution.*

It wasn't until the 1970s development of more durable, less expensive "cold cure foam" that PUs finally became the primary material in car interiors. Even so, high-end European automakers, Mercedes-Benz

---

* Sorry, I always have a hard time shaking IG Farben connections. That gang's legacy pops up in industrial family trees more often than your investment portfolio would like to admit.

notable among them, continued to use what they considered "luxury" materials, especially coconut husks, to pad seats and interiors. Remember those luxury-marketing lessons from chapter 1? Flaws and tradition count as much as reliability and modernity. As recently as 2018, Mercedes' C-Class models were still advertising interior components made from coconut coir, flax, and olives, along with a promise that these ancient products would proffer "sustained indulgence" and "spa-like comfort." I'm not sure about flax and olives, but I've been rasped by coconut husks and even for brochure writers that description feels more borne of malarial fever than tropical epiphany.

In the early 1980s, Paolo Scudieri was thinking about all of this. His father made furniture cushions from PU, but his vision didn't extend much beyond the living room. Paolo saw a wave cresting and felt if he paddled hard enough there was still time to find a space in the polyurethane swell.

Scudieri saw another wave coming right behind: carbon fiber, a superstrong, thin fiber made of chainlike molecules of pure carbon with a unique aesthetic appeal, was increasingly being employed by leading auto designers. He wanted in on this wave, too. He had the technical expertise to manipulate modern materials. He had the artistic vision to see how they could shape the future of cars. He had the ambition and business savvy to make big things happen.

But he still had one problem and it was a doozy: Mezzogiorno.

SCUDIERI INITIALLY REACHED for social justice on behalf of southern Italians by means of stealth. Near Naples in 1983, not far from his father's shop, Alfa Romeo operated a large plant that was in the process of ramping up production of the Alfa 33. A compact family hatchback, the Alfa 33 would become a hugely successful mainstream car for the company well into the 1990s. But its launch was shaky. Calling in favors from contacts in Naples, Scudieri began playing hooky from the family furniture operation and hanging around the Alfa Sud factory. He visited the site "almost incognito, almost as a 'spy' on the assembly lines," he told me.

The young entrepreneur soon learned of a flaw in the Alfa 33's design. A difficulty had arisen on the factory floor when workers tried to align sheet metal exterior panels with the plastic pieces around the gas cap. The seal wasn't tight. Something was needed to integrate the metal and plastic materials. The solution lay in polyurethane. No person in Italy was better suited to solve the problem.

"I knew the Alfa 33 had a problem with the fuel cap," Scudieri says. "I studied the defect. I developed a mold and had a seal tested and approved at the factory. Then I went to Arese."

Near the famously snobbish fashion capital of Milan, Arese is the location of Alfa Romeo's corporate headquarters. Scudieri wrangled a meeting with an executive named Giuseppe Iorio. Terrone or not, Iorio couldn't help but be impressed with the young man's innovation. Scudieri closed his first deal to supply the company with expanded polyolefin panels.

"I fixed the problem and I got the order," he says, still proud of the moment. "It was a lot to learn for a young person. If someone tells you no, but you are technically stronger, you can beat that person. Or at least change their mind."

Paolo Scudieri was finally out of the shirts and seats business. But it'd take another bit of nerve—and luck—to make him the King of Comfort.

AS WITH PICKUP artists, all good salespeople will tell you it's not how many nos you get, it's how many yeses. Hit one jackpot and the pain of a thousand rejections is erased.

During his days trying to break into the car business, Scudieri made a lot of cold calls. Many were aimed at reasonable targets—local connections at nearby companies and factories, such as Alfa Sud. Like most big dreamers, Scudieri mixed in the occasional home run swing—he aimed one of these swings at Enzo Ferrari.

In automotive history—Italian or otherwise—few names are as legendary.

Born in 1898, Enzo Ferrari was a World War I veteran, car freak, and fearless driver. After returning from the war, he began racing cars, winning his first race in 1924. Turned down for employment by Fiat, he became a test driver for the small company that would soon introduce the world to Vespa scooters. By the 1930s he gained worldwide fame as manager of Alfa Romeo's highly successful racing teams. Enzo Ferrari became to sports cars what Sophia Loren became to the Mediterranean diet.

Devoted to speed and exactitude, Ferrari founded his namesake company in the late 1930s. By the 1950s, Ferrari cars, painted in the now universally recognized shade of *rosso corsa* (racing red), exploded onto the international racing circuit, then still considered by some carmakers an important part of R&D. Ferrari won its first 24 Hours of Le Mans in 1949. Since then, Ferrari drivers have won more than five thousand sanctioned races.

"Ask a child to draw a car, and he will certainly draw it red," Ferrari once famously said.

Rare as left-handed shortstops, Ferrari's 250 GTO has been called the world's most revered modern car—only thirty-nine were produced. In 2018, one established an automobile auction record when it sold for $48.4 million to an unknown buyer. The previous record for most expensive car sold at auction was $38.1 million. That was set in 2014 by another Ferrari.

"For automotive enthusiasts, the Ferrari symbol—a black stallion prancing on a yellow field—became synonymous with . . . fabulous exclusivity and expense," wrote the *New York Times* in its obit of Enzo Ferrari in 1988.

Despite enormous business success, personal problems, including the heart-wrenching death of his son from muscular dystrophy in 1956, turned Enzo Ferrari into a recluse. Though he remained an industry powerhouse, by the 1970s he'd become all but untouchable to those outside his tightly guarded circle.

This didn't stop the enterprising Scudieri from taking a run at the man he figured was the best car contact a guy could have in Italy. In 1983, on a whim, he sent the cloistered tycoon a birthday card, wishing him well and introducing himself and his small automotive technology company. Unsurprisingly, he received no reply. He hadn't really expected one. He went about his business, fulfilling the Alfa 33 contract.

A few months later, however, Scudieri opened his mailbox and found an envelope bearing a postmark from Maranello. A small town in northern Italy, Maranello is famous for only one thing. Scudieri opened the envelope slowly, careful not to tear the contents.

Inside was a short note handwritten by Enzo Ferrari himself. The racing legend thanked Scudieri for his birthday wishes and, to the young man's profound disbelief, summoned him to a meeting at the company's headquarters in Maranello. Ferrari provided the date and time of the appointment and said he'd be pleased to receive Scudieri in his office.

Scudieri read the letter with shock, excitement, and . . . horror. Shock and excitement because, well, obvious. Horror because the letter had been mailed more than a month earlier. Scudieri received Ferrari's invitation on the very evening before the meeting was set to take place. Mussolini may have made the trains run on time, but he knew better than to make any promises about the Italian mail.

Ferrari was expecting Scudieri at nine the next morning. Anyone who knew anything about the demanding Ferrari knew missing such an appointment, knew arriving anything less than ten minutes early, would mean banishment from the great man's notice forever. After a moment of panic, Scudieri gathered his wits, canceled obligations for the next day, and called his father.

"The Ferrari headquarters in Maranello was about six hundred kilometers away," Scudieri says. "So I borrowed my parents' car and drove all night. I arrived in front of a hotel at four in the morning, but no one was awake, so I slept in my car in the hotel's parking lot."

At six a.m., Scudieri was awakened by a soft tapping on his window. The owner of the hotel was peering in at him through a spring-morning fog. He wanted to know why the young man was sleeping in his parking lot. He seemed more concerned than angry. A rumpled Scudieri opened the door and told the man about the birthday card and the reply that had come a month late and the meeting now just three hours away.

"He let me inside his hotel to clean up, eat, and get ready, at no charge," Scudieri says. "That hotel owner was so kind."

Though he'd only just begun working on his gas tank seal for the Alfa 33, Scudieri pitched Ferrari with confidence. He spoke in detail about polyurethane, carbon fiber, and other technical innovations he believed could ensure the continuing success of the Ferrari brand in racing and luxury markets. Although he didn't come right out and say it, Scudieri knew Ferrari at the time was losing its edge on the competition. He presented ideas to vault the company back in front of the pack.

"Mr. Ferrari listened to me quietly, not for a very long time, and then simply said, 'Why don't you start supplying some of these materials for me?'" Scudieri recalls.

Perhaps the once-modest Enzo Ferrari—he'd shoed mules as a teenage serviceman in World War I—saw something in Scudieri others missed. I ask Scudieri about his own demeanor in the meeting. How had he presented himself? A luxury salesman with the perfect elevator pitch? A plucky kid from the south just needing a break?

"My attitude was neither that of a poor young man from the south, nor a rich man showing his wealth," he says. "Neither of these are useful attitudes for success. What I did was make my technical competence evident. I made a promise to him of technical superiority and a promise to maintain it. From his side of the table, he saw a determined young man who knew a certain part of the business better than anyone else."

SCUDIERI COULDN'T HAVE been in a better place at a better time. The mid-1980s to early 1990s was a period of substantial change for auto interiors. Interactive pieces like seats weren't just a technical challenge. Putting them together was labor-intensive. And expensive.

"Companies like Chrysler had to pay UAW wages for guys to sew up seat covers and squeeze each individual hog ring with a pair of pliers," says automotive historian Elton. "It's really tedious work. Tough people were getting carpal tunnel syndrome and other workplace injuries all the time doing this shit."

The solution? Outsourcing. Find companies who could get away with paying nonunion wages for the gruntiest of grunt work.

"Suddenly, interiors are a supplier responsibility," Elton says. "The fact was nobody had really given that much study to interiors before. Car seats were kinda made like couches. Big wide bench seats in front. The idea of comfort was make it as close to your favorite couch at home as you could. That was not good for a car.

"Johnson Controls, another one of these huge companies no one has ever heard of, hired a couple professors from Michigan State University and started creating guidelines on making comfortable seats. GM had some guidelines in place, but they were pretty crude." Updates included greater attention to lumbar support and enhancing ergonomic relief while complying with a rash of new safety regulations.

The transfer of interior manufacture from traditional automakers to third-party suppliers followed a similar progression in Europe as it did in the United States. On either side of the Atlantic, no third-party supplier had the technical end of car interiors—from seat design to latest material innovations—nailed down as tight as the young son of a furniture maker with a degree in industrial engineering, a knack for design, and a bond with one of the industry's most respected high-end brands. Nor an ache for the prestige he felt his entire community had been denied.

Soon after the auspicious meeting in Maranello, Adler interiors became synonymous with Ferrari. Though Scudieri's roster of clients expanded as his reputation spread, he kept his promise of technical superiority—to which he'd soon add luxury grace notes—long after Ferrari's death. When Michael Schumacher was driving Ferraris to the top of the Formula One world in the 1990s and 2000s, he was doing most of it surrounded by interiors conceived and manufactured by Scudieri's company.

Today, Scudieri is chairman of the Adler Pelzer Group. The company has over eleven thousand employees at more than fifty production facilities in twenty-two countries, and research centers in Italy, the United States, China, England, Germany, Japan, Mexico, South Korea, and Turkey. In 2020 its total sales were $1.3 billion. More than three hundred thousand parts made of polyurethane, carbon fiber, and other materials are shipped from its production facilities every day. If you drive one of the following makes (each an Adler Pelzer client), there's a reasonable chance Scudieri has had at least a tangential influence on its interior: Alfa Romeo, Aston Martin, Audi, Bentley, BMW, Chrysler, Citroën, Ferrari, Fiat, Ford, GM, Honda, Hyundai, Jaguar, Kia, Maserati, Mercedes-Benz, Mini, Mitsubishi, Nissan, Opel, Peugeot, Porsche, Renault, Rolls-Royce, Saab, Škoda, Subaru, Suzuki, Tesla, Toyota, Volkswagen, Volvo.

With its 2010 acquisition of a majority stake in German competitor HP Pelzer, Adler changed its name to the Adler Pelzer Group and became one of the world's largest designers and producers of vehicle noise-reduction and soundproofing systems. In 2018, it doubled the size of its production facility in Port Huron, Michigan, to over 170,000 square feet. The expansion was made to accommodate new CIM (Compound Injection Molding) technology meant to improve acoustic efficiency in vehicle dash silencer parts.

The company also has marine and aeronautics divisions that design and build yacht and aircraft interiors for high-end clientele with a neurotic demand for acoustic isolation. Quiet rides, a major part of the modern luxury sell, have become Scudieri's latest mission.

It's an empire that, had a truant mail carrier detoured for just one more espresso or afternoon glass of wine, might never have come into existence. Yet for all the company's success on the global stage, Scudieri still can't escape his countrymen's lingering chauvinism toward his birthplace. Upon Adler's successful takeover of HP Pelzer, Rome's *la Repubblica* newspaper couldn't help taking a shot in its business pages at the home-grown success just down the road: "It seemed almost a crime of lèse-majesté that an Italian company took control of a large German industry.

And that to do it was a southern enterprise, of Ottaviano, common of the populous and degraded Neapolitan province."

MY AUDIENCE WITH Paolo Scudieri begins in underwhelming style. The Hotel Tiempo—which had been recommended to me as conveniently located by an Adler Pelzer Group communications flack—is located in what appears to be one of Naples' most tumbledown neighborhoods. The hotel itself is fine—basic budget business traveler place—but it's surrounded by an industrial hinterland of broken concrete and shuttered storefronts.

This shouldn't be misconstrued as a blanket critique of Naples, which has one of the most undeserved reputations of any big city in Western Europe. Hit any Italy travel site and you'll find a lot of shade thrown at the gateway to poor old southern Italy. It's dirty. It smells. It's dangerous.

This is ridiculous. With Mount Vesuvius looming over one of the world's most historic ports, Naples' waterfront promenade along Lungomare Caracciolo can compete against any street in the world for Walk Score. The place simmers in romance. Has *The Bachelor* ever been here? Had producers sequestered Juan Pablo and Nikki here for a week, Juan-Pabs would probably have broken down and proposed, sparing everyone all the Chris Harrison snit drama. (I've seen almost every season of *The Bach*, no apologies.)

The Hotel Tiempo, however, sits in another Naples altogether. While booking online back in the States, I'd pictured swaying palms in oversized golden pots ushering me into a hospitality gem along a gilded street lined with "*Ciao, bella!*" cafés and coffee bars. Upon arrival it seems the property's principal selling point is location, romantically nestled, as they say, between a vacant lot and a noisy highway overpass.

Moral of this section: Don't believe what you read about Naples. It's fantastic. Even though, somehow like everyone else, I couldn't just help dumping on the place a little bit. What the hell is it about this city?

MY ESCORT AND translator for the day is a forty-two-year-old corporate communications manager named Alessandro Pavanati. Good dude, bespectacled, receding hairline, soft-spoken, and not just for Italy. He drove down from Milan to Naples for the day just to squire me around.

We meet in the hotel lobby. He tells me it'll take half an hour to drive to the corporate headquarters in Ottaviano. Alessandro's English is good, though occasionally janky. I mention this because all of the Scudieri quotes in this chapter come through him. I ask where he picked up his unique English accent, a pungent blend of old-world wool merchant with musty hints of Ozark preacher.

"In the 1990s, I was a high school exchange student for a year in Vicksburg, Mississippi," he tells me.

I ask how he got on in Vicksburg.

"It was very religious," he says. "I grew up in Italy. My family is Catholic, so I was not a stranger to religion. But this was something different than I had ever experienced."

Alessandro drives a four-door Škoda Octavia, a cheaper rival to the Volkswagen Golf or Honda Civic. I'd been hoping, not without reason, given the man and company I was going to see, for something sportier.

The ride isn't out of place in the Hotel Tiempo lot. On the way out we're delayed fifteen excruciating minutes because the parking lot's security gate is locked, the ticket machine is broken, and no one is manning the little attendant's shed. After schlepping back into the hotel for help, Alessandro returns to the car and informs me we'll have to wait a few more minutes while someone looks for a key to let us out.

"Things are like this in southern Italy," he says. "The people are wonderful, of course, but things like this always . . ."

The Milanese Alessandro suddenly remembers the sacred oath of the public relations professional. He lets the rest of his thoughts on conditions in southern Italy trail away like dirty dishwater swirling down a drain. I can tell he's a little off his game. Alessandro is based in a PR office up north in Milan, and he's nervous about making a good impression on Mr. Scudieri, whom he's met in person only once before.

Truth is, I'm a little nervous myself. My knowledge of luxury vehicles is limited. While I understand the lure of expensive machinery, and the freedom of the blacktop, I've never really been a car guy. Utility and affordability have been my primary automotive guides. My first rig, a 1973 Ford Torino I bought for $400 off some guy's front lawn—Starsky and Hutch drove the Gran Torino, so I've got some pedigree—pretty much set a lifelong pattern. Like Alessandro, I'm aware of being out of my element in southern Italy and keen not to come off like a dipshit in front of one of the most respected car men in the world.

I NEEDN'T HAVE worried. Signor Scudieri is as easygoing and low-key as his hometown of Ottaviano. Set amid low, forested foothills, the long two-story Adler headquarters and factory bears the institutional concrete form of an old public school building, complete with the stand of flagpoles out front that flies Italian, EU, and Adler standards. If you've seen *Ford v Ferrari*, it looks a lot like Ferrari's Italy HQ as portrayed in the film. In fact, it's an old assembly plant Scudieri purchased from Ferrari.

Flanked by a pair of casually dressed male assistants, Scudieri greets me at the entryway's double doors with one of those two-handed shakes you get from priests after Mass. Thin, but in shape, tastefully tan with those pale gray eyes that exist almost exclusively in Victorian literature, he wears a blue-and-white-striped shirt with a sport jacket, no tie, dark slacks, and immaculate white tennis shoes. The watch on his wrist is Baci & Abbracci, a respected Italian brand, though not one that regularly appears on lists put together by luxury trendspotters. His only concession to eclectic fashion is a blue-and-red-threaded bracelet that looks like something you'd find at an outdoor market in Santa Fe.

"It was made by a friend of mine, a man who breeds cows and spends his summers in Sardinia," he tells me.

Fortune has smiled upon Paolo Scudieri and he tends to smile back. *La vida dulce* is his. He's got that controlled rhythm of the rich. He takes his time, but he's not slow. He's instantly likable, though I'm aware the face industrial titans show to visiting scribes is generally different from the one reserved for corporate rivals or boardroom flunkies.

Inside a claustrophobic second-floor conference room—white tile floor, white walls with black scuffs, Samsung monitor, dry-erase board, tight butt room between a cheap table and dirty walls—Scudieri pours me an espresso from a thermos and slides a plate of almond cookies my way. The most interesting thing about the room is a larger-than-scale blueprint tacked to a wall. The blueprint is for a Maserati dashboard Adler Pelzer designed to the specifications of a special client. A nifty feature is a pair of lipstick slots the client asked the company to custom-build into the driver and passenger sides of the dash. Scudieri won't say who the client was, but confirms that, yes, the person is quite famous. In a room that could be used for wartime interrogations, it's the lipstick slots that finally make me feel I've pierced the walls of Euro luxury-car zeitgeist.

For the next hour Scudieri drives a discussion of straight-up car talk. I manage to hang in there.

"Our clients are mainly automakers, but since their primary focus is on the individual driver, we also pay attention to the individual driver," he tells me. "For instance, we have a full textile branch that works with the fashion industry. This keeps us on top of luxury-market trends.

"If one year women like a certain brand of leather for their purses, or if a particular jacket brand becomes popular, perhaps we can use this same leather to supply material for the interior of cars. Most of our leather comes from Tramontano." Alessandro adds that Tramontano is a longtime Naples brand.

Matching your car's interior to your Tramontano purse? I offer a sagacious nod. Me and my 2002 LeSabre know just what he's talking about.

"The mindset of a client who buys a super-luxury car is that he doesn't make a price-benefit calculation," Scudieri says. "You buy a car like that for the emotional value, the beautiful experience. You aren't concerned with the cost."

"You say 'he' isn't concerned with the cost," I interject.

"Right now, this market is a sixty-forty-percent split between men and women," he says. "But we are moving toward a fifty-fifty split. Generally, the luxury client, whether it is a woman or a man, looks at the same thing—they look at the beauty of the interior."

I'm curious about the future of cars as status symbols. Expensive cars still command attention. But kids are in less of a rush these days to get behind the wheel.

"It's true for the young generation the car is no longer the status symbol it once was," Scudieri says. "It used to be when you turned eighteen the first thing you did was get a license. With your first job you got your first car.

"Now young men and women spend much more on electronics and experiences. They would rather spend a lot of money on a vacation to boast about."

Despite this, Scudieri believes cars will reclaim their position as dominant markers of status.

"Right now, the car is not as technically advanced as other products. When cars get more connected, get smarter, they will become a social good. Young people want a social network dimension, a more technically connected experience. Cars will become more and more technically equipped and connected.

"Automated driving and autonomous vehicles are all moving in this direction. The car will remain a means of freedom and of separating yourself from others physically, even as you are connected to them electronically. This is luxury for the future."

Scudieri loves cars, but in many ways it feels as though his business is a means to a greater end. He continually steers the conversation toward rousing rhetoric about southern Italy. His most animated moments come when he's railing against those who traduce Mezzogiorno in general, and his home region of Campania specifically.

"When you start from almost zero you have strong determination," he says. "You have the strength to fight against consolidated ideologies that have been long-established as tradition. You have to be better than them to succeed. That was always my plan to uplift Campania and Mezzogiorno."

I'D BE HAPPY to escape the cramped conference room no matter what, but it's pretty cool to tour a 462,000-square-foot car factory alongside the company chairman. We start in a room where designers are working on Porsche and Audi interiors. It looks like any midsize design operation you'd find in Brooklyn or Dallas or San Jose. Fifteen casually dressed young men and women sit on stools hunched over large computer monitors, absorbed in their work.

"Many are from the University of Naples," Scudieri notes with evident pride. "Others come from schools all over Campania."

On the factory floor we're joined by Walter Landolfi. The fifty-two-year-old engineer oversees the company's aerospace projects. Currently, these include the custom redesign of the interior of an AgustaWestland AW169 helicopter.

"The owner of a private helicopter wants people to see that his helicopter is more beautiful than the helicopters owned by the people he plays golf with," Landolfi says in perfect English. "Once, we were asked to cover all of the aluminum surfaces of a helicopter interior with gold rose."

This was a major modification that, among other things, added significant weight to the machine, requiring a specific type of certification the company also obtained.

"Can I assume the client was Arab?" I ask.

"The client was Arab, of course," Landolfi says, as if telling me the sky is blue and Italy will never have a unified government. "The most extravagant requests come from Dubai, Abu Dhabi, Russia, and Australia."

One of the most surprising things about the factory is its lack of automation.

"We don't have robots in this plant," Scudieri says. "The geometry for this kind of work is too precise."

"The most precise machine is the man," adds Landolfi. "We had Chinese executives and workers from a motorcycle factory tour this facility. They saw the workers tightening screws by hand. Their eyes popped wide open."

The highlight of the tour is the chance to ogle an Abarth 124. Abarth is Fiat's racing brand and the little white-and-black sports car with red trim sits alone in a large room like a Roman trophaeum. It's not the fastest car on the track, but even sitting still it looks like it's in the process of overtaking the field at the Monte Carlo Rally.

I run an appraiser's hand over the carbon fiber top designed and produced right in this facility. Scudieri opens the driver's door and invites me to sit inside. Definitely the coolest car I've ever sat in, but it's about as roomy as an Apollo landing capsule.

"This car is made for a very narrow market," Scudieri says. "Even though they can afford it, this is not a car for NBA players."

It's actually a car for racing drivers. It's been a long day, and as this is the culmination of the tour I'm hoping to be offered a chance to take it for a spin at a nearby test track. Sadly, a posed photo with Scudieri in front of the car is as intimate an experience with the Abarth 124 as I'm going to get. The chairman and I say goodbye back at the factory entrance. He gives me a black carbon fiber bracelet as a parting gift and apologizes for not being able to join Alessandro and me for a late lunch, though he assures me the meal will be delicious.

BEFORE SCUDIERI DISAPPEARS in the rearview mirror I'm compelled to insert a mildy uncomfortable coda.

One thing I found researching this book, particularly this chapter, is that like politicians and gentlemen's club doormen, vendors of luxury are prone to apocrypha. Paolo Scudieri is no less immune to this instinct than any other company head.

You expect a certain amount of puffery any time you interview someone whose agenda is to promote their work or company. Cool. You listen and record their words politely, then go back and fact-check the quotes and information against neutral sources. This is the reason I'd contacted Bob Elton and other credentialed automotive sources before and after meeting with Scudieri.

It turned out, although Scudieri told me nothing egregiously wrong, he embellished certain innovations and procedures associated with his company. In the part of our discussion that centered on the histories of polyurethane, carbon fiber, and other technical breakthroughs, he erred on some dates and baldly undersold contributions of competing companies. Nothing nefarious. Nothing you wouldn't expect from a busy company chief rattling details off the top of his head in response to ad-libbed questions delivered through a starstruck interpreter jacked up on espresso, almond cookies, and proximity to eminence. I've corrected such mistakes in the text above.

But there are some parts of everyone's story that only the storyteller can know. And, given what we know about the capricious nature of memory, that no one can ever be completely sure of. British neurologist Oliver Sacks made a point of distinguishing between "fabulations" and "fabrications" when recalling the disappointment of being confronted with inaccuracies in some of his own most vivid childhood memories and stories. "It's startling to realize . . . that some of our most cherished memories may never have happened—or may have happened to someone else," Sacks wrote in his book *The River of Consciousness*.

Did the letter from Enzo Ferrari really arrive a few dramatic hours before the scheduled meeting in Maranello? Did Scudieri really drive all night and sleep in the car before his theatrical wake-up call in the hotel parking lot? Did his rise to fortune really pivot on the last-second whims of the Italian postal immortals? Was he really that far ahead of the PU and carbon fiber curves when so many others were already working with these materials? The cynical reader may detect a whiff of corporate mythmaking at play here. Only Scudieri knows for sure, and after all these years it's possible he's unknowingly rewritten part of his own history.

At one point, Scudieri told me he'd sent his birthday card to Ferrari in 1982. But if it was 1982, that would have put the meeting with Ferrari at a time before he'd inked his decisive deal to provide gas tank seals for the Alfa 33, which would set up a conflict with larger parts of his chronology. So, I'm assuming, with an assist from Adler Pelzer communications people, the meeting with Ferrari took place in 1983.

I offer this tortured disclaimer partly out of the "full disclosure" spirit that becomes more important as each passing year gives us an ever-more tangled media ecosystem and ever-more evidence of the triumph of PR, marketing, and outright propaganda over the flow of public information. But it's especially appropriate to keep in mind when dealing with the pooh-bahs and purveyors of luxury for whom fondling the brocade of fantasy is all but de rigueur. (Pardon my French.) At least for businesspeople, fabulation is a built-in feature of luxury's allure.

ALESSANDRO AND I debrief on the drive back to Naples. He's pleased with how the day has gone, confident we both acquitted ourselves well. He tells me Mr. Scudieri was impressed that I wore a tie to the interview. This feels a little patronizing, but I let it slide. I'm not here to get offended. Maybe the guys just expect sartorial negligence from Americans. Or journalists. Who could blame them?

More to the point, I'm still holding out for a taste of luxury and thinking maybe a hosted feast at one of Naples' finest Lungomare Caracciolo establishments lies at the end of this ride. With the exception of those almond cookies, I haven't eaten since breakfast and the laxative rumbling of that conference room espresso has me as twitchy as a cat in a car.

Instead, Alessandro pulls off the highway at a familiar exit. He wheels us past the Hotel Tiempo and parks a few blocks away, directly in front of the dinner place I'd scoped out the night before. Apparently this really is the only place in the neighborhood worth getting a bite to eat at.

It's called Eccellenze Campane, and it's a sort of high-end food mall, with separate areas for small restaurants dishing up regional Campania specialties and celebrating Mezzogiorno's contributions to Italian culture.

Inside, we're joined by a pair of attractive PR women. The bustier of the two—tousled blond hair, eyes as dark, deep, and devastating as your first divorce—leans across the table at me. It's hard to casually pretend not to notice her hypnotically tight-fitting and low-cut top. Alessia is the PR manager for the restaurant, which just happens to be owned by . . . Paolo Scudieri.

"The aim of Eccellenze Campane is to promote the agriculture and gastronomic excellence of the Campania region," she tells me. "Mr. Scudieri's mission is to lift up the business and people of the local area. We have already opened stores in Milan and London, and soon we'll be in Rome."

The pasta is exquisite. The Buffalo mozzarella superb. The vegetables fresh. The wine delightful. Every detail is outstanding. Exchanging Euro kisses outside, I compliment Alessia on her stylish handbag, thinking I might pick one up as a gift.

"It's Tramontano leather," she says.

Of course it is.

I shake hands with Alessandro and walk through sheets of midday industrial haze back to the Scudieri-endorsed Hotel Tiempo, whose louche location suddenly makes all the sense in the world. If the King of Comfort hasn't yet succeeded in enriching the status of his entire region, he's gonna die tryin'.

CHAPTER 6

Luxury at the end of the world:
STATUS AS AUTHENTICITY

I HAD NO INTENTION OF MEETING ROY VICKERS. IN FACT, I'D
tried to avoid it.

In fall 2017, I took a two-week road trip through British Columbia.
The entire way I'd been harassed by heavy rains, premature snows, and
washed-out roads. On the last day, I had a breakfast meeting scheduled
with a guy named Blaine Estby way up north in Terrace (population:
13,000). For most people, Terrace is a gas stop on the Yellowhead Highway. For me it was the final obligation of a drawn-out voyage.

The owner of Smithers Brewing Company in nearby Smithers, Estby
asked over coffee and hash browns if I'd like to meet Vickers. Estby was
a friend of the local legend. I was familiar with Vickers's reputation as an
artist and had seen his work, but that was about it.

No, thanks, I said. I had a long drive in front of me and the days were
getting short. I wanted to make the painful border crossing before dark.

"Roy's got this incredible house right on the Skeena River, you should
see it," Estby answered. "He's working on an interesting project."

We arrived at Vickers's place about ten in the morning. His wife,
Andrea, met us with tea and cupcakes. I planned on putting in a polite

twenty minutes. I didn't leave until almost dark. "Roy can have a powerful effect on people in a short amount of time," a man who's worked with Vickers would later tell me.

After a little gibble-gab, Vickers pulled on a pair of rubber boots and a puffy black jacket and walked Estby and me to his outdoor carving shed. On its side across two sawhorses lay a massive cedar tree trunk that had been stripped of all its branches and bark. Along the Pacific Northwest Coast, the perfume of fresh-cut cedar is an intoxicant. After a few minutes Vickers began using his fist to pound out a rhythm on a bald cedar trunk, using the tree as a drum. He sang a song of his ancestors about sons becoming their fathers and grandfathers. Afterward, he explained the song, then made a joke about his own age, which showed in his salt-and-pepper hair, eyebrows, and mustache.

I shot a ninety-five-second video of his impromptu performance. I've watched it many times since. To white ears, all Native American songs sound the same—droning hypnosis. Like all music, once you become familiar enough with it to anticipate the changes, it starts making sense. You develop a taste for it despite initial objections. Just ask Todd Storz.

The tree trunk and song were fascinating, but what ultimately drew me into Vickers's orbit was the way he talked about his work.

"A thousand years old," he said, running a hand down the smooth barrel of the tree, smiling at it as if it were one of his First Nations ancestors come to visit. "Isn't that crazy?"

When you imagine status and luxury you don't imagine Terrace, BC, an old logging town whose economy now relies on mining, liquefied natural gas, and other industrial development. You don't imagine standing in a pile of wood shavings in a muddy yard watching your breath pillow out of your mouth as you carry on a conversation with strangers on a damp autumn morning when you've got other places to be. You don't imagine the bludgeoning repetition of music in a difficult language that to untrained ears sounds as if it were invented by people moving large boulders through a forest.

If you're truly interested in status and luxury, however, you probably should imagine that scene. Or something similarly obscure. Because it's from situations like these that the new arbiters of taste and privilege are combating the scourge of mass production and status capitalization. And driving travel's rise as a measure of prestige.

IN MANY WAYS, the luxury industry has become a victim of its own success. A major factor is the consolidation of once-small entities under conglomerate umbrellas—LVMH now owns seventy-five brands, including Bulgari, Chaumet, Tag Heuer, and Tiffany. Estée Lauder Companies owns Bobbi Brown, Clinique, MAC Cosmetics, Michael Kors, and Tom Ford. Richemont has Cartier, Montblanc, Ralph Lauren, Shanghai Tang, and you get the picture.

More than craftsmanship, family tradition, or unique artistic flair, the financialization of the luxury industry over the past half century brought shareholders. With shareholders came a demand for dividends. With a demand for dividends came culture change, corner cutting, and sacrifices in quality. Then, for luxury brands, came the final insult. With every sale on a third-party website, with every opening of a shop in a "factory outlet" mall, prestige brands concede their most precious commodity—scarcity.

How do you hit a 15 percent increase in annual profits while not raising prices and maintaining your reputation for exclusivity? You don't. That's the reason that, while luxury brands may still communicate some amount of monetary advantage, they no longer confer prestige.

A decade or so ago, the luxury and fashion industries began looking at the glut of "luxury brand" products in the market and didn't like what it saw. Neither did its clientele. Robin Lent, coauthor of *Selling Luxury*, the how-to book for "sales ambassadors" that's been translated into six languages, offers an example.

"A wealthy, attractive Shanghai lady buys the latest prestigious handbag from LV," Lent tells me by email. "That day in the street, she walks by a peasant woman from the boom docks, obviously not dressed as she should be, but guess what she has on her shoulder? The same bag the sophisticated Shanghai woman has, and she is not happy because the exclusivity part of the game is over." (It's possible Lent meant "boondocks," by the way, but considering the explosive economic climate in the world's fastest-growing luxury market,* he might just as likely have been coining a new phrase.)

The antidote to surfeit is authenticity. A notoriously opaque quality, "authenticity" in the context of luxury consumption sits at the intersection of such attributes as honesty, "family" (loosely defined), organic or unalloyed ingredients, heritage, tradition, location, and, much of the time, national, ethnic, regional, local, or other historic forms of "purity." To convey their own authenticity, large companies often seek marketing cues from the smaller ones they once resembled, such as the Hatch Chile Store ("Keeping the Tradition") in New Mexico: "At The Hatch Chile Store we have a tradition of excellence. Our extended family currently farms over 1,000 acres of prime farmland in the Hatch Valley, and have been in the produce business for more than 100 years. Our history here in the Hatch Valley dates back over 5 generations to Joseph Franzoy, the first farmer to grow chile here. Headquartered in Hatch, New Mexico, our history and heritage ensure that when you buy our Hatch Green Chile, you're getting the very best you can find, straight from the family farm."

You've heard some version of that pitch a million times, because in our rapidly digitized world authenticity is desired by nearly everyone and the concepts behind it are supple. Glossier makeup and skin care products captured millennial and Gen Z market share by positioning itself as an authentic, "people-powered beauty ecosystem" with a preference for an easy, "no makeup" look. Its campaigns conjure a friend's advice, not some febrile Madison Avenue come-on.

With social media, luxury brands began pushing an angle that lev-

---

* In 2019, mainland Chinese consumers accounted for 11 percent of the global personal luxury market. Defying the coronavirus downturn elsewhere, in 2020 that figure nearly doubled, jumping to 20 percent. China is expected to surpass the United States as the world's largest luxury consumer by 2025.

eraged the stark reality of their business: "authenticity" was better than "exclusivity." A newfound appreciation for "genuineness" that had been gathering steam in the luxury world was finally outed in a 2019 *Guardian* feature explaining "Why the Online Influencer Industry Is Going 'Authentic.'" The piece announced a "new era of authenticity." It promoted the idea of "micro" and "nano" influencers and shared quotes from trend shapers like Sarah Penny, head of content at the London-based marketing agency Influencer Intelligence. In the article, Penny cattily dismissed old-world, multimillion-follower social influencers: "They worked with so many brands they couldn't possibly be authentic."

Take proclamations by PR firms whose idea of authenticity is a *blurry* photo of Kendall Jenner (as Influencer Intelligence was featuring on its home page last I checked in 2021) for whatever you think they're worth. Whether or not you're convinced that low-tech imagery equals the antithesis of a staged campaign, the message is indisputable—in the halls of luxury creation "authenticity" has shifted from last decade's buzzword to this decade's marketing strategy. In the 2021 documentary *The Curse of Von Dutch*, about the meteoric, early-2000s success of the clothing brand established in part by gang bangers and a convicted felon, fashion impresario Mike Cassel includes authenticity as a key piece of his "branding mantra." "Classic never dies. Ever," Cassel says. "Authenticity speaks for and sells itself."

An amusing illustration of the consumer quest for genuineness is the demand that surrounds "authenticity certificates" that come tucked inside Hermès Birkin bags. Something between a satchel and a 1950s ladies purse, Birkins have been called the most copied bag in the world. Each is handmade and takes three months to put together. About twelve thousand are made each year. According to CNBC, the most expensive handbag ever sold was a white Himalaya crocodile diamond Birkin, which Christie's auctioned in 2017 for $380,000.

There are hundreds of thousands—probably millions—of counterfeit Birkin bags in existence. The ubiquity of the knockoff market contributes to luxury saturation—a situation that's led a number of serious buyers to seek out "authentication cards," tucked inside new bags, assuring them their newly purchased Birkin is the real thing.

There's just one problem. Hermès doesn't issue authentication cards with its bags. Never has. Never will. The whole "Birkin authentication card" business is a hoax. Dozens of online articles warn would-be Birkin buyers that authentication cards actually prove the opposite—that the bag is a fake. Alas, the zeal for real has ensured the scam's persistence.

Similarly, glut begat a decline in international travel's distinction as a marker of status. Budget tickets to Bangkok, Barcelona, and Machu Picchu cast a similar hue on everyone's slideshow. The tourism industry went through the same process of self-examination as the luxury biz. And mimicked its evolution.

In its 2021 report on global travel trends, forecasters at the World Global Style Network, headquartered in New York and London, claimed a "focus on authenticity" would drive post-COVID tourism in tandem with a newfound appreciation for "neighborhood hotels" and "ancient rituals." Already attuned to luxury shopping as a venerable vacation activity (careful with those street-corner Birkins), travelers whose day-to-day lives are subsumed with on-screen tasks place intense value on accruing authentic "life experiences." Their manes of proof grow dark and thick on a billion Instagram accounts, not unlike those old Aztec priests whose blood-soaked hair stood as a testament to the ritualistic dramas they'd experienced.

People travel for many reasons, but two factors in particular motivate today's traveling elite. The first is to fulfill the braggart's obligation (see chapter 1 if you've already forgotten Peggy Klaus) in a screen-worthy and difficult-to-duplicate manner. The second and more powerful urge is to establish a personal connection to authenticity—that is to say "status." Because along with hatch chiles, just about everything can be shipped anywhere nowadays; products that once imparted exotic cachet have lost their globe-trotter juju. A dinner of freshly caught salmon in Ketchikan means relatively little when the same fish can be FedExed and served to diners in Los Angeles or San Antonio the same day. About the only thing you can't package now is a place itself, or at least the scenery. If you want to claim the authentic experience of the Taj Mahal, Austrian Alps, or an Indigenous village in British Columbia—and then post the proof—you have to go there.

THE DAY WE met, Roy Vickers wasn't selling anything, fake, real, or otherwise. But he was creating something status seekers are feverish to get their hands on.

Born in 1946 in a village in northern British Columbia, Roy Vickers is an Indigenous artist of Tsimshian, Haida, Kwakwaka'wakw, and English heritage. He's spent the past four decades building a body of paintings and carvings that's earned him a reputation as one of Canada's greatest living artists. His international reputation was sealed with major installations he created for the 1994 Commonwealth Games in Victoria. He'd do the same for the 2010 Winter Olympics in Vancouver.

His painting *A Meeting of Chiefs* was presented as an official state gift to Queen Elizabeth II. In 2006, he received the Order of Canada, the centerpiece of the country's system of official orders, decorations, and medals. Now seventy-six, he shows no interest in emeritus status. He was nominated for a 2019 Grammy Award for his bentwood-style box artwork that wrapped a Grateful Dead nineteen-CD box set. He recently designed a series of labels for some of his friend Blaine Estby's seasonal beers.

Far south of Terrace (where he now lives) in the little tourist town of Tofino, BC, on Vancouver Island, the Roy Henry Vickers Gallery is a commercial landmark. Built in the style of a First Nations* longhouse, its tall, vertical cedar boards and doors of beaten copper summon a deeper objective. Step inside and you're whisked into a world of Indigenous luxury. A mini-temple of cedar, the gallery is built around two massive ceiling beams. At each end, the ancient timbers rest atop four hand-carved

---

* In Canada, "First Nations" is the rough equivalent of "Native American." What Canadians call a "band," Americans call a "tribe." "Poutine," of course, is "moose vomit" south of the border.

raven and eagle house posts. The sunken firepit in the center of the room is reminiscent of those found in traditional longhouses along the BC coast. Altogether, the gallery represents the kind of pinnacle validation for which artists struggle their entire lives and pretend not to care about.

The gallery claims to attract five hundred thousand visitors a year from all over the world. Most are gawkers. Many of the original or limited-edition Vickers paintings that line the walls run well past $10,000.

On the first day I visit, the most expensive piece in the gallery is a twenty-nine-by-twenty-one-inch original painting done by Vickers in 1983 titled *Pacific Sands*. It's a sort of Indigenous-fantasy rendering of a mother and baby humpback whale breaching from a deep blue sea against a sky of undulating red, orange, yellow, and blue oscillations. Nice, but too pricey for the mother and two teenage boys soaking it in next to me.

"Look at this, forty thousand dollars!" one of the boys half shouts. "Who the fuck spends forty thousand dollars for a picture of a whale?"

It's a fair question, so I put it to Casandra, the gallery's stylish Finnish director.

"A select group of European collectors comes through this area periodically looking only for original paintings," she tells me.

"Why do they come to this area?"

"Of course, they are looking for something authentic."

The quest for authenticity is in some part a reaction against what a Verge critic reported as the "harmonization of tastes" that's emerged as a by-product of globalization. Architectural and service sameness is no longer limited to McDonald's or Starbucks. From Lisbon to Philly to Singapore you can drink craft beer in some version of the same "local" brewpub featuring the same faux-artisanal aesthetic; follow familiar corporate branding to shops whose layout you know by heart; check into a cookie-cutter hotel room or even an Airbnb or Vrbo apartment with the same Keurig coffee maker as the ones you visited in Columbus and Cabo; get the same reliable directions to the same reliable type of club whose music, style, and vibe you know you can rely on before you get the stamp on your hand at the door. In a homogenized world, the status value of unique little wonders like Tofino and the Roy Henry Vickers Gallery increase exponentially.

THE SECOND TIME we meet—again at his spread on the Skeena River—Vickers is in a state of high obsession. He's deep into what he tells me is "the biggest and scariest challenge of my career."

On the surface, the project looks like any other in a long line of major undertakings. Vickers is carving a totem pole using the huge cedar log I'd seen the year before. Granted, totem poles take a lot of work. But Vickers has done many of them over the years. The first one—an owl totem he carved as a student in the early 1970s—sits at the Ksan Historical Village ten miles down the road from his house on the river.

This one, though, is different. Not just from any other Vickers has ever carved. But from any totem pole anyone has ever carved. He's working on a replica of a historic pole whose authenticity made it the pursuit of men for more than a century, and whose unique form tied it to the status of an entire people.

For a work of art considered one of the most aesthetically advanced of its type, a lot of mystery surrounds the ancient totem pole that's been part of Vickers's life for the better part of fifty years. People can't even agree what to call it. At the University of British Columbia's Museum of Anthropology (MOA)—where the original pole commands pride of place amid one of the world's most important collections of Pacific Coast Native art—curators refer to it as the Raven Pole.

Vickers doesn't care for this designation. He's always insisted the totem, with its distinctive eleven-foot-long beak, depicts not a raven but a fearsome, mythical bird known as *hok hok*. Eventually Vickers took to calling it the Hosumdas pole. "Hosumdas" literally translates to "the first person to drink from the water at the head of the river" in the Oweekeno language. In a poetic context it denotes the chieftain of the BC coast's Oweekeno people to which Vickers belongs.

No one knows when the pole was carved, who carved it, or from which nation or band the artist came. The MOA says it was carved circa 1890. Vickers guesses it could go back to the mid-1800s. Other than raven and eagle images, no one knows the significance of the other emblems carved on it.

There's disagreement about how the pole got from the village of Oweekeno to the MOA. The museum's website uses the sufficiently vague term "transfer" to explain how it acquired the pole in the 1950s. Vickers and the eldest person in Oweekeno—his ninety-something Auntie Evelyn, who happens to be one of fifty living people who speak the critically endangered Oweekeno language—believe loggers may have taken the pole as late as the 1960s. No one can say for sure what the reaction in the village was when locals discovered their heraldic pole had been taken.

"If there was an emotion it probably would have been more of pain and confusion than anger," says Vickers. "Like, 'Why would anyone have done this?' Because that's how we think."

The first time I heard the story, the pole supposedly had been stolen shortly after the turn of the century. This is not implausible. Canada's Indian Act of 1876, and subsequent amendments, became the tacitly genocidal legal instrument through which the Canadian government suppressed First Nations cultures across the country until the 1950s. In addition to forcing children to attend residential schools, where they were forbidden to speak their native languages and compelled to adopt English, the Indian Act banned the custom of potlatch. This included raising totem poles, crucial to Pacific Coast Indigenous identity and status.

"Potlatch" means "to give" and comes from a trade jargon, Chinook, once common along the Pacific Coast of Canada. "Guests witnessing the event are given gifts. The more gifts given, the higher the status achieved by the potlatch host," says a Kwakwaka'wakw cultural organization in Alert Bay, a BC town famed for secretly keeping totem pole and potlatch culture alive during the darkest days of oppression.

The most well-known feature of potlatch among non-Natives remains the lavish gift giving. In order to display their wealth, chiefs of great houses would legendarily give away incredible riches. Gold, furs, meat, baskets of rare food, slaves. Hit a good potlatch in precontact days and chances were you were going home with some heady swag. Even more than winning a battle, potlatch was the most important way to preserve or transfer authority and signal status along the Pacific Northwest Coast.

But it was more than gifts. Outlawing potlatch was a particularly evil act of cultural suppression by the colonial British/Canadians.* There's no simple imagine-the-Super-Bowl-Fourth-of-July-Marvel-movie-premiere-and-family-reunion-rolled-into-one cultural analogy to be made. Unique to this part of the world, potlatch developed largely as a result of the environment. Soaring mountains, wild forests, and tempestuous waters make travel difficult along the BC coast, where small groups of interrelated people live in isolation most of the time. Potlatches were, and still are, epic gatherings of nations, bands, villages, and houses from up and down the coast convened to handle a laundry list of cultural business, from sharing news of births and deaths to settling disputes to singing, dancing, and agreeing on the historical record.

The period of art theft that followed the imposition of the Indian Acts in Canada—roughly 1876 until the Great Depression—is referred to as the Great Scramble. This is when the landmark museums of America and Europe—Chicago, New York, London, Berlin, Vienna—and a handful of private collectors ransacked the Pacific Coast, plundering its now "illegal" totem poles, masks, regalia, and almost all known First Nations art. With their representations of ravens, eagles, bears, killer whales, beavers, frogs, and other fauna, totem poles have long transfixed visitors. In most of the world the highest respect animals get is when they're barbecued.

In his book *Captured Heritage: The Scramble for Northwest Coast*

---

* The history of Canadian sovereignty is bizarre and confusing and I still contend to my Canadian brothers and sisters, whose country I love and whose legal residency I covet, that any country that displays another nation's queen on its currency isn't fully disengaged.

Artifacts, Douglas Cole grimly describes the white world's locust deter-mination to "salvage in the last hour a residue of a dying culture." By 1882, one art prospector on the Northwest Coast complained that his competitors had "cleaned out the Indian market entirely and the agents of foreign Governments have swept away what the tourists have left."

At least according to white collectors, by the 1930s authenticity had pretty much disappeared from the art of Native peoples. In the 1950s, a group of anthropologists became so profoundly concerned about this that they assembled a group called the British Columbia Totem Pole Pres-ervation Committee. A university and government enterprise supported by major logging companies of the day, the committee was formed to survey, purchase, and conserve whatever authentic totem poles were left in the province.

First Nations people "were at the point of cultural change where they wished to abandon their places in the potlatch system and had no wish to hold on to materials of the potlatch, which had lost its importance," wrote a museum curator in 1967, an impeccable distillation of the co-lonial obliviousness (or hostility) to the reasons such cultural ennui had metastasized in the first place. Or just another lie to justify genocide.

"It was called the 'salvage period,'" says Pam Brown, a member of BC's Heiltsuk Nation, now curator of Pacific Northwest collections at the MOA. "At the time, people thought First Nations people were liter-ally dying out."

In 1956, as I eventually discovered by sifting through rarely visited records kept in the basement of the MOA, the British Columbia Totem Pole Preservation Committee sent a twenty-three-year-old anthropology grad student named Mike Kew to Oweekeno. His mission: remove the Hosumdas pole from the village and deliver it to the University of Van-couver.

AT ABOUT THE same time Mike Kew was traveling to Oweekeno another young man from rural Canada was beginning his own adventure on the coast of British Columbia. Howard McDiarmid had just completed a one-year internship at Vancouver General Hospital. By his own admission he hadn't distinguished himself as a medical student at the University of Manitoba.

"My academic record was very average," he later wrote. "I was not wildly enthusiastic about the study of medicine."

Upon graduation, McDiarmid wasn't exactly fending off job offers from the Royal Jubilee Hospital. It was thus in a state of mild desperation that he agreed to take a job as the only doctor in what was then the obscure village of Tofino. Local lore has it that the equally fraught and doctorless locals managed to persuade McDiarmid to take the gig only after plying him with copious amounts of liquor. The story is false, but its enduring local popularity illustrates how frantic everybody was for medical help in such a remote outpost in the 1950s. At the time, the population of Tofino was four hundred. The broader area's First Nations population was three or four times that.

Landing in Tofino on a drizzly day in January 1955 in a Queen Charlotte Airlines Canso floatplane, McDiarmid wondered who should be more fearful, himself or the townspeople. His new patients were a rough-looking collection of First Nations locals, loggers, miners, and fishermen. Scattered about the area like tendons and ligaments, a rangitang troupe of drifters, dreamers, squatters, and scofflaws maintained a fringe existence whose primary purpose was keeping a safe distance from modern society.

Furnishings in McDiarmid and his wife Lynn's first house consisted of a mattress on the floor and a refrigerator in the bedroom. The kitchen was too small to accommodate the fridge. Their humble beginnings weren't much different from those of Ralph Lauren (who started life as Ralph Lifshitz) and his wife, Ricky, who in the 1960s plotted a takeover of the fashion industry from their tiny Pullman apartment beneath the train tracks in the Bronx. The Laurens' refrigerator was in the living room.

Almost as soon as he'd arrived in Tofino, McDiarmid had become transfixed with the magnificent arc of sandy coastline south of town. During med school summers he'd worked at the Banff Springs Hotel. While training in minor surgery in England he'd visited the famed tourist beaches of the UK and southern France. The first time he saw Chesterman Beach just south of Tofino he thought it was every bit as beautiful as any stretch of coastline in the world. Reached only by a rough trail through dense forest, the beach was mostly empty, not counting a couple nondescript huts and houses. His mind's eye conjured a hotel. He began saving money. Eventually, he purchased a piece of waterfront property on the largely undeveloped beach.

There was a catch. Acquiring the land meant acquiring a strange figure that had attached himself to the property like a barnacle to a dock—a strikingly handsome man of narrow build with flowing hair, a snarled beard, and thickly muscled arms who most of the time walked around without any clothes on. The dedicated nudist's name was Henry Nolla. He'd been squatting on a piece of property down the coast for several years. Somewhat like a grizzly, however, he considered Chesterman Beach part of his ranging territory.

AS A COLLEGE student, Roy Vickers visited the MOA regularly to educate himself on the art of his ancestors. Each time, he felt an inexplicable pull from what the museum called its Raven Pole. Something in the strange design and remnant spirit within the wood wouldn't let him go.

"In those days, you could walk right up and touch it," Vickers says. "Growing up in Kitkatla we used to climb on the old totem poles. No one told us not to. No one said they were sacred."

In 1994, an unexpected development launched Vickers into the orbit of what he now sees as his appointment with status destiny. After a long and close association with an Oweekeno family, Vickers was adopted into the House of Walkus, hereditary chieftains in Oweekeno. Along with the chief's name of Tlagwikila, the honor conferred upon him all the responsibilities that come with that exalted status. Vickers had suddenly become the adoptive grandson of Simon Walkus, the chief who'd probably originally commissioned the Raven/Hosumdas pole, and certainly the man in front of whose house it had once stood.

By this time, Vickers was a highly successful artist. His Tofino gallery was averaging a million dollars a year in sales. (It still does.) Time slipped away as it tends to do when you're in demand. It wasn't until 2014 that his thoughts began turning regularly back to the totem pole. It simply refused to leave his mind. He'd come to resent its presence in the university's museum as a literal representation of cultural theft. (And, yes, there's an undercurrent of social justice in this tale Paolo Scudieri would appreciate.)

Canada's Truth and Reconciliation Commission was then in full swing, promoting explicit acts of healing between the government and First Nations. Petitioning the museum to repatriate the pole back to Oweekeno made sense as a symbolic gesture. But exposing the badly deteriorated one-hundred-and-twenty-year-old carving to the region's harsh marine climate would have amounted to another kind of gloomy Indigenous death sentence.

Gradually, the idea of carving a new, full-size replica to replace the original pole back in the village began taking shape. A new pole would embody a reborn spirit. It also fit the current fashion for "reconciliation." You hear that word a lot in Canada these days, though when I suggest the theme to Vickers, his usually cheerful countenance clouds over.

"Reconciliation is a political word some people have put together to mean something," Vickers tells me in his open-air workshop, carving blade in hand. "It's not even possible in this world to reconcile the cultural genocide that's happened to our people. You can't fix it. You can't make cultural genocide better.

"What is possible, what I want, is to regenerate a new culture, a new strength for people who seem to have lost their power. It's not lost. I'm proof."

VICKERS MIGHT HAVE had the will, but even for a man of limitless vision the way seemed dark. The original pole had been carved from a red cedar so massive Vickers estimates its age at possibly one thousand years. In addition to permission and costs, the logistics of finding, felling, and hauling a millennia-old cedar out of the dense BC backwoods seemed beyond even his considerable ability to move mountains.

It wasn't until a fishing trip that, as Vickers sees it, the spirits of the ancestors intervened. On a sunny summer evening in 2015 at the Good Hope Cannery in Rivers Inlet not far from Oweekeno (the old cannery is now a private lodge), Vickers was introduced to a couple of middle-aged logging men in from Vancouver on a fishing weekend. Because he's a storyteller, he began telling the strangers about the Hosumdas pole. They listened with interest.

"If I wanted to find a really big cedar for a totem pole, who would I need to talk to?" Vickers eventually asked.

"How big?" one of the men replied.

"About a thousand years old," Vickers said.

"Well, after jumping through a lot of hoops, eventually you'd have to talk to me," the man said. "I'm Ric Slaco, vice president and chief forester at Interfor." The Canadian company is one of the world's largest lumber producers.

When I repeat this piece of remembered dialogue for Slaco in a downtown Vancouver coffee shop, he confirms that's the way it went down.

"You could just see it was something special. I bought into Roy's dream right away," Slaco tells me. "I said, 'We'll get a log for you.'"

In February 2016, Interfor flew Roy and his adoptive brother and hereditary Oweekeno chief, Ted Walkus, into the Great Bear Rainforest to look at seven monumental cedar trees identified by field crews as totem candidates. None was quite right. Not straight enough, not wide enough, not . . . sincere enough, to borrow from Linus van Pelt.

After a frustrating day watching the brothers shake their heads at various forest giants, the Interfor crew mentioned a final tree they'd identified. But it was by far the toughest to access. Getting to it would require a perilous bushwhack, hopscotching across downed logs concealed with a shin-snagging network of brush.

Vickers was walking on a twice-broken, sixty-nine-year-old ankle and a couple cracked neck vertebrae, the result of recently being thrown from a horse. Both eyes would soon require laser surgery. He didn't hesitate. The group picked its way through the woods. Once in front of the tree he had no doubts.

"As soon as we saw it, Ted and I put a hand on the tree and started crying," Vickers says. "We knew it was the one." After his brother delivered a traditional blessing, a crew moved in and dropped the ancient tree in less than an hour.

Slaco was aware he was taking an enormous leap of faith. He might have bought into Vickers's dream, but he was still a circumspect timber exec with four decades in the business. When I ask Slaco what a tree like the one he arranged to have felled for Vickers cost to harvest and donate he takes on the look of a man who's just been told what his daughter's Ivy League education is going to cost.

"I don't want to tell you how much," he says, and not in a convivial way, more in an our-shareholders-don't-need-to-know-that way. "Clear-grade cedar prices have been at the top of the market for a long time. I don't want to go any further than that."

In fact, the prestige factor of products made with authentic old-growth cedar continues to skyrocket. This is because much of the best stands of old growth have either been logged or protected. The majority of all trees harvested today are, depending on species, between twenty-five and a hundred years old; secondary plantings put in after clear-cuts. Younger trees don't have the board dimension, density, or decay-resistant properties of centuries-old cedar trees.

As a result, many contemporary "wood" products are actually fakes. The "wood" siding that adorns most new residential houses today is actually something called fiber cement siding. It's made with water, wood pulp, fly ash, or silica sand, and Portland cement, which itself is made with limestone, clay, and iron. In other words, an inauthentic material, a wood facsimile. Fewer than 5 percent of new houses built in the United States today use wood or a wood-product siding, and virtually none of that wood can be classified as "old growth" (which has no official definition, but which the U.S. Forest Service describes as trees at least 150 years old). For scarcity, prestige, and luxury, a few hundred board feet of centuries-old Canadian red cedar is on par with diamonds and moon rocks.

BY HIS OWN accounting, Vickers has carved some thirty totem poles. But when he began picking apart the Hosumdas pole—multiple trips to the MOA, which let him in before opening hours to take measurements and photos—he noticed something he'd never before appreciated.

"The artist who carved this pole was way ahead of his time," Vickers says. "When I began trying to copy his work it twisted my mind. This brilliant artist also had the courage to do something totally out of the ordinary. There was no carver alive who could help me understand what this carver did." Without the aid of a computer, much less tracing paper or a ruler—Vickers guesses the carver probably did his designing with a pencil, string, and pieces of bark—the artist had rendered a 2D design onto a 3D pole with supernatural accuracy.

Back in his workshop with the new Hosumdas pole three-fourths of the way complete, Vickers walks me around the pole, which I'd originally seen in its raw form the day we'd first met. Now it was supercharged with carved images of ravens, eagles, and more unfamiliar motifs. What's known to carvers as the ABCs of Pacific Northwest Coast carving style— ovoids, nested ovoids, the U, split U, and elongated S—are the building blocks of a long-standing orthodoxy. In warping those rules, Vickers believes the unknown artist behind the masterpiece imbued the pole with an unprecedented vitality.

"He took the totally rigid forms of Northwest Coast art and bent them to his own way of design," Vickers says. "I am certain this pole is one of the most powerful statements a chief on this coast has ever made."

Vickers knew he couldn't carve the new Hosumdas pole alone. Using spoon knives and chisels to chip away at a twenty-one-foot-long log demands Sasquatchean strength and endurance. Cut to length and stripped, the log alone still weighed a couple tons. After a lifetime abusing his body, Vickers has no business carrying a load of laundry down to the basement.

To complete the pole, Vickers assembled a dream team of carvers. These include Latham Mack, a Nuxalk sculptor whose original masks sell for well into five figures, and Dean Heron, an artist and instructor of gallery renown throughout BC. The linchpin of the operation—the first person Vickers called for help—is a local timber framer named Matt Lewis. Anyone who's ever employed the hit-or-mostly-miss services of an independent contractor quickly learns to stand in amazement of Lewis's brute strength, feather-touch artistry, and beers-can-wait work ethic.

"Who the beep uses a Husqvarna 350 with a carving bar? This guy!" Mack captions an Instagram post of Lewis cutting out the raw form of the pole's eleven-foot beak from a leviathan section of tree trunk with a chain saw. The Insta post illuminates a number of nontraditional elements Vickers employs—chain saws, computers, social media, and . . . a white dude.

"It's a mindfuck to get it right," says Lewis, whose father was a conscientious objector from California who moved to Canada to escape being drafted during the Vietnam War. "We measured it and broke it down into sections, but this isn't the same piece of wood as the original pole. You can spend a lot of time chasing a knot around."

Lewis's centrality to the project raises another knotty point: authenticity. Vickers has heard grumblings within the community.

"No one has the nerve to say something like that to my face, but someone will tell me so-and-so said this-and-that about my methods," he says. In fact, he's been defending the use of chain saws, computer-aided design, and non-Indigenous carvers as far back as the 1990s, when he started using Macromedia Freehand to draw totem templates.

"To me, it's almost like one of the ancestors created that program, it's so suited to this type of design," he says. "These are the tools of our time and we utilize them for our traditional art just as past generations used the technology available to them."

"Our ancestors weren't dumb," adds Mack. "When they got steel introduced, the first thing they did was make knives and blades."

Vicissitudes of history aside, paternalistic worries about the "ethnological integrity" of Native art are almost as old as the market for that art. By the 1870s, white collectors were already expressing concerns about Philistine influence on aboriginal art, as though Native cultures should remain preserved in amber for the cognoscenti's aesthetic pleasure. "One can only shake his head sadly to see [Native] art so corrupted and debased," tut-tutted an 1880s travel writer named Miss E. Ruhamah Scidmore of the evolving state of Indigenous art along the Northwest Coast.

A commercial artist himself, Vickers knows the prejudices of the marketplace have scarcely changed. When I posit an example, he finishes the scenario before I can complete it.

"If a novice Indigenous carver makes a halfway decent Haida mask, he might sell it for a thousand dollars in a Vancouver gallery," I say. "But let's say a Jewish woman from New York studies Northwest Coast art for decades and masters the form . . ."

"She can't even give her work away!" Vickers shouts. "There are millions of people who think this way—including many First Nations people—but there's no substance to it. Stopping a white man from carving a totem pole isn't protecting the culture. It's dividing people."

Vickers is describing a common response to the purity test. Even if they might fail a Cava vs. Clicquot blindfold test, plenty of drinkers still sneer at "sparkling wine." Champagne isn't champagne unless it's from France. An American-made Fender Stratocaster guitar runs from about $1,200 to more than $2,000 off the shelf; a new Strat made in Mexico goes for about $700. Western aficionados will tell you it's not an authentic Stetson hat unless it was made before 1970, when the original company was sold.

Not everyone shares Vickers's the-more-the-merrier view of Native art. One Indigenous associate trying to explain Vickers told me, "Roy's a radical Indian." Bringing the matter of cultural misappropriation full circle, Mack takes note of my Seattle Seahawks ball cap. The team's logo copies Northwest Coast Native art motifs. Mack shows me pictures on his phone of a First Nations Seahawks mask he custom-carved for a collector based on the distinctive design of the team's helmet.

"I sold it for fifteen thousand dollars," he says, appearing none too displeased with anybody's role in the process.

"I notice it's never anyone with a tool in their hand complaining about authenticity," Lewis says, noting this is the fifth pole he's worked on with Vickers. "This pole was logged with a helicopter, eh? So where are we going with this?"

HOWARD MCDIARMID QUICKLY discovered building a place on the storm-swept promontory he'd purchased on Chesterman Beach presented a greater challenge than he had the skills to match. Fortunately, along with the beach he'd inherited a partner. A peculiar energy infused Henry Nolla. And not just the nudist part.

Nolla's father was Catalan. His mother was Swedish. He was born in Barcelona in 1930. During the Spanish Civil War, he and his three sisters were sent to the safety of Sweden. There the preternatural boy worked alongside his grandfather, a talented furniture maker who worked in the traditional style of Swedish carpentry. The pair spent hours with heavy adzes and homemade tools chipping out everything from shoes to tables from great blocks of wood.

Back in Spain as a teenager, Nolla apprenticed as a blacksmith. He mastered wrought iron and learned to make his own tools. Self-sufficiency was his mantra. In 1957, he immigrated to Ontario, Canada, and worked as a welder. By 1965 he'd made his way to Vancouver Island, initially settling in the capital of Victoria. He worked for a while in a nearby iron ore mine, mostly as a handyman fixing anything that needed it, including heavy equipment. In the mid-1970s he discovered Chesterman Beach and immediately knew his wandering days were over.

McDiarmid, a business-minded doctor, and Nolla, a dedicated nudist with hair below his ass, might seem like the kind of unlikely pairing you'd find in a cheesy network detective series. But after Nolla agreed to help McDiarmid build his cabin, the two men quickly settled into what would become a symbiotic and lifelong friendship.

Nolla brought materials to the beach on a flat-bottomed, aluminum herring skiff. The approach was rocky and treacherous. Twice, the skiff capsized with all its freight. From the beach, he hooked up a generator to a winch and elevated a tramline to haul supplies up to the building site.

When it was finished, McDiarmid's cabin was a humble affair. With a brick fireplace, the main room functioned as living room, dining room, and sleeping area. Separate kitchen, bathroom, and deck. No water. No electricity aside from a propane-fired generator. Not a hotel, but a start.

During construction, McDiarmid had given Nolla permission to throw up a temporary shelter on his property while work was underway. A short walk from the cabin, in a clearing in the forest with a panoramic view of the ocean, Nolla built a four-hundred-square-foot A-frame and separate carving shed, largely with scrap wood and repurposed materials. It took him two weeks to put it together.

Instead of booting him off the property after the cabin was completed, McDiarmid offered Nolla a deal. He could stay on the property as ad hoc caretaker and security guard. They shook on it, McDiarmid in his red windbreaker and wool pants, Nolla bare as birth, not counting his tool belt.

For more than a decade, McDiarmid and his family enjoyed the cabin while he hustled to find partners to build a luxury property on his beach at the edge of the continent. "We approached many private investors and every financial institution known to man, to no avail," McDiarmid wrote. "All thought it was far too risky a project."

The doubters seemed to have the final say. In the late 1980s, a bucket of rags soaked in linseed oil McDiarmid had been using as a wood preservative spontaneously combusted, setting off an explosion of nearby propane containers. The flames spread in seconds. McDiarmid stood on the beach and watched his cabin burn to the ground.

ROY VICKERS GREW up dreaming of being a Canadian Mountie—save the day in the Red Serge and campaign hat. Shortly after turning eighteen he submitted his application. But the Royal Canadian Mounted Police rejected him. During the selection process, the RCMP discovered something Vickers himself had not been aware of. He was partially colorblind. The artist who became famous in part for painting ocean sunsets and colorful skies into which whales breached has problems seeing color. That's irony. (Right?)

After recovering from the disappointment, Vickers took up art. For a while he studied at a university in the provincial capital of Victoria. In 1973 he transferred north to Ksan, near the place he was born, to study traditional Native art. Right away he showed a natural ability to create magic with just about anything you put in his hand—carving knife, paintbrush, pencil.

Vickers quickly became popular with gallery owners in Victoria. By the mid-seventies he was making a decent living pumping out paintings, prints, carvings, and other inexpensive art. After a while, though, he began feeling like a human assembly line. And he still hadn't found his artistic voice.

"I was a commodity for art galleries," he says. "Nobody was interested in my stories, nobody was interested in the culture. All they were interested in was how fast they could sell my stuff. I got discouraged with galleries and said, 'To hell with you all,' and bought a fishing boat."

In the late seventies, Vickers put art on a shelf, deciding to become a commercial fisherman. With money he'd saved from art sales, he bought the *Native Bride*, a gillnet boat that belonged to his uncle. But even back then, with far more fish under the water, making a living as a commercial fisherman was brutal business. The May 18, 1980, eruption of Mount St. Helens in Washington State that belched ash across a dozen states had a devastating effect on the fishing industry in the Pacific Northwest. In September 1980, at the end of his second full summer fishing, Vickers was despondent. "Fishing sucks," he told himself. Dieseling down the coast to Victoria, he tied up in Tofino for fuel and food. Walking into town from the dock, he idly wandered into a small gift shop.

Something on a shelf attracted his eye. A hand-carved alderwood bowl. Vickers flipped it over. On the bottom he found the initials *HN* carved into the wood.

"I said to the owner at the register, 'Hey, is this one of Henry Nolla's bowls? How do you know him?'" he recounts. "She said, 'Well, yes, he lives out on Chesterman Beach.'"

Literally at that moment, as Vickers tells it, the shop door opened. In walked the naked hippie himself—albeit mostly clothed. Vickers had crossed paths with Nolla nearly a decade before in Victoria. He'd liked him, admired his abilities, but never expected to see him again.

"He and I give each other big hugs and that was it," Vickers recalls of the gift shop reunion. "He said, 'Let's go get something to eat.' So I went out to his place and after a long visit he said, 'Gee, it'd be nice if you could stay the winter and teach me to carve totem poles.'"

For Vickers, the timing made sense. His second marriage had recently bottomed out. Fishing had lost its appeal. Nolla helped Vickers find a place to spend the winter a quarter mile down the beach from his shed. Vickers stayed fifteen years.

"I lived in a beautiful house right on Chesterman Beach," Vickers says. "It's gone now. There's a big multimillion-dollar, ugly mansion sitting there today. I could walk out on my porch and see Henry's house and he could see mine. We were both bachelors, and we had these yellow raincoats. If we saw a yellow raincoat hanging outside it meant don't bother me."

Vickers and Nolla became more than partners. Vickers taught Nolla the ins, outs, and ovoids of Northwest Coast art. Nolla showed Vickers how to "move wood" in great chunks and delicate slivers with old-world tools. The two spent countless hours in Nolla's shed, developing what Vickers calls "*kul-m-needsk*," which means "both looking as one." Together they carved more than twenty totem poles, including a thirty-foot Salmon Totem for the 1994 Commonwealth Games that still stands in Victoria.

NOLLA AND VICKERS'S houses became the nexus for beach parties that attracted small groups of locals. Many evenings Howard and Lynn Mc-Diarmid would wander down the beach from their cabin, which was still standing at the time. In Tofino, Vickers had hurled himself back into his art—eight to ten hours a day refining his style. Between beers and smoke at the beach parties, he'd bring out his latest work to show off. The locals recognized exemplary First Nations art when they saw it and snapped it up quickly.

By this time, tourism was on the march in Tofino. With the extraction industries largely played out, the town needed a new way to survive. With each season a newer, bigger hotel or additions to existing properties appeared. No matter how many rooms were added, each year the town was booked to capacity.

Then as now, visitors came to Tofino to be spiritually renewed by the natural surroundings. These included the newly established Pacific Rim National Park. But there wasn't much going on in town and it rained a lot. Business leaders worried the town's offerings weren't sophisticated or diverse enough to build a truly sustainable industry around tourism.

So they hatched a plan. Headed by McDiarmid—who was burned out after three decades as the town's primary physician and who was still chasing his vision for a hotel on Chesterman Beach—a coalition of businesspeople lobbied Vickers to build an art gallery in the middle of town. Vickers would have a place to sell his art, they told him, and the hoteliers would have a place to send their customers when it rained.

"After a lot of pressure from Howard and all the hotel owners, I finally caved in and bought the property across the street from the Schooner Motel and built the gallery," Vickers says.

By now nearly forty, Vickers knew what he wanted. Not some glorified, owner-operated swap-meet table. He envisioned a citadel. A space to showcase his art, but also a palace to stand as an authentic totem of a once-canceled culture (literally) and a collection of stories those gallery owners in Victoria had neither understood nor embraced.

Vickers knew only one person capable of helping him turn his vision into reality: Henry Nolla. Along with Vickers's brother, a construction contractor, Vickers and Nolla designed and built the longhouse-style gallery. All the wood was cedar, felled and milled on Vancouver Island. The pair carved all four of the eagle house posts. Nolla adzed every plank in the gallery by himself with a tool he'd fashioned out of the leaf spring of an old truck, a piece of metal that had contour, strength, and give. Even when using a chain saw, Nolla worked naked and barefoot.

The gallery transformed Tofino.

"Oh, hell, yes, I was over the moon!" Vickers says, recalling the job they'd done.

Right away he knew it was special—a world-class art gallery in a place that a few decades before could barely hire a doctor. The Eagle Aerie Gallery—since renamed the Roy Henry Vickers Gallery—opened in 1986.

"My career shot up like a rocket," says Vickers.

OWEEKENO IS STILL a one-dirt-road village sited in a cliff-stacked fiord on the hard-charging Wannock River. About eighty people live in town year-round.

To get to the totem-raising there, I join forty or so potlatchers in Port Hardy on the north end of Vancouver Island for a ten-hour trip on the "Buttle Shuttle," a converted 1950s, open-deck ferry that crawls up Rivers Inlet. The captain makes a pot of chili and serves it in Styrofoam bowls. We stand in the rain and eat it. Otherwise, there's no food or amenities. The only head is up a narrow flight of metal stairs. Or over the gunwales. First Nations carvers Mack and Heron spend the trip working on two small replicas of the Hosumdas totem to be given away as gifts.

July rains weather us out of some of the most epic scenery on the coast, but when we land in Oweekeno the skies lift, revealing a landscape of vertical valleys and mountain peaks shaped like cedar hats. Standing beneath a roaring two-hundred-foot waterfall called "piss-piss falls," Vickers waves us in.

"It's always like this before a potlatch, thunder and lightning," he tells me. "That's the Thunderbird welcoming visitors."

Family and friends from up and down the coast hug, then form a fireman line to haul the dozens of bins and boxes of potlatch goods from the deck of the boat to a phalanx of muddy trucks. Vickers's eyes go red and puffy.

"I've been like this all week," he says, his voice abruptly hesitant and thick. "It's really happening."

Potlatch is said to have been abolished because the Canadian government decided one of its functions—giving away wealth to demonstrate status—was bankrupting Indigenous villages. This, of course, is malarkey—as if the colonial government cared about any harm Native groups might bring themselves. Vickers laughs off the suggestion.

"What it was to me looking back is governments realizing the beauty and pricelessness of the artistic creations coming out of these people," he says. "They outlawed potlatch and took away all the beautiful art and put it in a fucking museum. It was just greediness, it had nothing to do with giving a shit about people bankrupting themselves."

The giveaways—which were subsequently reciprocated, thus keeping wealth flowing through the region—were always only a small part of the tradition. The Walkus family potlatch is typical. Over the course of two near-nonstop days—endurance is a big part of the potlatch program and newbies are rightfully terrified by the endless speechifying of old geezers—ceremonies are dedicated to honoring ancestors; noting recent deaths and births; settling disputes; commuting history and culture through song and dance; fostering business relationships; conducting coming-of-age initiations; gossiping; meeting potential mates from other villages; and lots of eating. In Oweekeno this means successive meals of salmon, elk, halibut, and crab.

The unveiling of the Hosumdas pole kicks off the potlatch. When a shroud is cut away and the golden cedar pole shines in front of the village's big house, the 250 or so guests break into a sustained cheer and trilling whoops.

"We want to gift this to the community," says tribal chief Ted Walkus. "This isn't us, the Walkus family, putting our pole up there. This is us bringing something home that will enrich every one of us."

On its side on wooden horses back in Vickers's carving shed, the pole was impressive. Standing up it seems three times larger and more powerful. All weekend, people gather at its base to talk. As if by instinct, children keep returning to play in its imposing shadow, as if gathering strength from the manifestation of status returned to the town, transmuting history, family, and legacy into power in a way that transcends ersatz marketing appeals.

During the potlatch, Interfor executive Ric Slaco is presented with a six-foot-tall replica pole and invited to join a dance around the fire. Everything at the potlatch moves counterclockwise around the great fire in the center of the dirt-floored big house, building a steadily entrancing aura around the proceedings.

The village matriarch, Auntie Evelyn, sits at a front-row table throughout the ceremony, surrounded by family members. At age five she'd been sent to residential school in Alert Bay.

"You didn't see your family or anybody when you were at the school, it was too far away," she tells me.

The 1950s was a particularly dire time for First Nations in Canada. Most were assumed to be on the verge of extinction. In that decade, a spate of suicides among First Nations youth—notably the suicides of three Saskatchewan Métis girls aged twelve to fourteen—shocked the country. Mike Kew, the University of Vancouver anthropology professor who as a young man had been tasked with removing the Hosumdas pole from Oweekeno, would later write that there was in the work of even well-meaning whites "nothing to offer for the future of young Indigenous people . . . no alternative to suicide."

This was the atmosphere in which the Totem Pole Preservation Committee was conceived, and which inevitably led to the mixed attitudes toward its work that still persist. The committee took pains to fix terms and secure written agreements for relics from rightful owners. But the negotiating table between whites bankrolled by timber companies and First Nations people on the edge of disappearance was hardly level. The committee typically paid $150 for a pole, far less than the peak price of $1,000 demanded in the 1920s. Family possessions were sold—"stolen" is the word many First Nations members use—out of desperation. Union carpetbaggers trawling southern plantations for bargains on the family silver offer apt comparison.

"A lot of First Nations people come to this museum and feel that way," says Pam Brown, curator of MOA's Wuikinuxv collection, which includes the original Hosumdas pole. "It can lead to some very difficult conversations."

"There are a lot of different perspectives on that committee's agenda," Katie Ferrante, an MOA archivist, tells me. "The balance of power in those transactions was so tilted it can be difficult to characterize any exchange as fair."

Auntie Evelyn has a vague childhood memory of the pole in the village, but isn't sure when it was removed. "So many things are gone," she says. "They took everything when the village was out fishing or at work in the canneries. The loggers would come and they would take whatever they pleased. So much has been taken."

Vickers is hurt by the memory, but his focus remains on the present. "It doesn't matter how or why the pole was taken from the village," he'd told me before potlatch festivities got underway. "I'm glad it happened. The museum acquired it and valued it. If not for that we wouldn't have created this monument today.

"Think about this: not so long ago it was illegal to do what I'm doing, just carving a pole for a potlatch! It feels like I was meant to do this. It feels like everything I have done in my life is all about getting this pole done."

The work of the totem committee was profound. But its legacy was temporary. The status of the Hosumdas pole is no longer history. Through Roy Vickers it's been returned to the future.

AFTER MORE THAN a decade badgering investors, Howard McDiarmid finally succeeded in raising enough capital to break ground on his dream hotel on Chesterman Beach. Contractors were brought in. But McDiarmid, as with Roy Vickers and his gallery, knew only one person who could turn his vision for an authentic tribute to Northwest Coast heritage into reality: Henry Nolla. From the hand-adzed cedar beams to the carving shed down the beach, the signature of the thrifty hippie whose entire wardrobe might fit in your sock drawer is all over what would become Tofino's first luxury hotel, and eventually one of the most prestigious destination properties in the world. The Wickaninnish Inn's entryway double doors, into which Nolla carved a pair of Native-style eagles, opened to the public in 1996.

There are no bad rooms at "the Wick." No windows overlooking the hotel's HVAC organs. No glorified closets set aside for Hotwire suckers. Each of the seventy-five rooms at the Relais & Châteaux–approved property has a fireplace, cedar furnishings, a soaking tub, a balcony, and picture windows facing the ocean. Two full-time woodworkers occupy a large, on-site wood shop making custom furniture and keeping everything from the Douglas fir trim in the rooms to the yellow cedar table for twenty in the wine cellar looking like they were milled this morning.

The panoramic views help justify the $600-to-$1,800-a-night rack rate. On a rocky promontory overlooking a mile-and-a-half stretch of Chesterman Beach, the hotel occupies the high ground above a primeval forest, a five-thousand-year-old First Nations fishing ground, and, especially in winter-storm-watching season, the thrashing of heavy breakers.

The waves are a spectacular reminder of the property's privileged position at the edge of the world. Or at least the edge of the New World, which, not that long ago, sufficed as the edge of the known world insofar as Western explorers understood it. The word most often used by visitors to define the vibe around Tofino is "magical." After that it's "authentic." Even the most cynical world travelers tend to straighten their backs upon arrival.

The Wick is almost as heavily awarded as Meryl Streep—not a confirmed visitor, though you wouldn't be surprised if she were. The property regularly shows up on best-hotels-in-the-world lists. In 2018, *Condé Nast Traveler* readers named it number one on its list of Top Resorts in Canada. By 2021 it was merely number two for readers of both *Condé Nast Traveler* and *Travel + Leisure*. In 2002 *T+L* ranked it the number three hotel worldwide. After hearing this, the Rolling Stones called to book the entire place. They canceled after being informed if they wanted to land their 747 on Tofino's dinky airstrip they'd likely wind up in the Pacific Ocean.

That Relais & Châteaux thing is actually a big deal. The French hotel-rating organization, which lists about five hundred properties in forty-five countries in its annual guide, is religiously followed by the kind of people you'll never meet, and whose idea of luxury might surprise you. Earnestly elegant, the Wick is far from ostentatious. Its authenticity is what makes it an elite staple. "Luxury is immaterial," explains Relais & Châteaux president Philippe Gombert. Instead, the company's rankings rely on "a custom-tailored, human relationship along with expertise, and the local culture and distinct heritage that a place can offer."

Most travelers will never attend a potlatch. The Wickaninnish Inn is a proxy for that and other distant experiences. Remember the World Global Style Network's promotion of "neighborhood hotels" and "ancient rituals"? This is what they were talking about, a place that provides a coveted connection to cultural authenticity.

Although in the same price range, it's clear upon arrival you're not staying at a Four Seasons or Ritz-Carlton. There's a birthright aura here that's impossible to fake. Guest books in each room are filled with comments from people actually thanking the hotel for allowing them the privilege of spending a night.

Yet there's one detail most customers* miss and it's the key to understanding the whole place. With its commanding view of Chesterman Beach, the small, second-floor library is as perfect a place as you'll find

---

* I refuse to play the game of calling people who stay at hotels "guests." Sorry, hospitality industry jargoneers, what kind of asshole makes a "guest" pay for anything?

to curl up on a rainy day with a copy of the *Robb Report.* Hand-textured old-growth beams. Comfy leather chairs. Telescope on tripod. Sextant in trophy case. Nautical charts from Captain George Vancouver's 1790s surveying expedition of the Pacific Northwest. Original letter from Vancouver to King George III breaking down his efforts to find the Northwest Passage preserved under museum-quality glass. This is high-octane bookworm Viagra.

Given all the maritime bric-a-brac and sea mammals breaching beyond the wall of windows, it's easy to miss the most important piece of art in the whole resort; an item that in one small package synthesizes the story of Tofino, totem poles, hotels, history, Hosumdas, and art that travelers still come from the other side of the world to collect. Above a desk in a corner of the library, a 13-by-18½-inch serigraph is mounted in a simple black frame. In muted grays and blues, the print replicates the view of the ocean as taken in from room 25. It depicts the rocky coastline and six or seven islands in a dewy distance. Hovering in the sky, gazing upon it all in a sort of 20 percent black-screened grace, is the ghostly visage of Henry Nolla. He has deep, mournful eyes, long hair, and a beard that hangs like seaweed over the coastal idyll. A pair of glasses is pushed atop the old handyman's head in a position of cockeyed repose.

Nolla died of cancer in 2004. In 2006, Vickers returned to Chesterman Beach and created this serigraph featuring his old friend's ethereal expression.

"The new addition to Wickaninnish Inn now stands where Henry's house used to be in what all the locals and thousands know as Henry's Corner," Vickers wrote of his work. "I stayed at the Wickaninnish Inn last fall and woke up in the morning to a scene I was used to looking at from Henry's front window. The rain was falling on a rising tide where we spent so many hours working and laughing and I miss him so."

I spent an hour in the library late one evening nursing the glass of complimentary port left at my bedside. I watched customers, couples mostly, taking quick laps through the library, giddy from the hotel restaurant's loganberry gimlets, gourmet meals, and post-dinner coffees laced with maple whiskey and Baileys. A couple guys examined the maps and sextant, but not a soul paused to look at the serigraph before lurching off to their rooms for the evening.

Henry Nolla wouldn't have minded the lack of attention. Neither would Roy Vickers. Like me, they already knew the mist-begotten yarn of how three unlikely figures—Vickers, Nolla, McDiarmid—came together to breathe spirit into one of the world's great hotels. Along with the Hosumdas pole recently raised in a village just up the coast, it's a story that says as much about the origins of status, and the importance of authenticity, as it's possible to find at this end of the world or any other.

CHAPTER 7

Rebels of Philanthropy:
STATUS AS DISRUPTION

JETS, YACHTS, AND JEWELRY ARE FINE, BUT THE ULTRARICH REALLY keep score with buildings. Concert halls. Colleges. Cancer wards. You may have noticed the things wealthy people value most bear the names of the donors and families who help keep the lights on. Buildings are the single most important way the wealthy flex.

The most misunderstood signifier of position and power among the global elite, "philanthropy" is central to the lives of the .01 percent and most of their poorer cousins. I put the word in quotation marks because the majority of people have no idea what modern philanthropy means or how disingenuous the entire enterprise is. Beneath the guise of mega-charity operates a murky world that has nothing to do with generosity or civic duty and everything to do with protecting wealth, promoting power, and preserving privilege. Astoundingly, the rich pull off their most public status plays under the guise of civic munificence.

Following in the charitable footsteps of 1800s banker George Pea-body, Andrew Carnegie and the Rockefellers established institutionalized American philanthropy around the turn of the twentieth century. But it didn't receive its official seal as a form of status signaling among the super-stacked until 2018, when the Forbes 400, a list of the wealthiest Americans, unveiled a new feature in its annual rankings: the Philanthropy Score. Measuring what it calls a billionaire's generosity, *Forbes* came up with the scores by deploying thirty-two journalists to scour public filings, tax forms, and press releases from nonprofits. Final scores were determined by weighting findings of their reporting against the percentage of each fortune given away. This included an icon for the Giving Pledge, the showy commitment by the world's wealthiest individuals and families to donate the majority of their money to charitable causes.

"I would argue philanthropy is high on the list of status signals among the wealthy, probably the highest," says Alan Davis, a legacy 1 percenter and philanthropist from whom we'll hear more in a minute. "You can't get into some country clubs if you're not giving lots of money away. The Giving Pledge is really just a club. . . . You have to show you're capable of giving that kind of money away. I've been told to get on the board of the Metropolitan Museum of Art, you have to give one million dollars to the Metropolitan Museum of Art."*

Because it affects the entire world, especially those who live beneath median income lines, the trend toward industrial-strength philanthropy is one of the more consequential shifts in status signaling since the times of Thorstein Veblen and Vance Packard. Back in their days, dropping a hundred-dollar bill in the Salvation Army bucket at Christmas or tossing your teenage caddy an extra sawbuck counted as brother's-keeper benevolence. This began to change with the establishment of the federal income tax in 1917. Then as now the wealthy reacted to tax like poison. They quickly invented an antidote—tax deductions.

The craftier tax avoiders understood the benefits of the philanthropy deductions dodge immediately. It took a while for the rest to catch on. In 1930, the United States tallied about 200 private foundations with total assets less than a billion dollars. By 2014, the number had exploded to about 100,000 foundations, with assets of more than $800

---

* I was unable to confirm Davis's claim about the Metropolitan Museum of Art.

billion. There are now 1.54 million different charities in the country—not local chapters, separate organizations—employing more than 12 million workers (10.2 percent of total U.S. private sector employment) and holding assets of about $3.8 trillion. As laws and protocols around this universe have codified, "philanthropy" has morphed into a national shadow economy. Call it status as tax evasion.

"Charitable activity accounts for 10 percent of the economic life of this country," says Ken Stern, former National Public Radio CEO and author of *With Charity for All*. Since World War II, he writes, charities have grown at "a rate that far outstrips the growth of private businesses, government, and national economic activity in general."

Virtually every billionaire nowadays is fronted by a private foundation. Galactic donations—not the annual Operation Rice Bowl dimes and quarters I chipped in as a dutiful church kid—dominate the field. The phenomenon isn't confined to the United States. From the UK's Wellcome Trust to Denmark's Novo Nordisk Foundation to Hong Kong's Li Ka Shing Foundation to Mexico's Carlos Slim Foundation, mega-philanthropies have quietly assumed an increasingly important role in world affairs. With the Bill & Melinda Gates Foundation's more than $50 billion in assets and its emphasis on funding school programs, Stern says, "It's hard to overstate the influence the Gates Foundation has on American education."

But buildings are where the real money goes, and where the real status is recognized. "When I went to USC, maybe half a dozen buildings had names of donors," says Davis. "Now almost every building on the USC campus has a name on it. This is where you see the class system of philanthropy." Davis should know. Within the University of Southern California's Leonard Davis School of Gerontology (named for his father), you'll find the Sophie Davis Art Gallery (named for his mother) and the Ethel Percy Andrus Gerontology Center (named for his father's most important business partner).

When I began looking into ways the wealthy commute ideas of

status and privilege on the popular imagination, I called Davis.* After assuring me he resides "comfortably within the 1 percent. . . . In a good stock market year I might cross over into the .01 percent," he invited me to a convention of philanthropists he was hosting called the Hunter Gathering, which took place in Washington, DC, in summer 2019.

Originally from New York, Davis is a quixotic seventy-three-year-old who earned a law degree from USC in the 1960s, made a small fortune in the recycled-paper business in the 1970s, and has spent the last few decades engaged in various business and philanthropic enterprises. He's part of the Patriotic Millionaires, a group of wealthy Americans who lobby for higher taxes on the rich, meaning higher taxes on themselves. In recent years, he's penned a number of class-traitor editorials excoriating the greedy behavior of his privileged peers.

"America's billionaires have a hoarding problem," he wrote in a 2020 *Fortune* article. "America's billionaires might seem generous when you look at the absolute amount they give, but percentages are much more telling when it comes to measuring generosity. Bill Gates, for example, is giving $300 million for COVID-19 relief, a number too large for most of us to fathom. But here's the thing: According to his estimated wealth as of this writing, Gates is giving just 0.3 percent of his net worth. It's a big number, but it's pocket change for him."

In a 2019 op-ed for Fox Business, Davis coined the term "Excessive Wealth Disorder" to describe a range of social, economic, and political problems created by extreme concentration of wealth in the hands of a fraction of society. EWD describes not so much a personal pathology as a societal disorder. "With income inequality at record levels, underfunded government programs, and unprecedented political and philanthropic

---

* I first met Davis in 1998 in the lobby of the Hilton in Port of Spain. I was in Trinidad covering Carnival for a travel magazine. Davis was in the midst of a global working vacation, planning the launch of a publishing house specializing in travel guides aimed at the wealthy. We struck up a conversation on our way to one of the Carnival parades. In 2002 and 2004, his Greenline Publications put out my two-volume set of books documenting World War II sites around Europe and the Pacific. Several established publishers had rejected my book proposal as a worthy undertaking that'd cost far more to produce than it could possibly earn in sales. Davis put out the books anyway. The established publishers were proven right.

giving, the excessively wealthy have outsize influence in vital parts of civic life," he wrote. "They influence who gets to run for office, what issues are discussed, and how Congress votes. They shouldn't."

America's philanthropy machine is a significant part of this dysfunction, Davis and others believe, which is why they convened in Washington. At the Hunter Gathering, a lot of ideas about fixing philanthropy are thrown around, but a central theme emerges: the upper echelon of philanthropy is dominated by men. That's bad.

"There's very much a gender gap," agrees Farhad Ebrahimi of the Boston-based Chorus Foundation, a private entity he founded based on inherited wealth. "I think it might be worst in family philanthropy."

"Rich men are hoarders. Ultra-wealthy, so-called philanthropists are pinching pennies while asking for praise," Davis says. "There's a gender gap in philanthropy. It's women who do most of the giving and women who are most open to new ideas."

A well-known example is Melinda Gates, who's regarded for nosing her former husband toward philanthropy in the first place, and for being the force behind the Bill & Melinda Gates Foundation's more humanistic approaches to development. "The question now is whether Ms. French Gates's influence will outlast the pair's divorce," wrote a worried *Economist* following the couple's 2021 split.

The good news, according to Davis, Ebrahimi, and other foundation heads, is that a histrionic shift is underway. "Women may be the last hope we've got for real reform in philanthropy," says Davis. If he's right, that would involve a major shake-up in the way the wealthy signal status to the world, and perhaps more consequentially, to each other. "It's coming," says Davis. "The question is, will it come fast enough?"

DAVIS'S CONTENTION THAT women represent philanthropy's best chance for change is rooted in family history. Now lost to most Americans, it's a story of two of our country's most influential status disruptors—Davis's father and his father's business partner.

Leonard Davis, Alan's father, spent most of his twenties as a small-time accountant and insurance broker in Poughkeepsie, New York. In 1956, standing in line to vote at a polling station, Davis fell into a conversation with a man who told him the New York State Retired Teachers Association was scrambling to find a way to provide health insurance to its members. In the 1950s, it was nearly impossible for senior citizens to buy health insurance. What plans that existed were outrageously priced. As older people are generally those with the most money and the greatest need for medical care, the situation struck Davis as an opportunity.

Using his highly developed actuarial acumen he devised a health insurance plan for New York's retired teachers. He took the plan to Continental Insurance and convinced the company to underwrite it. Davis was also a skilled marketer. Astonishing the industry, his insurance program became an unqualified success. Today it's recognized as the first large-scale health insurance plan for older Americans.

On the opposite coast, another visionary, a retired school administrator named Dr. Ethel Percy Andrus (of the eponymously named Gerontology Center at USC), was obsessing over similar issues. Born in San Francisco, Andrus began her career in education as a schoolteacher in 1903. She became the first woman to run a major urban high school in California when she took over as the principal at Los Angeles' Abraham Lincoln High School in 1916. After retiring in the 1940s, Andrus established the National Retired Teachers Association (NRTA) to promote her philosophy of productive aging. She was gravely concerned about the lack of health insurance available to retired teachers. Too many graduated from decades of wrangling adolescent recalcitrance—"Grammar? Whom cares!"—to live out their shuffleboard years on dog-food pensions with little or no coverage.

"As it is, when you leave a job, they often just give you a gold watch, and all you can do is look at it and count the hours until you die," she cheerfully told an interviewer in 1954. Not the anti-frantic type you'd want to be partnered with at bridge club, Andrus wasn't going meekly into her golden years. Between 1949 and 1954, she approached forty-two different insurance companies for help covering members of her organization. Each turned her down.

Connected by common interests—Davis was selling health insurance to retired teachers, Andrus was buying—the two eventually found each other. In 1956, working with Andrus to cover five thousand NRTA members, Davis created and brokered America's first nationwide health plan for a large group of retired people.

Two years later, still unhappy with the lack of social status afforded older Americans, Andrus began contemplating an advocacy group for all people fifty-five and older. More disruptor than traditional philanthropist, she was still devoted to aiding the underserved. Andrus recruited Davis as the key member of a team that would launch her little upstart idea. She called it the American Association of Retired Persons. Initially, the organization's primary mission was to provide insurance to retired people. Today, the lobbying juggernaut, officially named AARP, claims some 38 million members, 60,000 volunteers, more than 2,300 employees, and offices in all fifty states. Andrus led the organization until her death in 1967. Leonard Davis went on to found the Colonial Penn group of insurance companies in 1963 and make lots more money. After his death in 2001, his full-floor Manhattan apartment overlooking Central Park was purchased by Charles Kushner, father of Donald Trump son-in-law Jared, and reportedly became the midtown residence of one of the Kushner daughters.

This chin-wag nugget has no direct bearing on the story that follows. I share it partly because I find it mildly salacious, but mostly because after a couple hundred pages featuring rescue dogs, penile anxiety, and naked hippies, I want to offer evidence that I can clip on a tie and trade harrumphs with the smart set when offered the chance.

BEFORE WE GET to contemporary reformers, it's important to understand a little more about why philanthropy has become the essential measure of status among the rich, why that's a problem for the rest of us, and why the women disrupting it may just turn out to be national heroes in the tradition of Ethel Percy Andrus.

In Palo Alto, California, Stanford University sits on an endowment of $25 billion. This makes it the third-richest university in the world, behind Harvard and Yale. Yet from the school's Center on Philanthropy and Civil Society, one of the world's most erudite members of a growing community of what critics call the Charitable-Industrial Complex has emerged. With sandy-brown hair, black-frame glasses, pullover sweaters, and the mainstream nerd appeal pioneered by Bill Gates, Rob Reich (no relation to Clinton administration labor secretary Robert Reich) is a Stanford political science professor whose mission is to debunk pretty much everything you think is gallant about charitable donations. As he explains in *Just Giving: Why Philanthropy Is Failing Democracy and How It Can Do Better*, foundations don't actually often serve charities. They bear almost no connection to traditional views of tithing. And they're never just about donations.

The chief function of large foundations, says Reich, is to serve as tax shelters that allow platinum power players to solidify their positions of influence behind a veil of fawning public relations. America's "painfully inegalitarian" tax structure encourages the wealthy to circumvent the IRS and allows them to impose their own values on the rest of society.

In the United States, Reich calculates subsidies for charitable contributions cost citizens at least $50 billion a year in federal tax revenue. At best, maybe 30 percent of all charitable donations truly provide for the needy. Donations to education (elite alma maters that crank out dependably elite leaders are a favorite), religious groups, private foundations, the arts and humanities, and vanity projects constitute at least 60 percent of American charitable giving. Relatives placed on boards are often paid extravagant salaries to manage family trusts.

"The tax advantages that go to philanthropy massively advantages wealthy people as opposed to middle-class and poorer people as a mathematical function of what a deduction is," Reich says.

Large-scale philanthropy, in his view, is more accurately viewed as a plutocratic exercise of status, frequently with the goal of influencing public policy and attracting invaluable media hosannas. After the Notre Dame Cathedral in Paris burned in 2019, for example, luxury-world notables such as Jean-Nöel Kapferer instinctively praised the biggest names in the French fashion industry for pledging up to a billion euros to rebuild the scorched heritage site. He compared their benevolence to the fulfillment of a sacred charter to protect the nation's legacy of ordained opulence.

Reich singed eyebrows with a slightly more cynical take.

"In France (tax deductions) can amount to up to sixty-five percent of the contribution that you make," he told Southern California's KCRW radio in the aftermath of the blaze. (In the United States, comparable deductions equal about 60 percent of adjusted gross income.) "So a one-hundred-million-euro contribution might actually only cost the donor thirty-four million euros. And the French government, and French taxpayers by extension, are subsidizing the rest of that donation.

"So here we have an example where more than half the donation of one hundred million euros is actually being paid for out of what would otherwise be tax revenue for everybody. And yet the donor as it were gets all the credit for it and gets to direct the donation where he or she wishes to put it."

A fundamental tactic of big donors is to attach strings to their largesse. Naming rights are an obvious ploy, as anyone knows who's ever attended the Cheez-It Bowl at Camping World Stadium in Orlando or the Duke's Mayo Bowl in the Bank of America Stadium in Charlotte, North Carolina. But access to politicians is a far more valuable concession.

Philanthropy has become the currency of soft power. Numerous Koch Family Foundations exist to promote a far-right-wing political agenda and discourage government regulation of multinational family businesses, which range from petroleum to commodities trading. These efforts often start with the tax-exempt establishment of think tanks or university programs, which help give their political views academic legitimacy, launch them into the world, and eventually turn them into bills to be voted into law by compliant elected officials. In her 2016 book, *Dark Money: The Hidden History of the Billionaires Behind the Rise of the Radical Right,* *New Yorker* investigative journalist Jane Mayer outlines the "weaponizing of philanthropy" and dissects how Koch foundations and other sources co-opted politicians such as Texas senator Ted Cruz to do the legislative bidding of the über-wealthy. In his 2017 book, *The Givers: Wealth, Power, and Philanthropy in a New Gilded Age,* author David Callahan outlines the way former New York mayor Michael Bloomberg regularly imposes his vision of acceptable public policy through philanthropy. One of many examples Callahan uses is the one-time Democratic presidential hopeful's donation of more than $100 million to a Sierra Club effort aimed at eliminating coal plants.

Reich wants the media and public to stop with the knee-jerk tongue baths for people engaging in philanthropy. He prefers we see the PR bonanza and influence peddling for what it is: "An exercise of power that's often tax subsidized by the rest of the citizens to use private assets for some public influence."

In the United States, where the IRS is pretty much a rubber stamp, approving 99.5 percent of all charitable applications, the situation rises to absurd heights. As Stern notes, the cash cows that are college football bowl games—I didn't drag Cheez-Its and Duke's Mayo into this fight for no reason—are mostly nonprofits that, believe it or not, operate under the same charitable designation as outfits such as Habitat for Humanity.

The business end of bowl games is slimier than the inside of a pumpkin. In Stern's view, the Sugar Bowl, held annually in New Orleans, is the most egregious. "The Sugar Bowl . . . took in over $5.4 million in federal government subsidies from 2007 to 2009," he writes, this despite the fact that most bowl games contribute less than 2 percent of their annual revenues to charities. Out of net assets of $70 million in 2014 to '15, the Sugar Bowl paid its executive director $761,439—that's three-quarters of a million dollars to oversee a single football game. More stupefying is the Outback Bowl. As of 2021, that Florida game's CEO, Jim McVay, was scooping in more than $1 million for his annual ardor, even as the organization touted its Charitable Giving Initiative's commitment to donating at least $500,000 to organizations pulled from a list of more than 120 nonprofits.

"There is such a thing as authentic generosity, but when a mercenary hedge fund manager gives money to his alma mater business school, that doesn't automatically mean he's a good guy," says Chuck Collins, great-grandson of Chicago meatpacker Oscar Mayer, prep school classmate of Mitt Romney, cofounder of the Patriotic Millionaires, and author of *Born on Third Base: A One Percenter Makes the Case for Tackling Inequality, Bringing Wealth Home, and Committing to the Common Good.*

Collins, who I met at the Hunter Gathering in DC, is speaking theoretically. But the nation's top schools are typical targets of scumbag PR drives concealed by a cape of applause-generating generosity. Before he died in a jail cell, criminally wealthy sex criminal Jeffrey Epstein contributed millions to Harvard, MIT, and other schools in what the *New York Times* called "a campaign by Mr. Epstein to polish his image and get back into the good graces of the academic and corporate elite." Convicted of procuring underage girls for prostitution? If you're very wealthy, a series of donations to the universities that graduate the daughters and sons of your most important peers may buy you a ticket out of social purgatory.

The Sackler family—whose wholly owned Purdue Pharma pled guilty to federal charges of fraud and kickback conspiracies related to the national opioid crisis—trafficked in the same ruse. In its initial complaint, the New York attorney general maintained, "The Sacklers used their ill-gotten wealth to cover up their misconduct with a philanthropy campaign to whitewash their decades-long success in profiting at New Yorkers' expense." According to the Associated Press, over the years they donated more than $60 million to elite universities, including Yale, Brown, Cornell, NYU, the University of Connecticut, the University of Washington, Oxford, Tel Aviv University, and Columbia. The latter established the Sackler Institute for Developmental Psychobiology with money sanctimoniously provided by the family responsible for destroying the psychobiology of millions.

Schools are important targets, but buildings and other property remain the most audacious philanthropic ruse. "Where my family has spent years along the coast of central Maine, wealthy families will donate the land surrounding their homes to a conservancy, taking huge tax deductions for its appreciated value, and removing the properties from the tax rolls," says Collins. "Often these holdings have no public access, so they effectively create a taxpayer-subsidized buffer zone."

Turning the land around your home into a bird sanctuary, thus blocking any development around you while lessening your own tax burden and reaping journalistic fellatio from the local press and applause from environmentalists? As cabin scams go, that's slicker than deer guts on a doorknob. No surprise that after more than a century of American-style philanthropy there's little evidence that charitable organizations produce much of lasting social value. The game, however, may finally be changing.

THE UNQUALIFIED STAR of philanthropy entering the new decade was MacKenzie Scott. In 2019, in a tabloid-drenched divorce settlement after twenty-five years of marriage to Amazon founder and CEO Jeff Bezos, the forty-nine-year-old Scott received $37 billion in Amazon stock. Her estimated net worth ballooned to more than $60 billion, making her, according to *Forbes*, the third-wealthiest woman in the world.

In the months leading to and following their split, Bezos embarked on a high-life bender. As *Vogue* reviewed it, the peripatetic mogul bought "mansions in Washington, D.C., and Beverly Hills, as well as a multi-apartment complex on Manhattan's Central Park South and a 300,000-acre property in Texas; partied in St-Tropez and St. Barts with [girlfriend Lauren] Sanchez; showed off his newly buff body in $260 Vilebrequin swim shorts that quickly became an internet sensation; and has methodically squeezed every last dollar out of his Amazon employees while fighting their efforts to unionize." Eventually he'd make showy space voyages with such luminaries as William "Captain Kirk" Shatner.

Scott mostly remained out of the public eye until July 2020 when, via a short post on *Medium*, she announced she'd donated $1.7 billion to a variety of organizations. Many of her donations were directed at obscure community groups, historically Black colleges and universities, and women's and LGBTQ+ equity organizations. A few months later, again via *Medium*, she announced an additional $4.2 billion in donations to hundreds more nonprofits in all fifty states, Washington, DC, and Puerto Rico. The $5.9 billion giving spree represented almost 10 percent of her net worth. It likely was the single largest expression of charitable giving ever made by an individual, certainly by an individual under sixty. She's since pledged to give away all of her wealth.

Scott's unexpected giveaway hit Big Philanthropy the way Trump hit Fox, CNN, and MSNBC. No one talked about anything else. "Upended" was the word most often used to describe her impact on the Charitable-Industrial Complex. "MacKenzie Scott's bold and direct giving puts shame to the billionaire class and their perpetual private foundations," Collins wrote in December 2020. *Barron's* opined she'd "set a new standard of philanthropy." The Crisis Charitable Commitment—an organization Davis founded to pressure fellow 1 percenters to give more to ameliorate the impacts of the COVID-19 pandemic—named her Philanthropist of the Year.

The amount of Scott's giveaway was shocking. What made it transformative, what "upended" the philanthropy establishment, was the way in which the donations were made. Many were sent to organizations that hadn't even applied for grants, that didn't even know they were on Scott's radar. More significantly, as Scott explained in her *Medium* post, all donations were "given with full trust and no strings attached." Understood by everyone in the philanthropy trade, "full trust and no strings attached" were code words that scared the shit out of traditional foundations whose habit of sitting on millions and billions in assets, while annually parsing out the legal minimum 5 percent of their endowments to pet projects with more strings than a marionette, was suddenly cast into an unwelcome spotlight.

Scott's out-of-the-blue commitment to "trust-based philanthropy" shocked just about everyone. This was especially so for a woman named Pia Infante, who less than a decade earlier had coined the phrase and led the charge to push the concept into the public consciousness.

THE FIRST TIME I heard the term "trust-based philanthropy" I assumed it referred to charity doled out from trust accounts, those financial accounts held or managed by a trustee for the benefit of a third party. Rich parents and grandparents often set up trust accounts for their heirs, hence the phrase "trust-fund baby" used to disparage the cosmically fortunate but presumably underserving spawn of inheritance.

It turns out trust-based philanthropy has nothing to do with trust accounts. Instead, the phrase describes the apparently avant-garde concept that wealthy people should actually "trust" the organizations they do business with, and further "trust" that the downtrodden recipients of their aid are intelligent enough to know how to use that money to solve their own problems. This may sound obvious, but in old-world philanthropy it's anything but. Trust-based philanthropy—especially at the tectonic level practiced by MacKenzie Scott—is a sensation bordering on sedition.

The process by which large funding bodies typically deliver grants is a spaghetti of red tape. Hopeful organizations fill out detailed applications, justify need, provide reams of support materials, explain accountability measures, and jump through endless hoops (a theoretical impossibility, that's the point!) for the privilege of being rejected by committees that often look for as many reasons to say "No" as to say "Yes." It's an onerous process that stresses the entire system and forces nonprofits into doing things they aren't designed to do. A cottage industry of "grant writers" has arisen to guide charity-obligate do-gooders through the process of prizing a few rupees out of the local maharajas. Then, if they're successful, to do it all again next year.

Trust-based philanthropy eliminates all of that. Getting rid of restrictions, requirements, and reporting mechanisms, it puts the focus of giving on the recipient as opposed to the bestower. It also gives back time (which is money) to organizations that they can use to actually do the work they were established to do. Boiled to its essence, it's a profession of faith made by the donor that states: "Take this money freely and without strings. I trust you to know your own needs better than I. Go to thine realm where Audemars Piguet and Viking Ranges are known not and dispense good."

The concept of simplifying grant giving has been kicking around the philanthropy world for decades. But the "trust" idea appeared only in 2013 when the San Francisco–based Whitman Institute invented it. (Founded by a descendant of one of California's wealthiest families, Whitman supports "advances in social, political, and economic equity.") A year or so before that, Whitman had made the even more radical decision to become a "spend-down foundation." This is another newish operating model that dictates a foundation should spend down or "spend out" all of its capital reserves within a designated period of time and then, once all the money is gone, simply cease to exist. The give-it-all-away rationale is that if a foundation's true goal is to help alleviate a particular social ill it should damn the torpedoes and throw everything it has available at the problem. If all goes according to plan, the thirty-eight-year-old organization will be dissolved by the time you read this.

Like the trust-based model, "spend-down" is antithetical to the way large, perpetual foundations operate, which is to sit on a massive endowment* and give out the legally required minimum 5 percent of its assets each year. In this way, fortunes continue to grow (foundations tend to earn more than 5 percent a year on investments); PR campaigns attesting to the gentry's bigheartedness are waged and won; and an impregnable system of consolidated wealth is bolstered and preserved. Deployed in an asymmetric attack by MacKenzie Scott, who has pledged to give away all her money, the spend-down approach seeks to obliterate this entire system.

---

* When an endowment exceeds $1 billion it is considered "large," a category that in the United States accounts for about 14 percent of all endowments.

The Whitman is by no means the nation's largest nonprofit. Its decision to become a trust-based, spend-down foundation nevertheless sent a tremor through wainscoted boardrooms. Its ideas represented massive potential disruption to the protection-of-wealth-through-philanthropy ideal most foundations quietly absorb as part of their mission. As the executive director of another well-known foundation told me, "The Whitman Institute is a relatively small foundation with a huge voice."

Central to that voice is Pia Infante. If one person can be called the mother of the trust-based movement it's Infante, the Whitman Institute's co–executive director. Following an audit of the foundation's partnerships in 2013, it was Infante (along with co–executive director John Esterle) who led the push for the novel strategy and convinced the foundation's board of the proper messaging. The terms "equity-based philanthropy" and "relationship grant-making" were floated, but Infante wanted something more disruptive. Putting "trust" in the name announced a kind of revolt. "Trust-based philanthropy isn't rocket science," Infante tells me, but initially that didn't stop some from approaching it like an alien invader.

"It still hasn't been adopted by a wide swatch of philanthropy because of issues of power and control," she says. "There is a sense of benevolent power that all huge philanthropic entities have. The poor people we're helping—whatever you define as 'poor'—there's a patriarchal sense of 'We're helping you, we know what's right.'"

Infante is an unlikely figure to have gained such outsized influence over ways the superrich donate their fortunes. The daughter of Filipino immigrants, she was born in Olongapo near the former U.S. Naval Base Subic Bay in the Philippines and grew up in Southern California in a lower-middle-class environment. Her father worked janitorial and maintenance graveyard shifts for aeronautics companies, her mother worked in hospital offices. "When I came out [as gay] to my Catholic mother, that kind of blew the house down for a while," she says. She moved to Berkeley at age seventeen and has been in the East Bay since. "I don't come with my own wealth, so when I'm with wealthy folks themselves I'm certainly a fish out of water."

Her business savvy resonates, however, especially when she summons the muse of the Bay Area's biggest sharks. "In venture capital the founders of some little tech start-up will get thrown millions of dollars by angel investors who say, 'Go out and fail a bunch of times and find out what works,'" she says. "Philanthropy should work the same way. But instead of saying, 'Here, go out there and figure it out,' they say, 'Here's a twelve-month grant. If you can show ten percent less homelessness by this time next year we'll give you another grant.'"

The trust-based movement Infante and Whitman kicked off cruised along for a few years, attracting scattered disciples. It required a convergence of unforeseen events to push it into the mainstream.

"Trust-based philanthropy proliferated due to a combination of Trump's election and COVID," Infante says. "Those two devastating events were a wake-up call to philanthropy to operate differently. There was a lot of activity in philanthropy right after Trump's election in 2016—a sudden fear for the sanctity of democracy. With COVID, as well as the awakening around racial justice, it was more of an operational crisis. This has led to a lot of philanthropy looking at itself and agitating around the way power is operating."

Infante was gratified when Scott elevated the "Whitman Institute Model"—another handle for trust-based philanthropy originally bandied around—but not surprised by the inevitable elitist reactions. "I did see a lot of responses that were very patronizing, like, 'Here's the new kid on the block, she doesn't know what she's doing, she didn't do her research,'" says Infante. "But there was also a ton of support." As an agent of change, trust-based philanthropy is coming into its own, she says, because women like Scott are going out of their way to avoid "the same Harvard or Stanford people" who may have good intentions but nevertheless infect philanthropy with entrenched elitist tendencies.

"If we change the idea of a status symbol to trust-based philanthropy, if MacKenzie Scott is seen as the new model for how to be a good rich person, that will change a lot," Infante says.

If this happens, the drive to reform philanthropy would be at least a quarter complete. It would also greatly improve the chances of success for still another onslaught on the citadel.

THE THIRD PIECE of the assault on provincial philanthropic doctrine is, shocker, also spearheaded by a woman. It's called DivestInvest. As with trust-based and spend-down models, the push to shame foundations into divesting endowments from fossil fuel industries remains a boutique effort, but one that's catching a spark due to its chief proponent, a firebrand named Ellen Dorsey.

When I speak to her shortly after Joe Biden's election triumph over Donald Trump, Dorsey is riding high on 2020 rhetorical jet fuel—"You can't be in philanthropy and not interrogate privilege," she pronounces over Zoom—but her disruptor cred goes back decades. After completing a doctoral thesis on strategies employed by the apartheid movement, she lived in South Africa during the transition to democracy there. Each day she'd wake up, walk outside, and tell herself, "Oh my God, this is so exciting!"

In 2009, when student activists at Swarthmore College outside Philadelphia began demanding their school stop investing endowment funds in fossil fuel businesses, Dorsey, ever the friend of long shots, conceived a broader opportunity. By this time the executive director of the Washington, DC–based Wallace Global Fund, she backed the Swarthmore kids with Wallace muscle. She then helped launch DivestInvest, a program that lobbies organizations and individuals to withdraw investments from fossil fuel industries and redirect those investments in support of climate solutions such as renewable energy and sustainable agriculture. In 2014, she cofounded a subsidiary called DivestInvest Philanthropy to push the same agenda.

"I thought the model of the divestment movement [at Swarthmore] was analogous to when the United States government refused to impose sanctions on the South African government," Dorsey says. "It was U.S. activists, then students, who innovated the idea of divestment to fight apartheid. They took it to the corporations directly by going after investors and pressuring them to act."

There's an inescapable logic to applying the same leverage to philanthropy. Even eco-minded foundations reap hundreds of millions a year in profits from investments in fossil fuel businesses. Then they turn around and transfer a pittance of those profits—5 percent or less—to struggling nonprofits whose job it is to combat the negative climate effects those same companies are creating. At best it's a deeply cynical cycle; at worst a profoundly insane one. "We should not be funding the destruction of the planet. We should not be investing in those companies that are destroying the conditions for life on earth," says activist godhead Bill McKibben, an advocate of Dorsey's movement.

In 2009, the Wallace Global Fund began the process of divesting from fossil fuels. Within a year, Dorsey had persuaded seventeen foundations to join the movement. Today, more than two hundred philanthropic organizations have formally committed. Many more, according to Dorsey, have done so without publicly acknowledging the shift in order to preserve amity among board members and donors, who remain politically divided over the strategy. DivestInvest Philanthropy's influence is growing. In a TED Countdown talk released in late 2020, Pope Francis called for investors to divest from fossil fuels in order to speed along the world's transition to a renewable energy future.

As significant within the realm of privilege is the personality driving the movement. Dorsey is a hard-nosed, impeccably prepared, and pugilistic negotiator. "Please see me if your foundation has not already divested from fossil fuels," she recently began an online philanthropic reform town hall, like a dyspeptic vice principal summoning delinquents to her office. One imagines the puckered-sphincter scions of consolidated wealth facing her across plates of croissants and carafes of orange juice on boardroom tables and muttering, "Jesus Christ, this broad," before being rag-dolled by her arsenal of facts and moral comeuppance.

Dorsey grew up in Pittsburgh in the 1970s and '80s. "The city was polluted, the steel industry was crumbling," she says. "Every day someone's mom or dad at school gets laid off. That shapes your thinking about what's working for people or not."

Dorsey recalls her 2019 arrest at the U.S. Capitol and being hauled off in handcuffs alongside Jane Fonda and other climate change activists. She and her daughter spent several hours in a holding pen with a group of "raucous women." She calls the experience one of the most powerful of her life.

Like Infante, Dorsey doesn't fit the profile of the type you'd expect to be welcomed by moneybags whose lives revolve around accumulated wealth and reinforced positions of status. "Does the fact that an agitator like you is making such a large impact indicate a change in the halls of privilege?" I ask.

"No! N. O. No!" she answers. "It says more about the Wallace Global Fund's commitment to systemic change."

A few minutes later, though, she revises this assessment. For the first time in more than a century, cracks have appeared in the structure that through public relations chicanery and legal jiujitsu has turned philanthropy in America into yet another bulwark against changes to the status quo.

"Most foundations would not be comfortable with having a CEO or executive director participating in protests, and I did that in my personal capacity," she says. "But I do think as a result of the climate emergency, threats to democracy, and growth of inequality, there are more foundations and philanthropic organizations understanding they need to be responsive to those movements.

"I'm not going to handicap it in terms of what it will look like in five or ten years from now. But if organizations are committed to change, and believe they have to put all their tools in service of systemic change, then most foundations would change the way they're doing business today."

AFTER TRUST-BASED, SPEND-DOWN, and divestment, tax reform is the last battering ram in the four-headed blitz on philanthropy. The Hunter

Gathering has two purposes. Pass the torch of philanthropic reform from a generation famed for its pot-and-peacenik strikes on authority to a younger crew who might finish the job; and lobby to reform the federal tax code to increase the tax burden of the superrich.

Trump still occupied the White House when about two hundred extremely wealthy philanthropists and Patriotic Millionaires (self-named for their desire to contribute more to state and federal coffers) convened at Washington, DC's Mayflower Hotel, a ten-minute drive from the U.S. Capitol, to attend the convention. Named for David Hunter—the "godfather of the modern philanthropy movement," who died in 2000—the Hunter Gathering was a combination dinner, social event, and symposium on the future of philanthropy. From battle-hardened crusaders to a new generation of social justice warriors, speakers told war stories and emphasized the need to overhaul the corrupt Charitable-Industrial Complex.

Wandering through the hotel's subterranean, 4,300-square-foot District Ballroom felt a little like bearing witness to a Givenchy-clad passing of a sacred vow from a generation of somehow-still-starry-eyed bleeding hearts borne of the phantasmagorical sixties to one of world-changers hardened by an increasingly fascist political right, a reality show president, an escalating wealth gap, and social and racial justice battle lines that have been expanding not shrinking.

Alan Davis's private foundation underwrote the Hunter Gathering, throughout which his graceful manner and generous nature were lauded by a string of well-to-dos who took to the podium between drinks, crudités, canapés, and the cow, salmon, or cauliflower steak dinner option.

"Welcome to the Billionaire Bash. You can take that any way you like," Davis said in opening the event on a decent laugh line. "I myself am a conflicted poster child for Excessive Wealth Disorder. I woke up this morning and couldn't decide whether to wear a Brunello Cucinelli T-shirt or an Armani suit. I decided to go Armani."

The bulk of the crowd looked like the kind you'd find at one of the nicer restaurants in any American burg—educated, well-mannered, business casual, middle-aged and older, mostly but not entirely white. Yet beneath the veneer of the mundane were enviable résumés and lives exotically lived. Third cousin to George Pillsbury, Tracy Gary has an exemplary, if not typical, story. Four months after attending Woodstock with her boyfriend in 1969, she "came out" at her debutante ball. A year and a half later, she "came out" with her girlfriend. Then worked alongside Cesar Chavez in California's agricultural communities. In the 1970s she cofounded Associated Rich Folk, an activist group with the engaging acronym ARF propelled by similar motivations as the Patriotic Millionaires. When a Boston chapter of the group was established it jauntily operated under the name BARF.

Gary grew up like Arab royalty. Her family owned homes in New York, Florida, Minnesota, Wisconsin, and Paris; employed more than thirty people to keep the houses functioning; and traveled in a fleet of Rolls-Royces, private jets, and helicopters. But in the wealthy people who surrounded her, Gary saw lives of avaricious isolation. When she turned twenty-one, she was given a trust fund of $1.3 million—about $6 million in today's money. She gave away all but $100,000 to charities and embarked on a career of activism.

"When I came to San Francisco in 1973, I had just finished a degree in mythology from Sarah Lawrence College. Joseph Campbell, who was one of my teachers, had basically said, 'You know, you really have to think about who you are,'" she told the *San Francisco Chronicle* in 2016 by way of explaining the decision to off-load her fortune.

Unlike the affable predinner speakers, the younger generation of activists who took over the stage to close the Hunter Gathering struck a testy posture. These wealthy newcomers offered a mostly "American carnage" contrast to the secular-humanist, all-together-now, residual hippie devotion embodied by their sixties dowagers.

Iimay Ho is a North Carolina native and executive director of Resource Generation. The group "organizes eighteen- to thirty-five-year-olds with access to wealth who are among the richest top 10 percent of individuals or families in the U.S." At the conference, Ho said she wants "young, rich fat cats" to redistribute their inheritances, with the aim that "one day there will be no one percent, there will be no ten percent."

The group of ultra-affluent young people from Resource Generation believe that "telling the truth about wealth and our class backgrounds helps expose how deeply unjust and racist the U.S. economic system is."

Ho agrees. "Growing up Asian American with immigrant parents in the South politicized me early—I got a lot of messages growing up that I didn't belong," she's written. "My experiences of racism were buffered by my family's wealth and class privilege and my strong ties to my large extended family. . . . I attended UNC–Chapel Hill and learned how my individual experience had been shaped by larger systems of oppression. I started growing into my whole identity as a Southern, queer, Asian American woman."

In the Mayflower's lobby bar after the event's formal conclusion I sat with some of philanthropy's new power generation. Rajasvini Bhansali was raised amid the upper tiers of society in Mumbai and other big cities in India before getting a master's degree in public affairs at the University of Texas. She's now executive director of the Solidaire Network, a collective of nearly two hundred donors and foundations promoting "racial, gender, and climate justice." Talk to anyone in the sector about young philanthropists and Solidaire comes up pretty quickly. I asked Bhansali what kinds of appeals work when trying to rally rich kids to work for policy changes that clash with their own self-interests.

"In a collective, in a community, people are willing to make heroic moves," she said between sips of an old-fashioned. "Folks are willing to do something heroic or out of the norm if they're part of a community or group."

That sounds pretty good on its surface, though the opposite is just as often true. People are also more willing to make supremely antisocial moves when they're part of a collective. Safety in numbers. Herd mentality. National socialism. Assaults on the U.S. Capitol. I've never been a big fan of groups. Including the younger generation. Name me one enduring institution—aside from maybe marriage and the New York Jets—with such a consistent record of failing to live up to its promise.

Ho, Bhansali, and their comparatively youthful cohort—many are in their thirties—are friendly and engaging as individuals, angry and up for a fight as a team. It's a fight everyone at the Hunter Gathering accepted as a given. Many attendees came from around Silicon Valley—belief in the redemptive power of disruption is internalized.

For now, though, even in emeritus status, the boomer kings and queens of social justice remain in control of the battle to reclaim, or at least reshape, the common clay prestige surrendered to the hyper-capitalist establishment they've become. At the close of the dinner, a pair of fellow millionaires called Davis to the stage to receive a thank-you gift for sponsoring the event. Even the unflappable Davis seemed taken aback when he was handed a familiar robin-egg-blue shopping bag, the color universally recognized (in this crowd, anyway) as a trademark of prestige jeweler Tiffany.

No one missed the symbolic implications of the bag. An uneasy silence descended as Davis carefully picked through layers of crinkly wrapping paper. A few attendees shifted anxiously at what appeared to be the kind of ostentatious show of wealth and privilege around which they'd gathered to abdicate allegiance.

When he finally got to the gift, Davis looked as relieved as he did amused. Over the moneyed clink of cutlery and crystal, he held up a pair of black boxing trunks with *EWD* (for "Excessive Wealth Disorder") embroidered in bold white lettering across the front. It was a good gag, and it got a pretty big laugh from the older half of the crowd, the kind you hear from underdogs who can afford to lose a fight. As Davis was striking a pugnacious pose to drag out the mirth, I stole a look over at the table where Iimay Ho and several other up-and-coming women philanthropists were sitting. None of them was smiling.

CHAPTER 8

Fitzgerald was wrong:
STATUS AS EGALITARIANISM

"LET ME TELL YOU ABOUT THE VERY RICH. THEY ARE DIFFERENT from you and me."

No presumed insight into the gulf between the rich and the rest has endured like that indiscriminately misquoted F. Scott Fitzgerald nugget. The prairie bard's flapper-era bon mot appears in a short story called "The Rich Boy," widely regarded among his finest work. Following the now-famous line, the unnamed narrator of the story elaborates on the profound complex that lurks in the amygdala of the blue blood:

> *They possess and enjoy early. . . . They think, deep in their hearts, that they are better than we are because we had to discover the compensations and refuges of life for ourselves. Even when they enter deep into our world or sink below us, they still think that they are better than we are.*

The pithier version of the Fitzgerald quote was recycled in its more familiar form by Ernest Hemingway in "The Snows of Kilimanjaro." "The very rich are different from you and me. They have more money," wrote Hemingway.* Natalie Wood got off a good line about bifurcated society in 1952's *Just for You*: "Ordinary people drink because they can't measure up to life; well-bred people drink because life can't measure up to them." But, misquoted or not, it's Fitzgerald's observation that's become canonic—and ubiquitous in these days of anxiety about broadening wealth and opportunity gaps. Google "the rich are different from you and me" and you get back more than 1.4 billion references from sources as varied as *Forbes*, the *New Yorker*, *Psychology Today*, the *Financial Times*, the Tax Policy Center, and something named Better Living Through Beowulf.

"A friend of mine, who is in fact the curator of manuscripts at Princeton and therefore interested in Fitzgerald, plays a game every Sunday when he reads the Sunday *New York Times*, and the game is how long it will take him to find a reference to Fitzgerald," says James L. W. West III, one of the country's foremost scholars of FSF (that's how they write it in the Fitzgerald trade). "And he says he always does. There might be something about 'there are no second acts in American lives.' Or 'the rich are different than you and me.' Or someone who is said to be Gatsby-like. It's always there. He says it doesn't take him that long to find it and he doesn't cheat by going to the book review first."

Given that it's become the first refuge of the self-styled class critic, Fitzgerald's immortal quip demands a twenty-first-century reexamination. If it was ever accurate, his statement no longer is. Yes, the wealthy often hoard their money and use it to insulate themselves against the appalling sepsis of modern humanity—but who wouldn't? Money doesn't turn people into assholes. It simply allows them to act on animal impulses to a greater degree than those less fortunate.

Patriotic Millionaire cofounder Chuck Collins believes the same. "People talk about wealthy people as if they're a separate alien species," Collins told me at the Hunter Gathering symposium in Washington, DC. "Privilege has a narcotic effect. But the rich are no different from the rest of humanity."

---

* Hemingway's terse comeuppance was actually lifted from critic Mary Colum. But like a beloved spitballer, the rogueish Papa gets a pass from fans for all sorts of indiscretions.

Human beings aren't born altruists and turned into monsters by money. From the cradle, we're greedy and needy. We turn to altruism as a result of penury, circumstance, or good breeding.

UP TO THIS point, my trek through the world of status and luxury has dealt largely with people who create, sell, and set the tone for popular views of prestige. Thanks to them we have rescue dogs, stylish cars, and magnificent hotels at which to park the latter and enjoy walks on the beach with the former. All of the above if you happen to be staying at the Wickaninnish Inn.

But what about consumers? The people who acquire products they believe will confer prestige upon them? For many of us, "luxury consumer" conjures a social obscenity known in days gone by as the "filthy rich." Today, we know that obscenity as "the 1 percent." Or, when things get down to platinum tacks, "the 0.1 percent of the 1 percent," a designation that covers about 140,000 tax filers in the United States.

According to the Survey of Consumer Finances from the Federal Reserve published in late 2020, an annual income of $531,020 breaks a U.S. household into the top 1 percent. But that figure represents the lowest rung of the ladder. Average income of the top 1 percent of Americans is well over $1 million and their average wealth tops $11 million. For the 0.1 percent, average wealth is a little over $43 million. The median income of the remaining 99 percent of households in 2020 was $68,400.

For years, we've been pummeled by statistics that are close to incomprehensible to anyone with a normal bank balance. The richest 1 percent own as much as the bottom 90 percent. They control more than half the national wealth invested in stocks and mutual funds, and more of the country's wealth than at any time in the past half century. The world's one hundred richest people own as much wealth as the entire African American population—more than 42 million people. The world's wealthiest two hundred own as much as the entire Latino population of the United States—about 55 million people. In 2021, the average Forbes

400 member had a net worth of $10.5 billion, more than thirteen times the 1982 average after adjusting for inflation. We're living in a Second Gilded Age, jingle, jingle, Tesla, Tesla, Gucci, Gucci, Prada, Prada. . . .

So in the quest for status, where does that leave the rest of us? If researchers like Steven Quartz and DevHog are right, we're all motivated by the same rank stimuli. But in a world where money still talks and bullshit still walks (honestly, I've never understood what that means; isn't walking better than talking?), where are we possibly to find status on a roulette wheel tilted far beyond most of our abilities to break even?

This brings us to some welcome news. For the first time in history, social status is becoming available to the masses. Alert John Fogerty: You don't need to be a fortunate son to get it. Status, luxury, even prestige, are now commodities within everyone's grasp.

How can this be? Doesn't the definition of "status," or the idea of an "elite," exclude all but a comparative few from the rewards those notions proffer? "Status is for everyone" may sound fashionably inclusive, but isn't it an impossibility?

Not anymore.

"Millennials feel luxury is not just for the wealthy few, they feel it is for everyone." This oxymoronic game changer comes to me from Milton Pedraza, CEO of the Luxury Institute, a premium goods and services consulting firm in New York.

"The democratization of luxury is in people's minds," Pedraza tells me.

A bald, bespectacled gadfly in his sixties, Pedraza is the quintessential example of our evolving yardsticks of status. Born in Colombia, he grew up in Flushing, New York, "alongside Jewish and Irish kids," yet another self-described fish out of water that would grow legs and learn to walk or be chopped into sushi. Pedraza's working-class edges have since been smoothed by decades of rubbing against Brioni-clad shoulders. He's given talks at Columbia University and Harvard, and been recognized as a top Latin Entrepreneur by Stanford Business School. According to its website, "the Luxury Institute has conducted more quantitative and qualitative research on affluent consumers than any other entity . . . and Pedraza is the most quoted global luxury industry expert in leading media and publications."

After working in personal finance and marketing, Pedraza launched the Luxury Institute in 2004. Right place, right time, right gadfly. Having morphed from individually owned, artisan operations into interchangeable pieces of globally owned conglomerates, high-end brands were at the time desperate to expand their customer bases. Pedraza created a service to facilitate the luxury world's shift to mass-market commodification.

"One thing I saw at the time was there was no research, okay?" he tells me. "Many of my friends would buy a car and, let's say it was a BMW, and it was a terrible experience.* They liked the car but the buying experience was terrible. Or the real estate agent didn't really care about me when they sold me that million-dollar house. I realized luxury needs to be influenced by the voice of the customer."

Pedraza's breakthrough upended a static truism of high-end consumer marketing. Luxury brands no longer dictate the rules of the game. The clientele now has a voice. What's more, thanks to expansion of the consumer base through lower prices and glut-level distribution, the clientele is huge and getting huger.

"We work hard, we have stress, we put out to help our parents and friends and significant others, it's a tough commute to work, we sometimes get taken advantage of," Pedraza goes on. "You say, 'I deserve that. Yeah, it's not rational, but I want to give myself that indulgence.' That's a perfectly natural and good thing."

Grinding commutes and being snookered by the world aren't bothers we typically associate with the prestige set. Certainly not with the rich and privileged. Could our evolving attitude toward luxury as proletarian birthright be the result of the participation-trophy generation that grew up with levels of personal affirmation previous children did not? Are adults of the day more conditioned to receive rewards—or confer rewards upon themselves—for comparatively mundane achievements?

---

* I realize this is the third or fourth time in this book BMWs have appeared as a gratuitous metaphor for generic wankerism, but I swear each reference popped up organically.

The answers to these questions—yes, yes, yes—validate an oxymoron like "Status is for everyone."

"Women and men surveyed consistently say, 'I buy luxury for myself, I want the best of something, I want to feel good and special,' and we all need that feeling," Pedraza says. We all understand what he means when he says that, but it's a relatively new understanding. My parents would never have felt entitled to self-indulgence. Their parents couldn't have afforded it. Their parents wouldn't have known how.

Opening themselves to customer influence has worked for luxury brands because the strategy is rooted in a new social reality. Part of this is a pervasive mindset that values "inclusion" and "diversity" above strictly monetary means as measures of a healthy, functioning capitalist society. As *The Luxury Strategy* coauthor Jean-Noël Kapferer noted back in chapter 1, "There is a luxury industry because luxury does not mean anymore being accessible to a niche of richest people."

GERMAN SOCIOLOGIST KARL Mannheim defined the "democratization of culture" in 1956 (posthumously). Daniel Boorstin subsequently identified the "democratization of luxury." This has over the past decade come into vogue as a catchphrase among high-end marketers. This is the process by which luxuries became necessities—washing machines, toilets, ice, cars, $240-a-month phone/Wifi/streaming bills.

"Since the dawn of humanity right up to the turn of the nineteenth century, the world of luxury has been virtually totally isolated from the rest of the economy, its pleasures and delights reserved for a very small elite," Kapferer and Bastien wrote in *The Luxury Strategy*. "From the twentieth century onwards, this world of luxury gradually ceases to be a world apart. An ever-growing slice of the population is beginning to have access to it."

These are big ideas, but in recognizing them, Boorstin, Kapferer, and Bastien were ahead of their times. Without the international social upheavals of the past decade, these concepts couldn't find a true, multiethnic, proletarian footing—or constitute a consolidated global market. The global societal awakening around the Occupy, #MeToo, Black Lives Matter, and other social justice movements are turning revolutionary ideas into reality, starting with a reassessment of "privilege" and who should have it (everyone). So has the social-media-driven zeitgeist that says exposure, clicks, and influence are more important than salary. As a marketing principle, the "democratization of luxury" now exerts measurable commercial influence. Proponents are using it to boost worldwide sales and change popular ideas about elite status, which they insist now anyone can attain.

"How do you define a luxury customer?" ask Robin Lent and Geneviève Tour in *Selling Luxury*. "It is very simple. We are all luxury customers."

If bringing the trappings of privilege to the world means broadening the definition of privilege, so be it. Alexa von Tobel, founder of the personal finance software company LearnVest, goes so far as identifying brands and services like Uber, Blue Apron, Handy, Glamsquad, and TaskRabbit as part of the new luxury ecosystem, on-demand minions attending to the whims of an unrestricted swarm of Visa-wielding baronesses and barons.

Several generations ago, a classic indicator of wealth was a maid or personal servant. Now well more than half of Americans employ them. Paying gig-economy gofers to do everything a servant would—shop, cook, bring food, drive, do laundry, book appointments, give you a massage—may not feel as elitist if it's done through an app. But having a small army of paid help on call at all times puts many of us in the same echelon and ethical strata as someone who employs a man Friday.

The democratization of luxury is repeated even in nondemocratic places. China provides an example. After the 2008 economic crash, Chanel and other luxury companies there committed what once would have been considered an elitist no-no. They lowered their prices. This angered longtime brand loyalists, but gained companies many more new customers en route to expanding their global footprint and plebeian base.

ONE OF THE more stubbornly entrenched barriers between the general public and the status it craves is the perception of "privilege." Evident to anyone paying attention to homeless encampments on prime downtown real estate across the United States or wealthy St. Louis urbanites waving handguns and semiautomatic weapons at racial justice protesters, the whole idea of privilege is under heavy scrutiny.

In the United States, privilege is almost always preceded with the words "white" or "white male." This is understandable since it's mostly white and mostly male people who on average have the most money and wealth in the United States and who have set up long-standing finance and governance structures to benefit their own cohort. But in a global context, "white male" is a localized feature and insufficient as a way of understanding the dramatic changes afoot. From Cambodia to the Congo, Croatia, and Caracas, the same public outrage greets poohbahs who flaunt entitlement. Elitism is a state of mind as much as it is a bank balance or ethnic legacy. Spend a week among the grandees of China, India, or Dubai if you don't believe it.

Here's an example of how that plays out in real life.

The most flagrant encounter I've ever had with the elite mindset came in the mid-2000s during the Songkran water festival in Chiang Mai, Thailand. If you haven't experienced this peculiar Buddhist holiday-tourist event, you've probably seen photos or video. To mark the Thai New Year, Thais traditionally sprinkle water on each other by way of bestowing positive omens. The custom has evolved into a countrywide water fight, particularly in the northern city of Chiang Mai, where tens of thousands of rowdy celebrants take to the streets armed with water cannons, buckets of ice water, and garbage cans filled with brown liquid drawn from local canals to be used in drive-by hydro-assaults launched from the beds of speeding pickup trucks.

The bedlam in the center of Chiang Mai is difficult to overstate. Imagine yourself at the fifty-yard line of a football stadium hemmed in on all sides by the student body of some Division III school that's stormed the field after upsetting Alabama or Ohio State. Throw in a cattle stampede, Mardi Gras, and the Who's 1979 concert in Cincinnati. You're dressed in shorts and flip-flops. Now try to escape this anarchy and be back home and dry, reclining on your couch, glass of Scotch in hand, in under fifteen minutes.

That's pretty much the situation I found myself in at Songkran when the stupendously wealthy associate I happened to be with (I'll call him Cravat) looked at me and said, "This is nuts, I gotta get outta here." I concurred and began scanning building tops for bearings.

"It'll take some pushing and shoving, but I think if we head toward that Singha billboard we can get on a wider street and force our way down the canal," I suggested. As I was half shouting (Songkran is as loud as it is wet), I was taking a German elbow to my ribs and a water balloon to the back of my head.

Cravat appraised me as one might a dim child. He whipped out his phone.

"I'll have the hotel send a car," he said, ducking another water balloon.

"You're insane," I barked. "First of all, the hotel is not going to send a car for you. Second of all, even if they did it'd be impossible to get a car through this mob. We're shoulder to shoulder with two thousand people on this block alone. This party goes on for miles."

Cravat is a really good guy, but his breeding shows up on occasion.

"This is why you stay at the Four Seasons," he said.

Even though I knew no one at the hotel, when I heard him ask for the concierge and demand a car at once, I felt embarrassed in that white-man-in-the-tropics way—and Cravat isn't even white, strictly speaking. I was far more shocked, however, when a few minutes later a Mercedes-Benz sedan came honking through the crowd. The swarm of humanity parted. Cravat and I lunged into the back seat.

"You have some things to learn about life," Cravat said as the driver shot away.

He wasn't wrong. Theoretically, I could have made the same call. It's just that I'd have never contemplated doing so. Cravat's move was a window into the privilege enjoyed by a caste that lives with the certainty that other people are always available to solve their problems. As von Tobel noted, Uber, Blue Apron, Handy, Glamsquad, TaskRabbit, and hundreds of other new companies have tapped into the same expectation, putting shocking privilege, white or otherwise, within reach of the common herd.

AMUSING AS IT is to some, my story of Cravat's behavior enrages about half the people who hear it. Well-organized elements of society have declared war on privilege and privilege is losing.

But it's not the only long-standing tenet of wealth being twisted into more egalitarian shapes. For most of its history, humanity has made a fundamental assumption about the relationship between wealth and status. The assumption is usually wrong. "Money, although important, is not always the most important criterion of class," wrote social critic Paul Fussell in *Class: A Guide Through the American Status System.* "When John Fitzgerald Kennedy, watching Richard Nixon on television, turned to his friends and, horror-struck, said, 'This guy has no class,' he was not talking about money."

Like privilege, assumptions about the connection between wealth and status are being reformed. At the New School in New York, a sociologist named Rachel Sherman has been studying the presumed psychological differences between rich and poor, privileged and downtrodden. In fashioning an academic career analyzing the behavior of wealthy people, she's arrived at an entirely different set of conclusions than those that informed Fitzgerald. One of the most fundamental of Sherman's complaints against the established "rich asshole" canon is that the whole idea of categorizing "the rich" is absurd.

"Saying 'the rich' are X or Y is generally stupid," Sherman tells me. "There's so much variation in a group that defining them solely by their income and wealth, I don't think that's a meaningful category. The Poor. The Workers. The Women. I don't think these categories make any sense. I don't think they ever have."

Sherman was raised in Philadelphia. She graduated from Brown University in 1991 and completed her PhD in 2003. Professional notice arrived with the publication of her 2007 book, *Class Acts: Service and Inequality in Luxury Hotels*. For the book, Sherman logged time with the underlings of luxury hotel staffs—concierges, bellhops, housekeepers. What caught her eye were the relationships that played out between the serfs of the hospitality industry and their royal lords. A few nob-jobs aside, Sherman found that guests of upscale hotels invariably treat staff quite decently. Weeks of research at properties where guests paid between $500 and $2,000 a night—not a bad gig for a humble sociologist to fashion for herself—defied a number of the assumptions she'd carried into the project.

"I expected all the people who stayed in the hotels to be giant assholes," Sherman says. "In fact, it was less than ten percent of guests I interacted with at luxury hotels who were assholes. Mostly they're very polite and tip what they're expected to.

"We have a cultural tendency to assume the rich people we see are all the rich people there are, and draw conclusions based on the rich people who want to be visible in that way. It doesn't mean all rich people want to be visible. Obviously there are rich people who are literally criminals. Look at the entire Trump cabinet. But just the idea that having money makes you a terrible person, there's no point in thinking that. It's obviously not true."

Sherman readily disputes that touchstone of all knowledge of the leisure class—Thorstein Veblen. What people like Greg Berns, Steven Quartz, and Hilke Plassmann have done to the old bloviator's ideas about luxury consumption in the name of neuroscience, Sherman is doing in the name of modern sociology. Her 2017 book, *Uneasy Street: The Anxieties of Affluence*, is, if not sympathetic to the "plight" of the rich, at least understanding. For that book, Sherman interviewed fifty wealthy New Yorkers—incomes between $250,000 and $10 million—to find out what effect being outrageously rich has on the psyche. How different it truly makes the very rich from you and me.

In it, she dismisses traditional pillars of the gated set—the Social Register, debutante balls, ostentatious displays of wealth, keeping up with the Joneses—as relics of a bygone era. Her interviews with the well-to-do of New York—which she identifies as the most economically unequal large city in the United States—show a disinclination for public indulgence that "suggest[s] that Veblenian conspicuous consumption is not at work." Especially in the company of those who possess less material wealth, "interactions were largely governed by norms of civility that *effaced* class differences." (Emphasis hers.)

In other words, the world of luxury consumption is flat. Or, at least, getting flatter. As luxury is becoming more democratized, the legitimately wealthy (dickhead exceptions noted) prefer consumption that's less flashy.

The United States and other industrialized countries have changed immensely since Veblen's day, she says. For starters, women and non-white people have more legal rights, access to wealth, and individual agency. *Uneasy Street* wasn't written as an assault on Veblen. Or Fitzgerald for that matter. But Sherman doesn't stammer when I place it in that context.

"That book [*The Theory of the Leisure Class*] was written in 1899. A bunch of things have changed since then," she says. "In the past few decades . . . elites in the United States have become more diverse in terms of race, ethnicity, religion, and class of origin." The purchasing habits of new elites are under intense scrutiny, but one has emerged as commonplace—consumers will gladly desert brands that don't support their values and pay more for those that do.

Sherman is also sympathetic to my gripe about Veblen not citing a single authoritative source for his most bald-faced assertions.

"The early moments of social science, there was sometimes not a huge difference between social science and telepathy," Sherman tells me. "It's a lot of white men talking out of their ass."

THE OVERWHELMING TAKEAWAY from *Uneasy Street* is that "comfortable," "fortunate," and "high net worth individuals" (euphemisms the rich use to describe themselves and deflect projections of entitlement) genuinely see themselves as "normal" or "in the middle" of society. It bugs them when the rest of us don't view them that way as well. This goes back to Patriotic Millionaire Chuck Collins's remark about the widespread belief that wealthy people are an alien species. "The rich are no different from the rest of humanity," he told me. True, listening to people who own second vacation homes in the Hamptons or Sedona moan about not being considered normal or middle-class is like listening to people in their twenties tell you they're starting to feel old. But it doesn't mean they're entirely delusional.

Based on a survey of fifty-five millionaires, a recent *Business Insider* story reported on the five things the super-wealthy most consistently splurge on. Turns out, they're the same things everyday Americans splurge on. In order: travel, food/restaurants, cars, wine, and clothes. Honorable mentions include: bikes, books, concerts, dark chocolate, firearms, gardens, home decor, outdoor gear, sports, tech, and watches.

"You'll always find meats, cheeses, seafood, red wine, fresh fruits, and vegetables, and lots of dark chocolate in our kitchen," reported one exotic millionaire, as though his description didn't cover tens of millions of refrigerators across the country.

"We love cruises. . . . We're naturally frugal though and it comes into play with our cruises," responded a 1 percenter couple. "We dig around to find a really good deal, but we always get a balcony (once you go balcony, you can't go back!). We'll find a cheap flight and stay at a cheap hotel the night before. We don't buy any upgrades on the ship and very little in the ports." That simultaneously explains why locals hate cruise ship tourists and describes your grandparents' vacation strategy. Even if the filthy rich reside in a higher tax bracket than most of us, their habits come off strikingly proletariat.

Like volcanic eruptions, the blurring of class norms is the result of sulfurous burbles and imperceptible shifts. In retrospect, however, major big bursts are as obvious as casual Friday—the GI Bill, the sixties counterculture revolution, and the digital revolution being the biggies.

The GI Bill of 1944 opened the doors of higher education, giving America's common clay access to the lecture halls, laboratories, and theater arts programs that had heretofore been the near-exclusive dominion of old-money spawn. Within a decade the Ivy League was transformed from a refuge for mutton-headed elite who called themselves things like Tipper and Tad into something approximating a meritocratic proving ground for the best of the best.

The religious, military, political, and commercial institutions that ruled American life bowed in short order to what by 1964 author E. Digby Baltzell—the man credited with popularizing the term "WASP"—called a "campus community [that] has now become the principle guardian of our traditional opportunitarian ideals." More simply put, legacy still mattered, but test scores mattered more.

The 1960s youth revolution brought about the great leavening of fashion, pop culture, and even national culinary tastes. Rock went mainstream and eventually "adult." Bland and boiled palates happily turned on their mother's casseroles and transitioned to a cornucopia of cosmopolitan menus. As for fashion, as my friend Glasser likes to remind me, in addition to a stultifying religious aura that pervaded all aspects of everyday life, in the 1950s no one would ever mistake the bank manager for the bank teller. Not even if you happened to run into them buying Charles of the Ritz at the department store downtown on Saturday afternoon. Unofficial dress codes for labor and management tended to be followed even outside the office.

Cultural revolutionaries that challenged the segregated Protestant establishment arrived at the ramparts dressed in rags and paisley—memorably described by pedantic kvetcher Fussell as "amoeba-like foulard blobs." Hippie disruptors rejected Veblen's religion of conspicuous consumption and the rat race it charted. ("Only rats win a rat race!") By the turn of this century, quaint haberdashery mores that separated rulers from ruled had been obliterated by sixties kids who, upon attaining positions of power, wanted easy ways to signal they hadn't betrayed their roots. Ray-Ban–wearing sax addict Bill Clinton bleating out "Heartbreak Hotel" on *The Arsenio Hall Show* was just the start.

By the 1980s, as David Brooks wrote in his 2000 book, *Bobos in Paradise: The New Upper Class and How They Got There*, educated elites had "taken over much of the power that used to accrue to sedate old WASPs with dominating chins." A portmanteau of "bourgeoisie" and "bohemian," "bobos" is an inelegant term of derision Brooks coined with limited success for transmission into the mass vernacular.

Among the consequences of the information age Brooks believed a "status inversion" had "crushed the old WASP elite culture" by taking "the things the Protestant elite regarded as high status and [making] them low status," proving once and for all that "the Thorstein Veblen era is over." Brooks, too, was a little ahead of the curve. But by the time your CEO felt comfortable showing up in the boardroom in cargo shorts and a Foo Fighters tour tee, and Scott Cook, cofounder of financial software giant Intuit (they make TurboTax), would be profiled in the *Wall Street Journal* scarfing his lunch at Taco Bell, the status insurgents had become the establishment.

One of their more salient contributions to the democratization of status is called countersignaling. The countersignaler shows power by not showing it.

"The correct etiquette in today's plutocracy . . . is to downplay the personal impact of vast wealth," wrote Chrystia Freeland in her 2012 book, *Plutocrats: The Rise of the New Global Super Rich and the Fall of Everyone Else*. Bill Gates aligns his burger preferences with McDonald's. When Mitt Romney was CEO of Bain Capital, with a net worth of about $200 million, he drove a Chevy Caprice with a dented fender. As London mayor, and occasionally as UK prime minister, Boris Johnson did him one better by biking to work. In 2020, Netflix chairman and cofounder Reed Hastings showed up for his big profile interview with the *New York Times'* Maureen Dowd in khakis and bare feet. Granted, it was a COVID-era Zoom interview, but Reed's effort to modulate his celebrated position was a prime example of the shifting standards of elitism.

In his 2017 book, *The Complacent Class*, economist Tyler Cowen explained how countersignaling has downshifted fashion among the elite. "Jackets and ties are now anachronisms in most of Manhattan's top restaurants, and if anything, they are likely to reflect the relative poverty rather than the wealth of a visitor to Le Bernardin—maybe it's a very young man trying to impress a date or a middle manager dressing up so as not to offend a Japanese client," he wrote.

Like rock stars wearing ripped jeans and reeking of bong water in first class, not needing to impress anyone means not bothering to impress anyone. Cowen suggests Google has replaced Cartier, Bulgari, and Stefano Ricci. When one's status is a mere search away, the world has all the evidence it needs at its fingertips. No need for a $5,000 jacket, but, what, you don't have a Wikipedia page?

The rich aren't downplaying their wealth because they're ashamed of it. They're doing so because other displays of status have become more important. The further we move from the near-universal, uniformed military experience that defined postwar America (notably explicated by Vance Packard) the further we distance ourselves from the mores of the social hierarchy around which American life revolved through the second half of the twentieth century.

Yes, there are insufferable, superior twats out there. Even the tolerant Sherman must have to squelch a snort when some 1 percent tool starts whining about how hard it is to keep up with the kids' tuition and music lessons and summer vacations in Greece all while dropping six figures on a kitchen remodel. And I know it's uncool of me, but I'll admit to a big ol' eye roll when reading in her book about all the victims of success who spend years paying for counseling to talk through issues related to wealth-induced guilt, stress, and anxiety.

But most of Sherman's rich subjects sound a lot more similar to you and me than they seem different. They're creatures of fleshly desires, averse to stress, drawn to security, seduced by pleasures to which few of us are immune, and disinclined to turn their backs on fortune. The best quote in *Uneasy Street* comes from a woman called Eliana, who describes a phenomenon known as "luxury creep," a condition that occurs when an increase in wealth leads to an increase in spending to maintain a surging standard of living: "I don't think I fully live out all my values, I guess I would say. I used to say I was gonna be a revolutionary, and then I had that first massage."

Let she who is without sin cast the first hot stone.

AS I'D LANDED pretty firmly on the idea that Fitzgerald was wrong—the rich really are no different from you and me—I thought it might be a good idea to test my assumptions with one. From a universe of worthy candidates I chose eighties pop supernova Rick Springfield.

I wanted to speak with Springfield for a number of reasons. Not least of which is, unlike all the too-cool-for-school music snobs of the day, I liked "Jessie's Girl" the first time I heard it. I went out and bought the album. And the next two follow-ups. I've always enjoyed the dude's stuff without any sense of hipster irony.

More germane to the current mission, I sought an audience with Oz-Am music royalty because more than just about anyone I can think of he's experienced some of life's highest status highs and lowest status lows. He's been broke, then rich, then broke, then rich again. But unsteady finances are just part of Springfield's status odyssey.

"Jessie's Girl" will one day be mentioned in the lead of his *New York Times*, *Daily Mail*, *Asahi Shimbun*, and *Sydney Morning Herald* obituaries. But Springfield has charted seventeen Top 40 hits in the United States and plenty more around the world. His records, including four platinum albums, have sold in the tens of millions. He's headlined a huge stage spectacle, "EFX," at the MGM in Vegas to rip-roaring reviews. Been in TV shows and movies. Bonked hundreds if not thousands of the most attractive women the international groupie circuit has to offer.

At the same time, Springfield's road to excess success has been torturous. Most fans are unaware that his first big gig came as a seventeen-year-old guitarist with a band touring U.S. and Aussie military bases in Vietnam. 1968. Saigon. Da Nang. Quang Tri. Springfield had serious ambitions. But when he got back to the world, his *Tiger Beat* looks landed him in the pages of every teenybop fanzine in existence. He had a middling hit in 1972 with "Speak to the Sky" (folk bubblegum featuring banjo, tuba, and handclaps), but he became so distraught when his career as "the next David Cassidy" went tits-up, he underwent plastic surgery to restore his youthful vigor. At age twenty-three.

Short of opening for a puppet show, he's experienced all the personal obloquy the music business can muster. Hateful reviews. Broken contracts. Management betrayals. Record label abandonment. Bankruptcy. Private self-doubt. Public humiliation. Most hurtfully, at the height of his hyper-successful rise from obscurity, he became the butt of derision from the music cognoscenti, who took one look at his matinee idol face, and 20 million listens to "Jessie's Girl," and denounced him a lightweight, a soap opera confection, a nobody, and, finally, a has-been nobody.

"I've experienced being famous but not being respected," Springfield tells me when I reach him by phone to explain why I want to interview him. A low point, he says, came in 1989 when *The Oprah Winfrey Show* invited him to be part of their one-hit wonders special. Uh, seventeen Top 40 hits, bitches? That's how fast they forget. When even Oprah is taking a big dump on your career, you know you're in the shitter.

Springfield has danced on all sides of wealth, status, prestige, acclaim, and existential misery. This ought to give him, I'm hoping, insight into status and rich-guy psyche few others have.

In addition, he lives in Malibu and, when not tossing his BMW keys to valets at Nobu, drives a restored 1963 Corvette Stingray. And as he cops to in his international-groupie-laden memoir, *Late, Late at Night*, he has a weakness for "hand-painted leather jackets and $350 T-shirts that I wear only a few times a year." I didn't call in an Equifax report, but these are all pretty reliable indicators of a dude who's stacked an impressive amount of paper.

I've come to Southern California to find out what kind of impact excessive wealth and privilege have had on Springfield. What kind of guy they've turned him into. How late he arrives for the interview, or if he shows at all, will be my first indicator. Anything within ninety minutes of the scheduled time I'll chalk up to rock star noblesse oblige. After that the jerk-store clock starts ticking.

RICK SPRINGFIELD ISN'T on time for our interview. He's early.

By the time I arrive at the Starbucks at Trancas Country Market on the Pacific Coast Highway—a couple minutes early myself—the musician responsible for the song *Rolling Stone* once crowned the most-requested karaoke hit of all time is already set up with a drink at one of the high communal tables in the outdoor courtyard. Black Chuck Taylors. Black jeans. Black sweatshirt. Simple black bracelet, but otherwise no rings or jewelry. On his lap is Bindi. A toy mixed terrier sporting a red kerchief, Bindi clearly appreciates his status as a treasured child.

Springfield tells me he's always strived for success. Born in Australia, he spent a few childhood years in England, where he'd cut up pieces of newspaper in the shape of pound notes and walk around with them in a bag. At nineteen, he read and fell under the spell of *Think and Grow Rich*, Napoleon Hill's landmark Depression-era self-improvement book. In his twenties he consciously dropped his Aussie accent, forced himself to speak American, and, eventually, became a U.S. citizen. Even after achieving stratospheric success he continued to chase wealth and status.

"I've gone through all the Tony Robbins stuff, Lifespring, the self-awareness thing, always reading self-empowerment books," Springfield tells me. "I've always felt unworthy. I still feel unworthy."

Despite experiencing the kind of money, privilege, and sex most mortals only fantasize about—grown women were apparently throwing themselves at him by the time he was fourteen—he says that like most entertainers he's never felt he was "enough." Not that he hasn't enjoyed the adulation when it's come.

"High status is fun," he says. "It's like taking a shot or a hit of something. It was incredibly fun. It's still fun. I've done bad things that I regret deeply, but I never lorded my status over anybody."

The "hit of something" comparison draws a link to the research DevHog and Quartz are doing connecting status and prestige to changes in brain chemistry. I follow up with a question about life under the influence of status attainment. "I don't think money makes you an asshole," he says. "You're either an asshole to begin with or you're not. The people I've known who've made money have remained who they are through it all."

It's not important what you think of Rick Springfield's music; in person it's pretty much impossible not to like the guy. Though we'd initially agreed on a one-hour interview, we end up hanging at Starbucks for two and a half hours. Toward the end of the interview a female fan in her thirties who's been eavesdropping gathers the nerve to introduce herself.

We all know the "Don't approach celebrities at restaurants" rule. But there'll be no entitlement freak-out here. Springfield cheerfully signs an autograph and spends a couple minutes talking with the woman about Bindi and their mutual love of dogs.

I have a friend who says she's not interested in gossip about which celebrities are cool and which ones tip like Scottish widows. "I don't care if celebrities are nice or not, what difference does it make?" she says.

But I think it does matter, and I think most people agree with me. For better or worse, celebrities occupy the highest positions of public esteem afforded in U.S. society. As such, they're the most visible reflection of American values. We want, at bare minimum, for our celebrities to be decent people because we want to believe ourselves to be decent people. For those who agree with that proposition there's comforting news—the overwhelming percentage of the nation's celebrities are actually really nice people. A few might even deserve the accolades and treasure bestowed upon them.

I know this because from the late 1990s until about 2010 I worked for a variety of magazines and websites that occasionally assigned me interviews with big names from a variety of fields—Tom Hanks, Venus and Serena, Stephen Colbert, Mark Cuban, Shaq, Dwight Yoakam, Chilli from TLC! That's why I can say without hesitation that while their publicists, managers, and little Napoleon reps are by and large as responsive to your requests as a cat licking its ass on the dining room table, America's celebrities are almost always a pleasure to meet.

So are most rich people. In a fifteen-minute phoner I did with Donald Trump in 2007, the worst president in the history and future of the United States was actually borderline charming while sharing his secrets of financial success. Obviously, I'd never admit to such heresy today.

OUR UNDERSTANDING OF status, privilege, and wealth is undergoing radical change for the variety of reasons covered in this book. These changes have forced the rich—once sole doyens of prestige—to adapt. They dress down like everyone else, vacation in the same places, overspend on wine, eat at Taco Bell.

Even the old mid-Atlantic accent—that manufactured vestige of class anxiety among East Coast aristocracy reinforced by an army of British nannies who once raised the progeny of Ivy-covered elites—is a linguistic fossil. Kelsey Grammer and David Hyde Pierce resurrected it to award-winning comic effect in *Frasier*. But the thespian king of the Locust Valley lockjaw will always be Jim Backus as Thurston Howell III chivalrously maintaining standards on *Gilligan's Island*, a character now nearly as obscure as the Linnaean status classification he parodied.

Even so, Veblen, Packard, and Fitzgerald's elitists continue to haunt our egalitarian dreams. On occasion they pop up in real life. The most compelling recent symbol of American profligacy was captured in the quasi-pornographic 2017 photo of U.S. Treasury Secretary Steve Mnuchin with trophy-wife-and-Cruella-de-Vil-stand-in Louise Linton holding up a sheet of one-dollar bills at the Bureau of Engraving and Printing in Washington, DC. The image became an instant meme. Thanks largely to Linton's elbow-length black gloves and let-them-eat-shit sneer, it inspired howls of prole indignation and earned the couple comparisons to Bond villains.

The Mnuchins of the world will never completely go away. As Lovey once assured Thurston, "Even if you'd been born an ape, you'd still be a Howell. A bit hairy, but a Howell." The rich may be no different from you and me, other than having more money, but we can't help imagining they are, even if what we know about them mostly turns out to be at worst a lie and at best an anachronism.

It's time to discard the extravagant paradigm we've inherited from Veblen, Packard, and other social critics from centuries past, such as Fitzgerald and John Kenneth Galbraith, who himself once noted, "We are guided, in part, by ideas that are relevant to another world." In an era of identity politics, social justice, and celebrations of diversity, it no longer fits.

Yes, "elites" still exist. It'd be naive to make the case that a janitor with a rescue dog commands the same esteem as a powerful family with their names on buildings. But everyone can now attain "status." And a surprising amount of luxury. This is true because anyone can virtue signal; we now know everyone is neurologically wired to crave luxury; academic institutions that propagate such discoveries are socially diverse; as a result, recognition of status is more inclusive than ever before; global brands and the booming world of apps put luxury products and services within reach of the majority of people in Western countries; even when they have little money, civic respect can elevate the status of people from "lower tiers" of society; authenticity is available to anyone at little to no cost; and even political rebels can change the behavior, beliefs, and philanthropy habits of the rich.

"Belonging to the 'elite' . . . has nothing to do with how much money you have or how you obtained it," wrote New York–based brand strategist Arwa Mahdawi in the *Guardian*. "Donald Trump, Boris Johnson, and Nigel Farage all rail against 'global elites' without irony. The 'elite' has been redefined to reflect your politics, not your purse."

In "The Rich Boy," Fitzgerald describes "all the lies that the poor have told about the rich and the rich have told about themselves." The cartoonish perversity of the wealthy and privileged remains potent. But for those looking closely, the lies have been exposed. The secrets behind what David Brooks called "the hypnotic magic of prestige" have been revealed. The curtain is drawn. Everyone gets backstage. Everyone's a VIP.

Conclusion:
STATUS REBORN

WHEN I SET OUT TO UNEARTH THE BASIS OF OUR EVOLVING UN-
derstanding of status and luxury I had no idea of the gargantuan industry
that labored behind these concepts. The effort is so vast and complex that
even after seeking out status from obscure villages to the world's wealthiest cities I can't pretend to be an expert on the subject. I doubt anyone
can. Status and privilege surround us. Start looking for the signals and
you can quickly find yourself drowning in them, as adrift as an overboard
tourist from a luxury liner and with the same chance of catching up to
the gilded beast.

In our time of commercial disruption and social upheaval, status,
prestige, and privilege are no less shaken—indeed they've become even
more unstable—than other pillars of civilization. Profound changes in
them will continue to lead to profound changes in what we seek and
accept as their markers. Like toppled statues of Confederate generals and
Founding Fathers, it's possible that within a generation or two, traditional totems of status will have been rendered obsolete, and new ones
erected in their places.

It's easy, of course, to lean back, deliver a prophecy that "things will change," and be proven right. But that's not been my intent. My assertion is that things have already changed in ways most of us have yet to fully accept. Like that old left-brain-right-brain fable, a lot of misinformed dogma is reinforced in popular media. Stigmas and cliché are powerful and those surrounding the pursuit of status are entrenched. In a *New York Times Magazine* article about elite nannies I found this aside: "I've often assumed that a $40 bottle of wine is twice as good as a $20 bottle even though the American Association of Wine Economists has essentially proved that the price of wine has almost no bearing on enjoyment."

But that's not true. Neuroscientists like Hilke Plassmann have proven consumers enjoy expensive wine more than they do cheap wine. There's nothing artificial or embarrassing about that.

It's natural, as philosopher Alain de Botton noted, that we should be anxious about the place we occupy in the world. So why, as he writes, is this most ardent desire so often framed "in caustic, mocking terms, as something of interest chiefly to envious or deficient souls"? The answer is because a lot of people who should know better haven't caught up to the turn of the times.

Written by a respected university professor, a recent pop sociology book that for a time you could find at lots of airport newsstands—I'm not going to name it by title, my intention isn't to ignite a literary feud and the example here is one that could apply to many contemporary authors—begins with a lengthy quote from Thorstein Veblen and is steeped throughout in the old master's antiquated wisdom. It makes the case that, "in the 100-plus years since Veblen's book was first published, his theories apply more today than ever before, and they apply to all of us." This is sheer nonsense. The same book invokes the "caustic, mocking" moralizing of both ancients and moderns when it refers to conspicuous consumers as "culprits." This, too, is mistaken.

Status and privilege are changing in ways that each year push the boundaries of our collective wisdom about them to new frontiers. Forty or fifty years from now a young reader may stream this book into the memory function of her brain cloud and wonder why its author devoted so much time to automobiles. Those awkward contraptions born of the Industrial Age are still important to most people. One day they will not be.

THE LONGER VIEW of status is open to speculation. The best guess probably comes from historian and philosopher Yuval Noah Harari. In his 2015 book, *Homo Deus: A Brief History of Tomorrow*, Harari speculates on the rise of a "useless class" that will appear as the result of robots and nonconscious algorithms forcing humans out of the job market, creating mass unemployment.

"In the twenty-first century we might witness the creation of a massive new unworking class: people devoid of any economic, political or even artistic value, who contribute nothing to the prosperity, power and glory of society," he writes. "This 'useless class' will not merely be unemployed—it will be unemployable."

I've repeatedly made the point that as touchstones of wisdom, Veblen, Packard, and other familiar critics of status are already obsolete. But if the majority of humankind no longer needs to work, the world Harari envisions would invert the entire concept of a "leisure class." Such a world would make Dr. Steven Quartz's crusade to destigmatize luxury consumption look like the meditations of a prophet.

We may already be seeing the beginnings of this change in the much-publicized Great Resignation of employees from the workplace, when millions of people (especially younger ones) simply decided they no longer wanted their lives to revolve around nine-to-five jobs. Granted, disruption of the conventional concept of "workplace" and unprecedented government unemployment benefits fueled by the coronavirus pandemic ignited the movement. What's gone unnoticed, however, is an emerging public spirit that's taken a machete to work-world pyramids and made the slavish boss-worker dynamic intolerable for a sizable chunk of the population.

What happens to status when work is antediluvian—turning

everyone into the aristocrats of Veblen's ire—and money is divorced from all its historic purposes? I have no idea, but its symbols will probably look as ridiculous as beaver-felted top hats, bound feet, and Jeff Bezos's $260 swimsuit. Certainly its beginnings will be nearly imperceptible. Changes in status come in many forms, but they almost always start small. An ad in a newspaper. A birthday card. A dime in a jukebox. A chance reunion in a gift shop. A conversation with a stranger standing in line to vote.

While these events have often sowed the seeds of major social change, they've rarely done so in a way that dramatically shifts burdens or rewards between groups or individuals. Paolo Scudieri overcame prejudices to become the King of Comfort and elevate the fortunes of at least some of his southern cohort, but he didn't displace the Italian auto hierarchy in the process. Raising a totem pole on the coast of British Columbia restored prestige to villagers in Oweekeno, but the original Hosumdas pole still stands at the Museum of Anthropology at UBC. New players in the world of philanthropy are challenging the status quo but, as tax dodge or not, charitable giving hit a historic record of $471.44 billion in 2020 and last I looked the Ford Foundation was still sitting on well over $12 billion in assets. It turns out becoming rich—or just staying rich—doesn't mean you have to be an asshole about it.

Even the rise of rescue dogs, the most contentious example in this book, has had a limited impact on the status of their biggest competitors and objects of disdain. The Westminster Kennel Club Dog Show is as popular as ever—2.48 million viewers tuned in to watch the broadcast in 2021, the most in years—as are dogs from breeders. Adoption of rescues skyrocketed during the pandemic, but guess what? So did the pursuit of puppies from kennels, many of which reported a surge in sales that created waiting lists stretching for months, even years in the case of a Canadian breeder of "doodles." A report out of Rescue Dog Central (Portland, Oregon), where I'd met kennel advocate and Dalmatian breeder Patti Strand, included dog kennels among industries "swimming in cash" after a "pandemic puppy boom" that resulted in a 12 percent statewide uptick in dog-biz revenue. The story was the same across the country. "Puppies are in such high demand, many breeders have stopped taking deposits for future litters," reported the *Boston Herald*, as "demand for [kennel] dogs skyrockets during quarantine."

Not all that long ago someone famous asked, can't we all just get along? The status revolution answers that plaintive call for unity with an empathic, "Yes we can." Status is for everyone.

WHEN THEY WERE younger, our nephew and two nieces frequently spent the night at the house I share with The One and Only Joyce. This was simple enough, given they lived just around the corner from us.

Their overnight stays became so routine that at some point TOOJ bought each of the kids a toothbrush to keep at our house. She used a Sharpie to write each child's name on the handles—Jacob, the oldest; followed by Grace; then June, who was and still is several years behind the other two. TOOJ placed each brush in a little ceramic cup in the medicine cabinet in our downstairs bathroom. The cup with the kids' brushes stood next to a plastic caddy that held our adult-sized toothbrushes (no name tags required). We also kept slippers and other personal items for each kid at the house. All of this made impromptu overnight stays easier.

As they grew older and became consumed with middle school, then high school intrigues, Jacob and Grace made fewer and fewer overnight visits. Now maybe seven or eight, June, along with her stuffed doggy (someday she'll have her own rescue), remained a semiregular overnighter, banking lots of imaginary loyalty program points. At some stage she began casually referring to the guest room all the kids nominally shared as "my room."

One afternoon I opened the medicine cabinet and noticed something had changed. June's toothbrush, which had always stood alongside her siblings' toothbrushes in the "visitors' cup," had been moved into the adult caddy alongside the brushes belonging to TOOJ and me. We both laughed. It was one of those adorable things kids do that takes you by surprise because it indicates a mental development that feels beyond their years.

We didn't move the toothbrush, partly because it was so cute, but mostly because we recognized the powerful statement it wordlessly articulated. Like a cat scratching out its turf on the side of a sofa, June had made a public declaration—with this minor elevation of status by her own hand she was signaling herself as a more permanent or at least more prominent part of the household. She wanted everyone to know it, her older brother and sister every bit as much as TOOJ and me. As the years that followed have proved, it was the start of something bigger and better for us all.

ACKNOWLEDGMENTS

THIS BOOK WAS CONCEIVED IN JON KARP'S OFFICE IN NEW York, so it makes sense to start there in expressing gratitude to the people who've brought it to life—the esteemed and eminently patient Simon & Schuster publisher above all.

This book has benefitted from the wisdom of two of the best editors in the business. Jofie Ferrari-Adler applied a deft hand to early chapters until exiting for greener pastures. Stephanie Frerich not only stepped in with great skill and insight, imposing order on an unruly pile of notes, rough drafts, and poor jokes, but she saved me from myself on numerous occasions. I owe her and her circumspect eye an enormous debt.

Tremendous thanks is due to Simon & Schuster staff, including Emily Simonson and Jessica Chin.

Thank you to David Patterson, an extraordinary agent and editor himself.

I said this book had two editors. Given that it actually started many iterations ago as a book about foodie culture, it technically had three editors. Sarah Knight is currently somewhere "Not Giving a F*ck," but her influence is present here, along with my eternal gratitude.

Though not immediately involved in its production, editors and others who supported me during the process indirectly supported the book. Enormous appreciation to: James Heidenry, Dana Joseph, Ross McCammon, Rob Bernstein, Alex Heard, John DeVore, Jordan Burchette, and Brendan Vaughan. Frances Cha—who wrote a great book called *If I Had Your Face* about women striving for high standards of beauty and social status—has been a much-appreciated font of information on fashion breakthroughs and HABA products.

My boundless appreciation to Susan and Jurgen Hess, Buck Parker, and the entire *Columbia Insight* board and community.

I tend not to share unfinished work with readers, but in this rare case did solicit feedback on several chapter drafts from the inestimable Robert Glasser. Had I such power, I'd decree he spend the rest of his days ordering gratis room service from luxury hotel suites. Bob Hill, who actually has spent a fair portion of his life in luxury hotel suites, emails me far too many internet links. A few, nevertheless, pay off, including the greatest joke in the history of *Gilligan's Island* ("Heavens, a Yale man!"), the link for which is buried in the chapter 8 endnotes.

In L.A., undying multi-track mellow gold to David Gale (*Camo and Plaid* will happen!), Van Toffler, everyone at Gunpowder & Sky, as well as to Jon Katzman and David Garrett.

In Juneau, hugs to everyone named Davis, with particular nods to Randy, Merridy, Hanna, Jay, and Sue. Deep and repeated bows to the cabin crew of Mike Thompson, Dave "Speedster" Swansborough, Mike Studt, Hanna Davis, Randy Davis, Scott Evans, Rod Brink, and everyone else who has abetted that quixotic project. Shaun McCormick has read so many books over the years he deserves a mention in this one.

Sincere appreciation to everyone quoted in these pages for making time to speak with me, and apologies to those whose stories regrettably didn't make the final cut. The first draft of chapter 6 was literally forty-five thousand words—it wasn't quite six months in a leaky boat but grim choices were made. Thanks to Chris "Mr. Plywood" Stewart and son Felix for inviting me to the Bighorns, where everything began clicking into place; and Russell Okamoto for inviting me on a cross-country drive that turned up in print many years later.

I might as well thank the entire province of British Columbia, because everyone there is always so helpful. Special recognition, however, is due to Roy Vickers for allowing me such close access to his work and extending the privilege of an invite to an unforgettable potlatch experience in Oweekeno. Thank you, too, to Andrea Vickers, Dean Heron, Matt Lewis, Latham Mack, and families, and to Blaine Estby for introducing me to Roy. I'm indebted to Destination British Columbia, BC Ferries, and the UBC Museum of Anthropology, in particular Katie Ferrante for digging up long-forgotten documents about totem poles, then providing sensible feedback on what I was writing about them.

I wrote nice things about Alan Davis not simply because he ushered me into the rarified world of Patriotic Millionaires and heavyweight philanthropy, but because his inexhaustible humanity should inspire others.

Bob Elton at the Society of Automotive Historians was not just incredibly helpful, he was a joy to listen to talk about cars.

London research—and a brief stint working in The Shard, the most prestigious building in which I've ever sat at a desk staring out the windows—would have been impossible without the support of Peter Bale, Jimmy Wales, Ed Upton, and the excellent staff at the short-lived *WikiTribune*. Team Hagar executed its offbeat duties with brains and aplomb—thank you, Dr. Daniel Richardson, Rea Al Hallal, Annie Shiau, and Luyi Xu.

Intrepid Italian journalist Silvia Marchetti provided greatly needed tips and information about Italy—any mistakes I made in characterizing the country are mine, not hers. Even if he is from the north, I doubt there's a more helpful fixer in southern Italy than Alessandro Pavanati, who helped arrange an extremely enjoyable interview and factory tour without making me feel the least bit embarrassed about my lack of car-guy savvy.

Erik and Chuck 2.0 flexed their car-guy savvy in the service of deeper scientific understanding of the relationship between sports cars and the private lives of sports car owners. Dylan, Kyle, Carlos, Jacob, Grace, and June remain trustworthy guides to cultural minutiae that somehow elude me.

Despite going through life head and shoulders above the crowd, nothing could come less naturally to The One and Only Joyce than elitism or entitlement. As always, nothing remains possible much less worth doing without her.

NOTES

INTRODUCTION:
STATUS IN CHAOS

2 *"Zero Bark Thirty"*: Maureen Callahan, "Zero Bark Thirty," *New York Post*, April 14, 2013, http://nypost.com/2013/04/14/zero -bark-thirty/.

4 *"busy and overworked lifestyle"*: Silvia Bellezza, Neeru Paharia, and Anat Keinan, *Journal of Consumer Research* 44, no. 1 (June 2017): 118–138, https://doi.org/10.1093/jcr/ucw076.

5 *"The leisure class no longer exists"*: Elizabeth Currid-Halkett, *The Sum of Small Things: A Theory of the Aspirational Class* (Princeton, NJ: Princeton University Press, 2017), 14.

5 *"prestige-obsessed industries"*: Elizabeth Olson, "A Trump Bump for Law Firm of President's Lawyer," *New York Times*, June 23, 2017, https://www.nytimes.com/2017/06/23/business/dealbook/a -trump-bump-for-law-firm-of-presidents-lawyer.html?mcubz=0.

6 *$1.1 trillion global luxury industry*: Claudia D'Arpizio, Federica Levato, Filippo Prete, Constance Gault, and Joëlle de Montgolfier, "The Future of Luxury: Bouncing Back from Covid-19," Bain &

Company, January 14, 2021, https://www.bain.com/insights/the
-future-of-luxury-bouncing-back-from-covid-19/.

7   *$1,300 crystal-studded socks*: Liana Satenstein, "Are Rihanna's
$1,340 Crystal Gucci Socks Dry-Clean Only?" *Vogue*, Decem-
ber 6, 2017, https://www.vogue.com/article/rihanna-gucci-crystal
-sock-for-1340-dollars.

10 *"Apart from economic payoffs"*: Adam Waytz, "The Psychology of
Social Status," *Scientific American*, December 8, 2009, https://
www.scientificamerican.com/article/the-psychology-of-social/.

11 *"We believe in a particular order"*: Yuval Noah Harari, *Sapiens: A
Brief History of Humankind* (New York: Harper Perennial, 2015),
110.

11 *"divide humanity into two parts"*: Ibid., 195.

CHAPTER 1:
THE WOMAN WHO INVENTED RESCUE DOGS:
STATUS AS VIRTUE SIGNALING

16 *the richest county in America*: Alyson Shontell, "Facebook Employees Made So Much Money from the IPO, Their County Is Now
the Richest in America," *Business Insider*, July 3, 2013, https://
www.businessinsider.com/san-mateo-highest-paid-county-thanks
-to-facebook-2013-7.

16 *"the canine bathtub"*: Jennifer B. Lee, "Where They Used to Drown
the Dogs," *New York Times*, September 30, 2008, https://cityroom
.blogs.nytimes.com/2008/09/30/where-they-used-to-drown-the
-dogs/?mcubz=0.

16 *The gunslinger was renowned*: Merritt Clifton, "Street Dogs in
the U.S.? Nathan Winograd Has Gone Barking Mad," Animals
24-7, February 6, 2017, http://www.animals24-7.org/2017/02/06
/street-dogs-in-the-u-s-nathan-winograd-has-gone-barking-mad/.

17 *"animals have certain basic moral rights"*: Tom Regan, *The Case for
Animal Rights* (Berkeley: University of California Press, 1983), xii.

18   *"To persist in calling such practices"*: Ibid., 110.

18   *"It is no more true"*: Ibid., 116.

18   *"The animal rights movement"*: Ibid., 399.

19   *"public pet execution"*: Miles Corwin, "Pet Sterilization Becomes Law in San Mateo County," *Los Angeles Times*, December 19, 1990, https://www.latimes.com/archives/la-xpm-1990-12-19-mn -6411-story.html.

19   *"One reporter cried"*: Jane Gross, "San Mateo Journal: A Crusade to Save Unwanted Lives," *New York Times*, October 31, 1990, https://www.nytimes.com/1990/10/31/us/san-mateo-journal-a -crusade-to-save-unwanted-lives.html.

20   *Ninety-eight percent of animals killed*: Gaverick Matheny and Cheryl Leahy, "Farm-Animal Welfare, Legislation, and Trade," *Law and Contemporary Problems* 70, no. 1 (Winter 2007): 325, https://www.jstor.org/stable/27592172.

21   *Thought to be the first of its kind*: Corwin, "Pet Sterilization Becomes Law in San Mateo County."

23   *Pet euthanasia rates*: Emily Bowden, "Shelter Statistics," Final Project for INLS 541, University of North Carolina, spring 2013, https://sites.google.com/site/shelterstats/.

23   *down to 920,000 by 2021*: "Pet Statistics," American Society for the Prevention of Cruelty to Animals, 2021, https://www.aspca .org/helping-people-pets/shelter-intake-and-surrender/pet-statis tics.

23   *When the movement hit critical mass*: Jordan Tyler, "US Pet Owner-ship Projected to Increase to 71 Million Households," Pet Food Pro-cessing, August 31, 2020, https://www.petfoodprocessing.net/arti cles/14085-us-pet-ownership-projected-to-increase-to-71-million -households.

23   *38 percent of U.S. homes*: "U.S. Pet Ownership Statistics," Amer-ican Veterinary Medical Association, 2021, https://www.avma .org/resources-tools/reports-statistics/us-pet-ownership-statis tics.

23 *In the early weeks of the outbreak*: Allison Morrow, "New York Dog Rescues Report an Unprecedented Surge in Applications as Coronavirus Keeps Humans Isolated," CNN, March 30, 2020, https://www.cnn.com/2020/03/30/us/dogs-adoption-surge-trnd/index.html.

23 *4 percent increase*: Tyler, "US Pet Ownership Projected to Increase to 71 Million Households."

23 *More than 230 U.S. cities*: Joshua Emerson Smith, "California Could Become First State to Ban Stores That Sell Commercially Bred Dogs, Cats and Rabbits," *San Diego Union-Tribune*, June 12, 2017, https://www.sandiegouniontribune.com/news/environment/sd-me-puppy-bills-20170612-story.html.

23 *In 2017, California passed a statewide law*: Assembly Bill No. 485, Chapter 740, California Legislative Information, October 13, 2017, https://leginfo.legislature.ca.gov/faces/billNavClient.xhtml?bill_id=201720180AB485.

24 *Writing in the* Spectator *in 2015*: James Bartholomew, "Easy Virtue," *The Spectator*, April 15, 2015, https://www.spectator.co.uk/article/easy-virtue.

24 *"Brag doesn't have to be"*: Peggy Klaus, *Brag! The Art of Tooting Your Own Horn Without Blowing It* (New York: Warner Books, 2003), 18–19.

25 *"Luxury is culture"*: Jean-Noël Kapferer and Vincent Bastien, *The Luxury Strategy: Break the Rules of Marketing to Build Luxury Brands* (London: Kogan Page, 2009), 5.

26 *Serena Williams was the first to wallow in*: "Serena Williams Takes Most Expensive Bath," United Press International, February 27, 2005, https://www.upi.com/Odd_News/2005/02/27/Serena-Williams-takes-most-expensive-bath/55011109525338/.

26 *"must . . . be active at a cultural level"*: Kapferer and Bastien, *The Luxury Strategy*, 210.

26 *"Customers want to make a statement"*: Robin Lent and Geneviève Tour, *Selling Luxury: Connect with Affluent Customers, Create*

Unique Experiences Through Impeccable Service, and Close the Sale (Hoboken, NJ: John Wiley & Sons, 2009), 10.

27   *"Price on its own"*: Kapferer and Bastien, *The Luxury Strategy*, 29.

27   *"There is a luxury industry"*: Jean-Noël Kapferer, "Luxury After the Crisis: Pro Logo or No Logo?" *The European Business Review*, September–October 2010, https://www.researchgate.net/publica tion/265080236_Luxury_after_the_crisis_Pro_logo_or_no_logo.

27   *Bernard Arnault, CEO of Moët Hennessy–Louis Vuitton*: Benjamin Berghaus, Günter Müller-Stewens, and Sven Reinecke, eds., *The Management of Luxury: A Practitioner's Handbook* (London: Kogan Page, 2014), 72.

28   *According to a study by Niro Sivanathan*: Brad Tuttle, "Psych Study: When You're Bummed, You're More Likely to Buy," *Time*, May 7, 2010, https://business.time.com/2010/05/07/study-low-self -esteem-makes-you-more-likely-to-buy-luxury-goods/.

28   *$58,000 golf cart hovercrafts*: Petr H., "25 Crazy Things Rich People Bought Just Because They Could," List 25, October 4, 2015, https://list25.com/25-crazy-things-rich-people-bought-just-be cause-they-could/.

28   *Studies have shown acquisition of goods*: Peter Noel Murray, PhD, "The Emotions of Luxury: How Emotions Related to 'Self' and Brand 'Truth' Create Perceptions of Luxury," *Psychology Today*, October 12, 2016, https://www.psychologytoday.com/us/blog /inside-the-consumer-mind/201610/the-emotions-luxury.

29   *"precious object"*: Lent and Tour, *Selling Luxury*, 98–99.

30   *"The aim of an upper-premium brand"*: Kapferer and Bastien, *The Luxury Strategy*, 63.

30   *"improving force in society"*: Ibid., 8.

30   *"uplifting impact on their lives"*: Lent and Tour, *Selling Luxury*, 10.

31   *"a millennial fever dream"*: Hayley Hershman and Eliza Mills, "Everlane Is a Millennial Fever Dream and It's Making a Killing," *Marketplace*, June 9, 2017, https://www.marketplace.org/2017/06/09 /everlane-millennial-fever-dream-and-its-making-killing/.

228

228   NOTES

31   *top reasons to adopt a pet*: "Top Reasons to Adopt a Pet," Humane Society of the United States, https://www.humanesociety.org /resources/top-reasons-adopt-pet.

31   *Bartholomew understood how anger*: Bartholomew, "Easy Virtue."

32   *Strand served on the AKC's board*: "AKC Judges Biographies: Patti L. Strand," American Kennel Club, https://www.apps.akc.org /classic/nationalchampionship/judges/blocks/dsp_judge_bio .cfm?event_id=2009277101&id_stakeholder=12870309.

33   *NAIA's stated goals*: "Mission Statement—Animal Welfare," National Animal Interest Alliance, http://www.naiaonline.org/about -us/mission-statements/.

34   *Humane Society of the United States*: "2020 Annual Report: Achievements for Animals," Humane Society of the United States and Humane Society International, 31, https://www.humanesociety .org/sites/default/files/docs/HSUS-HSI_AR2020_LR_1.pdf.

34   *less than 1 percent*: "The Humane Society of the United States and Pet Shelter Giving," HumaneWatch, https://humanewatch.org/the _humane_society_of_the_united_states_and_pet_shelter_giving/.

34   *ASPCA CEO Matthew Bershadker*: Emily Brill, "ASPCA Under Fire Again for Lavish Spending, Fundraising, Executive Compensation," Canine Review, August 5, 2021, https://thecaninereview .com/2021/08/05/aspca-back-under-fire-for-outlandish-spend ing-on-fundraising-executive-compensation/.

36   *"The evolution of luxury"*: Jean-Noël Kapferer, *Kapferer on Luxury: How Luxury Brands Can Grow Yet Remain Rare* (London: Kogan Page, 2015), 90.

CHAPTER 2:
A RICH YET TASTEFUL HISTORY:
STATUS AS VICE

38   *"the idea that all humans are equal"*: Yuval Noah Harari, *Sapiens: A Brief History of Humankind* (New York: Harper Perennial, 2015), 109.

39　*lavish wedding ceremonies*: Ciara Nugent, "Why Chinese Authorities Are Cracking Down on 'Extravagant and Wasteful' Weddings," *Time*, December 3, 2018, https://time.com/5469153/china-wedding -crackdown/.

39　*Dr. Michael Scott*: "Guilty Pleasures: Luxury in Ancient Greece," pt. 1, BBC4, 2011, https://vimeo.com/25556379.

41　*problem with Veblen*: "Thorstein Veblen, 1857–1929," Econlib, https://www.econlib.org/library/Enc/bios/Veblen.html; "Thorstein Veblen: American Economist and Sociologist," Britannica, https:// www.britannica.com/biography/Thorstein-Veblen#ref124655.

42　*"odd man out"*: "Thorstein Veblen, 1857–1929."

42　*"conspicuous consumption"*: Thorstein Veblen, *The Theory of the Leisure Class: An Economic Study in the Evolution of Institutions* (1899; New York: Penguin, 1994), vi.

42　*"The commercial value of canine monstrosities"*: Ibid., 142.

42　*"The cat's temperament"*: Ibid., 140.

43　*Shang dynasty emperor Di Xin*: Ced Yong, "Top 10 Terrible Chinese Emperors," Owlcation, June 21, 2021, https://owlcation.com /humanities/Top-10-Terrible-Chinese-Emperors.

43　*beaver-felted top hat*: Veblen, *The Theory of the Leisure Class*, 132.

44　*"The possession of wealth"*: Ibid., 25–26.

45　*"Women and other slaves"*: Ibid., 53–54.

45　*"The pressure exerted"*: Ibid., 195–96.

46　*"law of conspicuous waste"*: Ibid., 93.

47　*"Machine guns, even mortars"*: Chuck Thompson, *The 25 Best World War II Sites: Pacific Theater* (San Francisco: Greenline, 2002), 205.

47　*Over just two decades*: Kimberly Amadeo, "US GDP by Year Compared to Recessions and Events," Balance, April 28, 2021, https:// www.thebalance.com/us-gdp-by-year-3305543.

47　*four times as many cars*: "The Postwar Economy: 1945–1960," U.S. Department of State, http://countrystudies.us/united-states/history -114.htm.

47　*seventeen thousand TV sets*: Ibid.

47   *personal-computing*: "Percentage of Households with a Computer at Home in the United States from 1984 to 2010," Statista, https://www.statista.com/statistics/184685/percentage-of-households-with-computer-in-the-united-states-since-1984/.

48   *80 percent of Americans*: "Employment by Major Industry Sector," U.S. Bureau of Labor Statistics, September 8, 2021, https://www.bls.gov/emp/tables/employment-by-major-industry-sector.htm.

48   *majority of workers held white-collar jobs*: Carol A. Barry, "White-Collar Employment: I—Trends and Structure," *Monthly Labor Review* 84, no. 1 (January 1961): 11–18, http://www.jstor.org/stable/41834419.

48   *entertainingly uppity*: John Kenneth Galbraith, *The Affluent Society* (Boston: Houghton Mifflin, 1958), 71–72.

49   *Vance Packard was an unlikely figure*: Daniel Horowitz, *Vance Packard and American Social Criticism* (Chapel Hill: University of North Carolina Press, 1994), 10-41.

49   *"new American aristocracy"*: Matthew Stewart, "The 9.9 Percent Is the New American Aristocracy," *The Atlantic*, June 2018, https://www.theatlantic.com/magazine/archive/2018/06/the-birth-of-a-new-american-aristocracy/559130/.

50   The Status Seekers: Vance Packard, *The Status Seekers* (New York: David McKay, 1959), 2, 41.

50   *"Call girls"*: Ibid., 94–95.

50   *Adapting wartime experiences*: Ibid., 6.

51   *"Our class system"*: Ibid., 32.

51   *2021 Bureau of Labor Statistics*: "Military Careers," U.S. Bureau of Labor Statistics, https://www.bls.gov/ooh/military/military-careers.htm.

51   *sixteen four-star generals*: "List of Active Duty United States Four-Star Officers," Wikipedia, https://en.wikipedia.org/wiki/List_of_active_duty_United_States_four-star_officers.

51 *eight admirals*: Erin Duffin, "Total Military Personnel of the U.S. Navy, from the FY 2020 to FY 2022, by Rank," Statista, June 21, 2021, https://www.statista.com/statistics/239345/total-military -personnel-of-the-us-navy-by-grade/.

51 *"upper uppers"*: Packard, *The Status Seekers*, 34.

52 *"The lower classes"*: Ibid., 62.

52 *"most of its potency"*: Ibid., 22.

52 *"funeral directors"*: Ibid., 84.

52 *"early settler"*: Ibid., 8.

53 *"An example of irrational discrepancy"*: Ibid., 81.

53 *one hundred jobs*: Ibid., 100.

53 *"The American Concept"*: Alison Griswold, "The American Concept of 'Prestige' Has Barely Changed in 37 Years," *Slate*, September 10, 2014, https://slate.com/business/2014/09/most-prestigious-jobs -in-america-the-short-list-has-barely-changed-in-37-years.html.

CHAPTER 3:
MUSIC, WINE, AND SEX APPEAL:
STATUS AS NEUROLOGICAL IMPERATIVE

56 *"Being popular is a marker for social status"*: Gregory Berns and Sara E. Moore, "A Neural Predictor of Cultural Popularity," Economics Department and Center for Neuropolicy, Emory University, December 17, 2010, https://ssrn.com/abstract=1742971; http:// dx.doi.org/10.2139/ssrn.1742971.

60 *Todd Storz*: Ben Fong-Torres, *The Hits Just Keep On Coming: The History of Top 40 Radio* (San Francisco: Backbeat, 1998), 37–39.

63 *"A major barrier"*: Steven Quartz and Anette Asp, *Cool: How the Brain's Hidden Quest for Cool Drives Our Economy and Shapes Our World* (New York: Farrar, Straus and Giroux, 2015), 9–10.

64 *"We intrinsically care"*: Ibid., 148.

64 *"[buying a] Prius"*: Ibid., 241.

65   *Plassmann's study*: Hilke Plassmann, John O'Doherty, Baba Shiv, and Antonio Rangel, "Marketing Actions Can Modulate Neural Representations of Experienced Pleasantness," Proceedings of the National Academy of Sciences, January 22, 2008, https://www.pnas.org/content/105/3/1050.

67   *"Although [Packard's] explanation"*: Quartz and Asp, *Cool*, 11.

67   *"Stigmatizing Materialism"*: Leaf Van Boven, Margaret C. Campbell, and Thomas Gilovich, "Stigmatizing Materialism: On Stereotypes and Impressions of Materialistic and Experiential Pursuits," *Personality and Social Psychology Bulletin* 36, no. 4 (April 2010), 551–63, https://www.researchgate.net/publication/42975757_Stigmatizing_Materialism_On_Stereotypes_and_Impressions_of_Materialistic_and_Experiential_Pursuits.

67   *"Expensive Wine Is for Suckers"*: Joss Fong, "Expensive Wine Is for Suckers. This Video Shows Why," *Vox*, May 20, 2015, https://www.vox.com/2015/5/20/8625785/expensive-wine-taste-cheap.

70   *left-right brain story line*: Maria Konnikova, "The Man Who Couldn't Speak and How He Revolutionized Psychology," *Scientific American*, February 8, 2013, https://blogs.scientificamerican.com/literally-psyched/the-man-who-couldnt-speakand-how-he-revolutionized-psychology/.

CHAPTER 4:
SPORTS CARS AND SMALL PENISES:
STATUS AS INCLUSIVITY

79   *In his memoir,* Shoe Dog: Phil Knight, *Shoe Dog: A Memoir by the Creator of Nike* (New York: Scribner, 2016), 42.

84   *The Paul bros*: "Our $400,000 Disaster . . . ," Logan Paul YouTube channel, September 26, 2017, https://www.youtube.com/watch?v=LnyiAofuHaE.

85   *about 25 percent of American sixteen-year-olds*: Katharina Buchholz, "Americans Get Driver's Licenses Later in Life," Statista, January 7,

2020, https://www.statista.com/chart/18682/percentage-of-the-us
-population-holding-a-drivers-license-by-age-group/.

85 *evolutionary psychologist Dr. Gad Saad*: Gad Saad, "Men: You're
Only as Good-Looking as the Car That You're Driving," *Psychology
Today*, December 6, 2010, https://www.psychologytoday.com/us
/blog/homo-consumericus/201012/men-you-re-only-good-look
ing-the-car-you-re-driving.

85 *citizens of the "bicycle kingdom"*: Xinhua News Agency, "Car Brands
Represent Status, Stereotypes in China," China.org.cn, April
21, 2014, http://www.china.org.cn/business/2014-04/21/content
_32166181.htm.

91 *doctoral degrees nationally*: "Doctor's Degrees Conferred by Postsecondary Institutions, by Race/Ethnicity and Sex of Student:
Selected Years, 1976–77 Through 2017–18," table 324.20, National Center for Education Statistics, 2019, https://nces.ed.gov
/programs/digest/d19/tables/dt19_324.20.asp.

91 *female faculty increased*: "Characteristics of Postsecondary Faculty,"
National Center for Education Statistics, May 2020, https://nces
.ed.gov/programs/coe/indicator/csc.

91 *first daughter of Norwegian immigrants*: M. Michael Brady, "Thorstein Veblen (1857–1929)," *Norwegian American*, October 29, 2018,
https://www.norwegianamerican.com/thorstein-veblen-1857-1929/.

91 *Sociologists for Women in Society*: Heather Laube and Beth B. Hess,
"The Founding of SWS," Sociologists for Women in Society, 2001,
https://socwomen.org/about/history-of-sws/the-founding-of-sws/.

91 *no women on the American Sociological Association's*: Pamela Ann
Roby, "The Women's 1969 Sociology Caucus, Sociologists for
Women in Society and the ASA: A Forty Year Retrospective of
Women on the Move," Sociologists for Women in Society, 2009,
https://socwomen.org/about/history-of-sws/the-women/.

91 *ASA's 2021 Executive Committee*: "Standing Committees," American
Sociological Association, November 15, 2021, https://www.asanet
.org/about/governance-and-leadership/standing-committees#EC.

91   *top five countries of origin for foreign students*: Elizabeth Redden, "Number of Enrolled International Students Drops," Inside Higher Ed, November 18, 2019, https://www.insidehighered.com/admis sions/article/2019/11/18/international-enrollments-declined-un dergraduate-graduate-and.

92   *Henri Tajfel*: Saul Kassin, Steven Fein, and Hazel Rose Markus, *Social Psychology* (Boston: Houghton Mifflin, 1990), 181.

92   *Seth Stephens-Davidowitz*: Seth Stephens-Davidowitz, *Everybody Lies: Big Data, New Data, and What the Internet Can Tell Us About Who We Really Are* (New York: Dey Street, 2017), 16.

93   *driving a Porsche Carrera*: Gad Saad and John G. Vongas, "The Effect of Conspicuous Consumption on Men's Testosterone Levels," *Organizational Behavior and Human Decision Processes* 110, no. 2 (November 2009): 80–92. https://www.researchgate.net /publication/46489134_The_Effect_of_Conspicuous_Consump tion_on_Men's_Testosterone_Levels.

93   *30 percent of sports car owners*: "Do Men with Fast Cars Really Have a Small Manhood?" Flexed, 2014, https://flexed.co.uk/men -fast-cars-really-small-manhood/.

95   British Journal of Urology International: "Am I Normal? Review Analyzes Data on Flaccid and Erect Penis Lengths in Men," *British Journal of Urology International*, March 3, 2015, https://www .bjuinternational.com/bjui-blog/normal-review-analyzes-data -flaccid-erect-penis-lengths-men/.

CHAPTER 5:
THE KING OF COMFORT:
STATUS AS SOCIAL JUSTICE

105 *Second University of Naples academic paper*: Amedeo Lepore, "The Gap Between Northern and Southern Italy from Its Origins to Its Current Status. Historic Evolution and Economic Profiles," Seconda Università di Napoli, 2012.

105 *"religious as fuck"*: M. E. Evans, "Northern Italians Versus South-ern Italians: Are They Really That Different?" *Surviving in Italy*, July 30, 2014, https://survivinginitaly.com/2014/07/30/north ern-italians-versus-southern-italians-are-they-really-that-differ ent/.

106 *"altered forever the basis"*: Alain de Botton, *Status Anxiety* (New York: Vintage International, 2004), 31.

107 *"rappers in junkyards"*: "Hype Williams on Working with Puff Daddy, California Love and Missy Elliott," Red Bull Music Academy, YouTube, June 5, 2018, https://www.youtube.com /watch?v=zSUav71UBmk.

108 *"The evolution of luxury"*: Jean-Noël Kapferer, *Kapferer on Luxury: How Luxury Brands Can Grow Yet Remain Rare* (London: Kogan Page, 2015), 90.

108 *fizzy mistake*: Layla Schlack, "The History of Sparkling Wine Includes Accidental Science and Exceptional Champagne," *Wine Enthusiast*, December 2, 2019, https://www.winemag .com/2019/12/02/history-sparkling-wine/.

108 *led in consumption*: Mike Epson, "These Countries Consume the Most Champagne," Smart Consumer, April 27, 2021, https:// www.thesmartconsumer.com/these-countries-consumes-the -most-champagne.

108 *Kihachiro Onitsuka*: Phil Knight, *Shoe Dog: A Memoir by the Cre-ator of Nike* (New York: Scribner, 2016), 86.

108 *Nobutoshi Kihara*: John Nathan, *Sony: The Private Life* (Boston: Houghton Mifflin, 1999), 28–30; "This Is the Product We Must Produce," Sony, https://www.sony.com/en/SonyInfo/Corporate Info/History/SonyHistory/1-02.html.

109 *"a pitiful, helpless giant"*: Studs Terkel, *The Studs Terkel Reader: My American Century* (New York: New Press, 2011), 32.

113 *interior components*: "C-Class: 2018," Mercedes-Benz, 2017, https://www.mbusa.com/vcm/MB/DigitalAssets/pdfmb/bro chures/2018-C-Class.pdf.

114 *Enzo Ferrari*: Doron P. Levin, "Enzo Ferrari, Builder of Racing Cars, Is Dead at 90," *New York Times*, August 16, 1998, https://www.nytimes.com/1988/08/16/obituaries/enzo-ferrari-builder-of-racing-cars-is-dead-at-90.html.

119 *Adler Pelzer Group*: "We Today," Adler Pelzer Group, https://www.adlerpelzer.com/about-us.

119 *homegrown success*: Patrizia Capua, "Adler Group, the Multinational of Dashboards, 58 Factories in the World with Its Head in Ottaviano," *la Repubblica*, May 3, 2011, https://ricerca.repubblica.it/repubblica/archivio/repubblica/2011/05/03/adler-group-la-multinazionale-dei-cruscotti-58.html.

127 *Oliver Sacks*: Oliver Sacks, *The River of Consciousness* (New York: Vintage, 2017), 107.

CHAPTER 6:
LUXURY AT THE END OF THE WORLD:
STATUS AS AUTHENTICITY

134 *Chinese consumers*: Danielle Wightman-Stone, "China's Share of the Global Luxury Market Reaches New High in 2020," FashionUnited, January 6, 2021, https://fashionunited.uk/news/retail/china-s-share-of-the-global-luxury-market-reaches-new-high-in-2020/2021010652819.

134 *the Hatch Chile Store*: "Keeping the Tradition," Hatch Chile Store, https://www.hatch-green-chile.com/pages/about-us-and-our-team.

135 *"Online Influencer Industry"*: Sophie Elmhirst, " 'It's Genuine, You Know?' Why the Online Influencer Industry Is Going 'Authentic,' " *Guardian*, April 5, 2019, https://www.theguardian.com/media/2019/apr/05/its-genuine-you-know-why-the-online-influencer-industry-is-going-authentic.

135 *"Authenticity speaks for and sells itself"*: *The Curse of Von Dutch*, Hulu, Episode 1, November 2021.

135 *Hermès Birkin bags*: Robert Frank, "Handbags Were the Hottest Investment for the Rich Last Year," CNBC, March 5, 2020, https://www.cnbc.com/2020/03/04/handbags-were-the-hottest -investment-for-the-rich-last-year.html.

136 *"Birkin authentication card"*: "How to Avoid a Fake Hermès Scam," Bags of Luxury, 2021, https://bagsofluxury.com/guides/avoid -fake-hermes-scam/.

136 *World Global Style Network*: "Travel & Hospitality: 10 Key Trends for 2021," World Global Style Network, January 5, 2021.

137 *Roy Vickers*: Julia Skelly, "Roy Henry Vickers," *The Canadian Encyclopedia*, April 13, 2018, https://www.thecanadianencyclopedia .ca/en/article/roy-henry-vickers.

138 *"harmonization of tastes"*: Kyle Chayka, "Welcome to Airspace: How Silicon Valley Helps Spread the Same Sterile Aesthetic Across the World," Verge, August 3, 2016, https://www.the verge.com/2016/8/3/12325104/airbnb-aesthetic-global-minimal ism-startup-gentrification.

140 *Canada's Indian Act*: "Indian Act," *The Canadian Encyclopedia*, December 16, 2020, https://www.thecanadianencyclopedia.ca/en /article/indian-act.

140 *"Potlatch"*: "Living Tradition: The Kwakwaka'wakw Potlatch on the Northwest Coast," U'mista Cultural Society, https://umista potlatch.ca/potlatch-eng.php.

141 Captured Heritage: Douglas Cole, *Captured Heritage: The Scramble for Northwest Coast Artifacts* (Seattle: University of Washington Press, 1985), 65, 100.

143 *Howard McDiarmid*: Howard McDiarmid, *Pacific Rim Park: A Country Doctor's Role in Preserving Long Beach and Establishing the New Wickaninnish Inn* (Tofino: H. McDiarmid, 2009), 21.

143 *obscure village of Tofino*: Ibid., 12–13.

147 *Fewer than 5 percent*: Ashok Chaluvadi, "Most Common Exteriors on New Homes Are Stucco and Vinyl in 2019," National Association of Home Builders, October 1, 2020, https://eyeonhousing

.org/2020/10/most-common-sidings-on-new-homes-are-stucco-and-vinyl-in-2019/.

150 *E. Ruhamah Scidmore*: Cole, *Captured Heritage*, 98.

151 *Henry Nolla*: Alva and Nuri Nolla, "Henry Nolla," Pacific Rim Arts Society, November 28, 2020, https://www.wickinn.com/on-pointe/henry-nolla/.

152 *build his cabin*: McDiarmid, *Pacific Rim Park*, 93–101.

154 *Vickers and Nolla*: Roy Henry Vickers, *Spirit Transformed: A Journey from Tree to Totem* (Vancouver, BC: Raincoast, 1996), 49–52.

158 *"no alternative to suicide"*: J. E. Michael Kew, "Reflections on Anthropology at the University of British Columbia," *BC Studies*, no. 193 (spring 2017): 175, https://doi.org/10.14288/bcs.v0i193.189198.

161 *Relais & Châteaux*: Amber Gibson, "What It Takes to Be Relais & Châteaux," *Forbes*, January 1, 2018, https://www.forbes.com/sites/ambergibson/2018/01/01/what-it-takes-to-be-relais-chateaux/#5653f4ee292d.

162 *"The new addition to Wickaninnish"*: Roy Henry Vickers, *"Henry's Corner*: Story," Roy Henry Vickers Gallery, https://royhenryvickers.com/products/henrys-corner.

CHAPTER 7:
REBELS OF PHILANTHROPY:
STATUS AS DISRUPTION

166 *Philanthropy Score*: Deniz Çam, "The New Forbes 400 Philanthropy Score: Measuring Billionaires' Generosity," *Forbes*, October 3, 2018, https://www.forbes.com/sites/denizcam/2018/10/03/the-new-forbes-400-philanthropy-score-measuring-billionaires-generosity/?sh=2831816e7e1d.

166 *private foundations*: Rob Reich, *Just Giving: Why Philanthropy Is Failing Democracy and How It Can Do Better* (Princeton, NJ: Princeton University Press, 2018), 9.

167 *1.54 million different charities*: "Nonprofits Account for 12.3 Million Jobs, 10.2 Percent of Private Sector Employment, in 2016," U.S. Bureau of Labor Statistics, August 31, 2016, https://www.bls.gov/opub/ted/2018/nonprofits-account-for-12-3-million-jobs-10-2-percent-of-private-sector-employment-in-2016.htm?view_full; "The Nonprofit Sector in Brief," National Center for Charitable Statistics, June 18, 2020, https://nccs.urban.org/project/nonprofit-sector-brief.

167 *"Charitable activity"*: Ken Stern, *With Charity for All: Why Charities Are Failing and a Better Way to Give* (New York: Anchor, 2013), 2.

167 *Gates Foundation*: Ibid., 49.

168 *"hoarding problem"*: Alan Davis, "America's Billionaires Have a Hoarding Problem," *Fortune*, July 14, 2020, https://fortune.com/2020/07/14/billionaires-philanthropy-coronavirus-crisis/.

168 *"Excessive Wealth Disorder"*: Alan Davis, "AOC, Sanders, Warren Should Think Bigger (and Wider) on Taxing the Wealthy," Fox Business, March 4, 2019, https://www.foxbusiness.com/politics/aoc-sanders-warren-should-think-bigger-and-wider-on-wealth-tax.

169 *"Ms. French Gates's influence"*: "The Gates Foundation's Approach Has Both Advantages and Limits," *The Economist*, September 18, 2021, https://www.economist.com/international/2021/09/16/the-gates-foundations-approach-has-both-advantages-and-limits.

170 *Leonard Davis*: Leslie Wayne, "Leonard Davis Dies at 76; Philanthropist and Insurer," *New York Times*, January 20, 2001, https://www.nytimes.com/2001/01/20/business/leonard-davis-dies-at-76-philanthropist-and-insurer.html; Zsa Zsa Gershick, "Philanthropist, Founder of AARP, Leonard Davis, 76," *USC News*, January 29, 2001, https://news.usc.edu/6049/Philanthropist-Founder-of-AARP-Leonard-Davis-76/.

170 *Dr. Ethel Percy Andrus*: "Dr. Ethel Percy Andrus Dies," *New York Times*, July 15, 1967, https://timesmachine.nytimes.com/timesmachine/1967/07/15/83617095.html?pageNumber=18.

170 *"count the hours"*: "Education: The Dignity They Deserve," *Time*, May 10, 1954, http://content.time.com/time/subscriber/article /0,33009,819857,00.html.

172 *"painfully inegalitarian"*: Reich, *Just Giving*, 69.

172 *Reich calculates*: "Philanthropy & Democracy," BOOKTV, C-SPAN2, January 24, 2019, https://www.facebook.com/booktv /videos/2198885133704927/.

173 *Jean-Nöel Kapferer instinctively praised*: Jean-Noël Kapferer, "Notre-Dame Fire: Why Luxury Brands Have Lined Up to Support the Restoration Process," Scroll.in, May 8, 2019, https://scroll.in/article /922492/notre-dame-fire-why-luxury-brands-have-lined-up-to -support-the-restoration-process.

173 *KCRW radio*: "Big Donors Are Funding Notre Dame's Restoration, but Is Philanthropy the Best Way to Deal with a Disaster?" *Press Play with Madeleine Brand*, April 19, 2019, https:// www.kcrw.com/news/shows/press-play-with-madeleine-brand /a-backlash-as-philanthropists-fund-notre-dames-restoration/big -donors-are-funding-notre-dames-restoration-but-is-philanthropy -the-best-way-to-deal-with-a-disaster.

174 *"weaponizing of philanthropy"*: "Jane Mayer: The Koch Brothers and the Weaponizing of Philanthropy," Stanford Center on Philanthropy and Civil Society, March 7, 2016, https://pacscenter.stan ford.edu/event/jane-mayer-the-koch-brothers-and-the-weapon izing-of-philanthropy/.

174 *Michael Bloomberg*: David Callahan, *The Givers: Wealth, Power, and Philanthropy in a New Gilded Age* (New York: Vintage, 2017), 11–14.

174 *"An exercise of power"*: "Big Donors Are Funding Notre Dame's Restoration, but Is Philanthropy the Best Way to Deal with a Disaster?"

174 *"Sugar Bowl"*: Stern, *With Charity for All*, 92.

175 *Jeffrey Epstein*: William K. Rashbaum, Benjamin Weiser, and Michael Gold, "Jeffrey Epstein Dead in Suicide at Jail, Spurring In-

quiries," *New York Times*, August 10, 2019, https://www.nytimes
.com/2019/08/10/nyregion/jeffrey-epstein-suicide.html.

175 *"ill-gotten wealth"*: Anand Giridharadas, "How America's Elites
Lost Their Grip," *Time*, November 21, 2019, https://time
.com/5735384/capitalism-reckoning-elitism-in-america-2019/.

175 *$60 million to elite universities*: Collin Binkley and Jennifer McDer-
mott, "AP Exclusive: Colleges Got Millions from Opioid Maker
Owners," Associated Press, October 3, 2019, https://apnews.com
/article/lawsuits-opioids-boston-ct-state-wire-england-fe455c8b
d8af41ca94ce0bcada92381a.

176 *peripatetic mogul*: Stuart Emmrich, "7 Things to Know About
MacKenzie Scott, the Woman Who Has Donated $6 Billion in
2020," *Vogue*, December 21, 2020, https://www.vogue.com/article
/7-things-to-know-about-philanthropist-mackenzie-scott.

177 *post on* Medium: MacKenzie Scott, "116 Organizations Driving
Change," *Medium*, https://mackenzie-scott.medium.com/116-or
ganizations-driving-change-67354c6d733d.

177 *"bold and direct"*: Chuck Collins, "MacKenzie Scott's Bold and Direct Giving Puts Shame to the Billionaire Class and Their Perpetual Private Foundations," *Common Dreams*, December 15, 2020,
https://www.commondreams.org/views/2020/12/15/mackenzie
-scotts-bold-and-direct-giving-puts-shame-billionaire-class-and-their.

177 *"new standard of philanthropy"*: Fang Block, "MacKenzie Scott
Sets New Standard of Philanthropy with Additional $4.2 Billion
Gifts," *Barron's*, December 16, 2020, https://www.barrons.com
/articles/mackenzie-scott-sets-new-standard-of-philanthropy-with
-additional-4-2-billion-gifts-01608159359.

177 *Philanthropist of the Year*: Alan Davis, "Philanthropist of the Year,"
Crisis Charitable Commitment, December 29, 2020, https://charit
ablecommitment.org/philanthropist-of-the-year/.

177 *"no strings attached"*: MacKenzie Scott, "384 Ways to Help," *Medium*, December 15, 2020, https://mackenzie-scott.medium
.com/384-ways-to-help-45d0b9ac6ad8.

179 *endowment exceeds*: Amanda Agati, "Endowments and Foundations: 2019 in Review," PNC Financial Services Group, March 18, 2020, https://www.pnc.com/insights/corporate-institutional/manage-non profit-enterprises/endowments-and-foundations-2019-in-review.html.

183 *"We should not be funding"*: "About Us," DivestInvest, https:// www.divestinvest.org/about/. Post viewed September 25, 2020.

183 *Pope Francis*: "In TED Countdown, Pope Francis Calls for Divestment from Fossil Fuels," Catholic Climate Movement, October 22, 2020, https://catholicclimatemovement.global/in-ted-count down-pope-francis-calls-for-divestment-from-fossil-fuels/.

186 *Tracy Gary has*: David Ian Miller, "Finding My Religion/Born into Great Wealth, Tracy Gary Finds Happiness in Giving Her Money Away," *SF Gate*, September 12, 2005, https://www.sfgate .com/news/article/FINDING-MY-RELIGION-Born-into-great -wealth-3302867.php.

186 *Iimay Ho*: Iimay Ho, "Meet Iimay Ho!" Resource Generation, https://resourcegeneration.org/meet-iimay-ho/.

187 *Resource Generation believe*: "Programs & Conferences," Resource Generation, https://resourcegeneration.org/what-we-do/.

CHAPTER 8:
FITZGERALD WAS WRONG:
STATUS AS EGALITARIANISM

189 *"different from you and me"*: F. Scott Fitzgerald, "The Rich Boy," *The Short Stories of F. Scott Fitzgerald: A New Collection* (New York: Scribner, 1989), 318; originally published in *Red Book Magazine*, January–February 1926.

189 *pithier version of the Fitzgerald quote*: Eddy Dow, "The Rich Are Different," *New York Times*, November 13, 1988.

191 *140,000 tax filers*: Aimee Picchi, "How Much Income You Need to Be in the 1%," CBS News, February 6, 2019, https://www .cbsnews.com/news/how-much-income-you-need-to-be-in-the-1/.

191 *Survey of Consumer Finances*: "Survey of Consumer Finances," Federal Reserve System, November 4, 2021, https://www.federal reserve.gov/econres/scfindex.htm.

191 *one hundred richest people*: Josh Harkinson, "America's 100 Richest People Control More Wealth Than the Entire Black Population," *MotherJones*, December 2, 2015, https://www.motherjones.com/poli tics/2015/12/report-100-people-more-wealth-african-american -population/.

191 *The average Forbes 400*: Chase Peterson-Withorn, "The Ups, Downs, Crashes and Comebacks of the Richest People in America," *Forbes*, October 9, 2021, https://www.forbes.com/sites /chasewithorn/2021/10/09/inside-the-most-elite-club-in-america -how-the-forbes-400-has-gotten-4-trillion-richer-since-the-1980s /?sh=26ca60f114fe.

194 *"There is a luxury industry"*: Jean-Noël Kapferer, "Luxury After the Crisis: Pro Logo or No Logo?" *The European Business Review*, September–October 2010, https://www.researchgate.net/publica tion/265080236_Luxury_after_the_crisis_Pro_logo_or_no_logo.

194 *"democratization of culture"*: "Mannheim, Karl, 1893–1947," Encyclopedia.com, May 18, 2018, https://www.encyclopedia.com /people/social-sciences-and-law/sociology-biographies/karl-mann heim.

194 *"democratization of luxury"*: Elizabeth Currid-Halkett, *The Sum of Small Things: A Theory of the Aspirational Class* (Princeton, NJ: Princeton University Press, 2017), 6.

194 *"dawn of humanity"*: Jean-Nöel Kapferer and Vincent Bastien, *The Luxury Strategy: Break the Rules of Marketing to Build Luxury Brands* (London: Kogan Page, 2009), 10–11.

195 *"How do you define"*: Robin Lent and Geneviève Tour, *Selling Luxury: Connect with Affluent Customers, Create Unique Experiences Through Impeccable Service, and Close the Sale* (Hoboken, NJ: John Wiley & Sons, 2009), xv.

195 *Alexa von Tobel*: Jeremy Goldman, "Why Brands Must Embrace

the Democratization of Luxury in 2016," *Inc.*, January 4, 2016, https://www.inc.com/jeremy-goldman/why-brands-must-em brace-the-democratization-of-luxury-in-2016.html.

198 *"Money, although important"*: Paul Fussell, *Class: A Guide Through the American Status System* (New York: Simon & Schuster, 1983), 69, 28.

200 *"Veblenian conspicuous consumption"*: Rachel Sherman, *Uneasy Street: The Anxieties of Affluence* (Princeton, NJ: Princeton University Press, 2017), 121.

200 *"effaced class differences"*: Ibid., 130.

201 Business Insider: John, ESI Money, "I Asked 100 Millionaires All About Their Money, and Found They Tend to Splurge on the Same 5 Things," *Business Insider*, March 27, 2019, https://www .businessinsider.com/millionaires-tend-to-spend-money-on-same -things-2019-3.

202 *E. Digby Baltzell*: David Brooks, *Bobos in Paradise: The New Upper Class and How They Got There* (New York: Simon & Schuster, 2000), 29.

202 *"foulard blobs"*: Fussell, *Class*, 67.

203 Bobos in Paradise: Brooks, *Bobos in Paradise*, 39, 94, 40, 33, 84, 114.

203 *"The correct etiquette"*: Chrystia Freeland, *Plutocrats: The Rise of the New Global Super Rich and the Fall of Everyone Else* (New York: Penguin Press, 2012), 235–36.

203 *Reed Hastings*: Maureen Down, "Reed Hastings Had Us All Staying Home Before We Had To," *New York Times*, September 4, 2020, https://www.nytimes.com/2020/09/04/style/reed-hastings-netflix -interview.html.

204 *"Jackets and ties"*: Tyler Cowen, *The Complacent Class: The Self-Defeating Quest for the American Dream* (New York: St. Martin's Press, 2017), 155.

204 *victims of success*: Rachel Sherman, *Uneasy Street: The Anxieties of Affluence* (Princeton, NJ: Princeton University Press, 2017), 77.

205 *"luxury creep"*: Ibid., 114–15.

206 *"hand-painted leather jackets"*: Rick Springfield, *Late, Late at Night: A Memoir* (New York: Touchstone, 2010), 324.

207 *most-requested karaoke hit*: Lauren Sher, "Rick Springfield on Battle with Depression, Promiscuity," ABC News, October 12, 2010, https://abcnews.go.com/GMA/morning_mix/rick-springfield-jessies-girl-singer-opens-battle-depression/story?id=11857669.

209 *always a pleasure to meet*: This goes back a ways. It's a story I've told often to friends, people always seem to like it, and it's a good distillation of celebs being decent human beings in the context of underdogs subverting status.

It's 1999. Venus and Serena Williams are living in Florida with their family, but it hasn't been that long since their adolescent years on the public courts of Compton. Hair still in those braids and beads they burst onto the tennis scene with, making everybody go "WTF?" back before anyone knew what WTF meant. And I don't mean World Tennis Federation.

They weren't dominating the sport yet—neither had won a Grand Slam singles title, though Serena would win the U.S. Open later that year and Venus would take Wimbledon the next—but they were already stars. Big enough to get a cover story in the inflight magazine of a major U.S. airline (and I can defend the honor of inflights if you need it), not yet big enough to turn it down.

The interview takes place just after an excruciating Australian Open. Serena had lost in the third round to a 14th-seed named Sandrine Testud. Venus lost in the quarterfinals to U.S. Open champ Lindsay Davenport. Then Serena and partner Max Mirnyi lost the mixed doubles final to a pair of South Africans in a wrenching third-set tiebreaker.

The interview takes place the day after the sisters arrive home from these disappointments and an exhausting flight from Australia. The two teenagers simply can't be in good moods or have much energy for a stranger who spent most of his flight cross-country devising probing interview questions and ordering them in a note-book for maximum impact.

I'm a little nervous because the parents, Richard and Oracene, have a reputation for being hard on the media. Yet they can't be more gracious when I show up at their home, tape recorder in hand. The ten-minute chat with them in the living room makes me feel a little like a prom date being vetted by protective parents, but they serve me iced tea and cookies and we establish an easy rapport. Richard is pretty cool and funny; Oracene is friendly and more laid back. After a while the sisters come down from upstairs, sit on a sofa, and talk with me like a new friend. Venus is poised and intelligent to a royal degree. Serena still has a bit of mischievous kid in her, but the charisma, brains, and drive are unmistakable.

The interview goes fine, but it's what happens afterward that makes the day memorable. A photo shoot has been arranged at the conclusion of the interview. The shoot location is a nearby studio compound owned by Burt Reynolds. Normally, freelance writers aren't involved in arranging details of photo shoots. For various reasons, however, I've been engaged as a helpmeet for this one.

From the beginning the Williams team has been flexible and accommodating, but adamant with one request. Since the shoot will require a couple wardrobe changes, and is for the magazine's cover, they've asked that whatever makeup artist is contracted be someone with experience working with African American women. Not specifically that the makeup artist be an African American woman. Just that he or she is familiar with the particular makeup needs of African American women. What I know about women's cosmetics you could stuff inside a dried-out tube of Bonne Bell Lip Smacker (gateway-makeup drug, so said *Allure*, for every girl in my junior high school). But this seems like a pretty reasonable request to me. Naturally the magazine agrees.

Following the interview, I drive to the studio twenty or thirty minutes ahead of Venus and Serena to check out the scene. This turns out to be a good decision.

The decor inside the hangar-like structure where the shoot is set to take place is retrograde Gator McKlusky. Confederate flag. Rifles mounted on a rack. Dixie Beer signage. Gridiron bric-a-brac. A pickup with the tailgate down is parked in a corner of the warehouse. Two large speakers in the bed are blasting Toby Keith to the point that some of the doors in the metal building are literally rattling.

Nothing at all wrong with the scene if you're looking to celebrate a big Seminoles win over Vanderbilt with shots and beers. (Sadly, as of this writing, Vandy constitutes a big win for FSU.) Just not the vibe most people would put together were they hoping to make two young Black women feel comfortable. The photographer isn't around, but the makeup artist and her assistant are. A pair of women in their early thirties, as best as I can recall, with pale skin and dirty blonde Jersey perms. My conversation with the makeup artist goes roughly like this:

Me: Any chance of turning those tunes down a little?

(Music notches down from "I Love This Bar" level to "Courtesy of Red, White and Blue" level.)

Me: Well, hey, big day, Venus and Serena Williams coming in a few minutes.

Makeup artist: I heard they're a couple of bitches.

Me: Really? I don't know where you heard that but I just spent an hour at their house and they're actually super nice.

Makeup artist: Uh-huh.

Me: So, you do a lot of celebrity makeup? You guys must get some big names through here. Ever meet Sally Field? Loni Anderson?

Makeup artist rattles off a few recognizable names she's worked with.

Me: Ever done makeup for any Black women?

Makeup artist: Nah.

Me: Cool, cool. Um, my understanding is that Venus and Serena had specifically asked for someone familiar with doing makeup for Black women.

Makeup artist: It'll be fine.

Now I notice something else, which is that usually at these types of things someone will have laid out bottles of water or juice, maybe a tray of veggies or donuts or something. But here there's nothing.

Me: Hey, so, is there no catering? I imagine we'll be an hour or two and it's pretty hot in here.

Makeup artist: Dunno.

So, great, two of the biggest stars in U.S. sports are gonna be here any minute, Toby Keith is fixin' to bust a gut on the loudest boom box in SEC country, there's no potable water in sight, and not only does the makeup artist have zilch experience with African American skin, she's got a chip on her shoulder the size of an alligator tooth and already has it in her head that her clients for the day are a couple of rags.

Not simply because I do my best to avoid all awkward social situations—I can't even watch *Curb Your Enthusiasm* anymore, too hard on me—but because I can't cotton to hosting guests without offering them something to drink, I sprint out to my rental car. Doing my best Bandit impersonation I haul ass to the nearest convenience store. In normal conditions this looks to be about a thirty-minute round-trip. With "Eastbound and Down," "Amos Moses," "Lord, Mr. Ford," and other Jerry Reed twangers screaming in my head I make it there and back in under twenty.

I jog back into the studio like 7-Eleven Santa. Plastic bags filled with Aquafina, Gatorade, iced tea, chips, nuts, pretzels, cookies, various counter caramels, and jerkies. Across the warehouse Venus, Serena, and their mother are talking with the photographer. When I approach the group the conversation is just getting to the part about the makeup lady not really "doing" Black people. There's a polite disagreement about matching outfits the photog really wants to shoot the girls in, something they're not particularly interested in doing.

Now, it should be said at this point that despite my one-hundred-percent positive interaction with them, Venus and Serena and their parents actually have been known to get testy when they don't get their way. And impatient and demanding even when they do. I'm cognizant of this reputation and because I'm the only actual representative of the magazine here, I really don't want this situation to go any deeper south than it already has. Although right now I don't see any other way it's likely to go.

I mean, put yourself in the shoes of these two young women. You've just suffered a major professional setback in front of the world. Endured a beast of a flight from halfway around the planet. Soldiered through a pleasant if perfunctory hour-long interview in your living room with some over-solicitous dude (I worry I come off that way in these situations) from a goddamn inflight magazine. Which, seriously, an inflight mag? You gotta be wondering at this point who in your camp thought booking that gig on the heels of a return flight from Australia was a good idea and can we get them doing something less schedule-oriented in the future? Now you've driven half an hour to some makeshift redneck disco in a warehouse in the middle of a swamp with no water or food to get your picture taken by a photographer who thinks teenage sisters enjoy dressing alike and the one fucking request you made for all of this—that being to enlist just one makeup artist in all of Gator Country who's dealt with your kind of skin before—isn't gonna be honored.

What do you do? Throw a tantrum like everybody expects and would love to see? Call all y'all a bunch of country-fuck dickshines and march out the door in a huff? Scream for your manager to fix all this right now or start looking for a new job? Go through with the shoot but sulk the whole time while lobbing snide cracks at everyone who comes near you with a hairbrush or pink tennis top? Or do you do what the Williams sisters did? Smile politely; say that's cool, we can do our makeup ourselves; go overboard thanking the hapless writer for running out to fetch water and snacks; allow the photographer to position you in poses you don't really care for; generally act like there's nowhere your jet-lagged butt would rather be on this muggy Florida afternoon than in Burt Reynolds's media ranch, where Randy Travis is now booming out of the stereo; and shoot a cover standing back-to-back with your sister that a couple months later will greet everyone contorting themselves into the crappiest seating assignment since their cousin's rehearsal dinner with a big smile on your face that says, *That's how winners do.*

I've never been more impressed with a pair of teenage girls than I was that afternoon. That was a one-percent-is-a-state-of-mind performance. As it turned out, one of many.

209 *photo of U.S. Treasury Secretary Steve Mnuchin*: Christopher Ingraham, "The Richest 1 Percent Now Owns More of the Country's Wealth Than at Any Time in the Past 50 Years," *Washington Post*, December 6, 2017, https://www.washingtonpost.com/news/wonk/wp/2017/12/06/the-richest-1-percent-now-owns-more-of-the-countrys-wealth-than-at-any-time-in-the-past-50-years/.

210 *"you'd still be a Howell"*: "Our Vines Have Tender Apes," *Gilligan's Island*, season 3, episode 20, January 30, 1967, https://www.youtube.com/watch?v=tCCCN-3NJiU.

210 *"We are guided"*: John Kenneth Galbraith, *The Affluent Society* (Boston: Houghton Mifflin, 1958), 2.

210 *Arwa Mahdawi*: Arwa Mahdawi, "How Do You Make Poverty Sound Better? Rebrand It!" *Guardian*, April 4, 2018, https://www.theguardian.com/commentisfree/2018/apr/04/poverty-kids-jobs-work-side-hustle-living-precariously.

210 *"all the lies"*: Fitzgerald, *The Short Stories of F. Scott Fitzgerald: A New Collection*, 318.

CONCLUSION:
STATUS REBORN

214 *"$40 bottle of wine"*: Adam Davidson, "The Best Nanny Money Can Buy," *New York Times Magazine*, March 20, 2012, https://www.nytimes.com/2012/03/25/magazine/the-best-nanny-money-can-buy.html.

214 *"caustic, mocking terms"*: Alain de Botton, *Status Anxiety* (New York: Vintage International, 2004), 5.

215 *"In the twenty-first century"*: Yuval Noah Harari, *Homo Deus: A Brief History of Tomorrow* (New York: Harper, 2017), 330.

215 *Great Resignation*: Jeff Cox, "Workers Quit Jobs in Record Numbers as Consumer Sentiment Hits 10-Year Low," CNBC, November 12, 2021, https://www.cnbc.com/2021/11/12/consumer-sentiment-hits-10-year-low-while-workers-quit-jobs-in-record-numbers.html.

216 *$471.44 billion in 2020*: "Giving USA 2021: In a Year of Unprecedented Events and Challenges, Charitable Giving Reached a Record $471.44 Billion in 2020," *Philanthropy Network*, June 15, 2021, https://philanthropynetwork.org/news/giving-usa-2021-year-un precedented-events-and-challenges-charitable-giving-reached-re cord-47144.

216 *2.48 million viewers*: "FOX Sports Records Most-Watched Westminster Kennel Club Dog Show Since 2016," *Fox Sports*, June 15, 2021, https://www.foxsports.com/presspass/latest-news/2021/06/15/fox-sports-records-watched-westminster-kennel-club-dog-show-since-2016.

216 *Canadian breeder of "doodles"*: Hallie Cotnam, "Year of the Dog: Pandemic Puppies in High Demand, Short Supply," *CBC*, October 29, 2020, https://www.cbc.ca/news/canada/ottawa/pandemic-puppies-ottawa-supply-demand-breeders-rescue-urge-caution-1.5778956.

216 *dog-biz revenue*: Aaron Mesh, "Can We Get a Pandemic Puppy? Dog Breeders Are Among the Businesses Booming Amid Oregon's

Freeze," *Willamette Week*, December 2, 2020, https://www.wweek
.com/news/business/2020/12/02/can-we-get-a-pandemic-puppy
-dog-breeders-are-among-the-businesses-booming-amid-oregons
-freeze/.

217 *"dogs skyrockets during quarantine"*: Maghan Ottolini, "Pandemic
Puppies: Massachusetts Sees Puppy Shortage as Demand for Dogs
Skyrockets in Quarantine," *Boston Herald*, June 19, 2020, https://
www.bostonherald.com/2020/06/19/pandemic-puppies-mas
sachusetts-sees-puppy-shortage-as-demand-for-dogs-skyrockets
-in-quarantine/.

INDEX

ABOUT THE AUTHOR

CHUCK THOMPSON is the author of the political screed *Better Off Without 'Em: A Northern Manifesto for Southern Secession*, comic travel memoirs *Smile When You're Lying* and *To Hellholes and Back*, as well as a two-volume World War II survey (*The 25 Best World War II Sites: Pacific Theater* and *The 25 Essential World War II Sites: European Theater*), regarded as the most comprehensive catalog of World War II sites in existence. He's been an editorial director and executive producer of CNN.com Travel; an editor with *Maxim, Travelocity,* and other magazines; and wrote and executive produced the Paramount+ documentary *Sometimes When We Touch: The Reign, Ruin and Resurrection of Soft Rock.* He's currently the editor of *Columbia Insight,* a nonprofit environmental news website covering the Columbia River Basin. Thompson's writing has appeared in numerous publications and websites, including *New Republic, Politico, Outside, Outdoor Life, Salon, Esquire, Popular Mechanics, Men's Health, Medium,* and the *Los Angeles Times.*